This is a astrologers
hand book.

D0335021

The ASTROLOGER'S
H A N D B O O K

Julia Parker

CHANCELLOR
PRESS

Previously published by
Mitchell Beazley

This 1993 edition published by
Chancellor Press
an imprint of Reed Consumer Books
Michelin House, 81 Fulham Road, London SW3 6RB
and Auckland, Melbourne, Singapore and Toronto

Edited and designed by
Mitchell Beazley International Limited

ISBN 1 85152 296 4

A CIP catalogue record for this book is available at
the British Library

Typeset by Vantage Photosetting, Eastleigh and London
Printed in China

Editor Margaret Ramsay
Designer Eric Drewery
Executive Editor Susan Egerton-Jones
Production Jean Rigby

Illustrations
Hilary Paynter: 9, 73, 80
Ronan Picture Library: 43, 49, 55, 59, 63

teach you to become an astrologer, for though we can consider the planets' positions, we cannot go into "house positions", "aspects", "midpoints" or dwell on the Midheaven in any detail. All that will come later on for you, if you decide to study the subject seriously.

Think of this book, then, as a stimulating apéritif, and allow it to speak to you and reveal areas of your personality which you may not so far have appreciated. Learn, for instance, how to counter your weaker personality traits by using your more positive, strong qualities. This is only one way in which astrology can really be of practical help to you in your life. You will not have read far before you realize that you are a far more complex human being than any one Sun-sign could possibly portray! And for those who want to look *through* the mirror, behind their outward appearance and behaviour, to try to fathom what makes them what they are, there is no better tool than astrology. It is perhaps the most revealing and rewarding of all the disciplines which help us to self-knowledge—and it makes use of an accumulation of data which has been assembled over four thousand years and more.

So you will find that in all probability this will be only an introduction to a subject which will be so interesting to you that you will never be bored again! There'll be no turning back; you'll not want to give up—especially if you start out with a natural interest in human nature, in what makes men and women tick.

To my fellow astrologers
It may be difficult to remember it, but there was a time when you, too, probably thought that astrology began and ended with the Sun-signs. It's easy enough to forget once one becomes conversant with the fully-calculated birth- and progressed charts.

This book is, I hope, a step ahead of others in the field, for in it I aim to build a bridge, teaching novice readers enough to give them the appetite to move on and eventually join the ranks of the millions of competent amateur and professional astrologers all over the world. In the process, maybe they will also be helped to come to terms with their own potential and motivations, as seen so clearly and particularly through the planetary influences which we study.

The interpretations are based on my own experience as a consultant astrologer, backed up of course by the empirical observations of many generations of astrologers since Ptolemy, and even before him. There may be individual points of interpretation with which you disagree, but perhaps at least some which may stimulate you to think again about particular influences and the way in which they work for individuals.

I feel very strongly that experienced astrologers should give some time and effort to stimulating the individuals who start out by knowing that "there's more to astrology than the columns in the papers", or who admit (maybe, even in the 1980s, a little sheepishly) that yes, they're interested in the subject. Among them are the people who will form the next generation of astrologers. It is up to us to assist the embryonic astrologers towards their birth, to become in a sense their parents.

Julia Parker

Contents

THE BASIC FACTORS

THE INNER PLANETS

THE OUTER PLANETS

THE MODERN PLANETS

SELF-EXPRESSION

General Characteristics   74

Friendship, Love and Marriage, Careers and Money:

THE TABLES

Your astrological profile

A full horoscope consists of a chart worked out by an astrologer showing the positions of the Sun, Moon and planets as they were seen in the sky at the moment and from the place of your birth. The astrologer also calculates the important "Rising-sign", that is the zodiacal sign which is over the horizon at the time of birth. These positions form a profile showing how the different parts of the solar system and the Zodiac work for the individual. You can work out an abbreviated version of your birth-chart by looking at the diagrams and tables at the back of this book. As these are constantly referred to in the text I suggest that you begin by looking them up and filling them in below.

Birth Date..

Birth Time..

Birth Place...

Rising Sign...

Sun Sign..

Moon Sign..

Mercury Sign...

Venus Sign..

Mars Sign...

Jupiter Sign..

Saturn Sign...

Uranus Sign..

Neptune Sign...

Pluto Sign..

The Zodiacal calendar

Aries Mar 21–Apr 20	**Libra** Sept 23–Oct 23
Taurus Apr 21–May 21	**Scorpio** Oct 24–Nov 22
Gemini May 22–June 21	**Sagittarius** Nov 23–Dec 21
Cancer June 22–July 22	**Capricorn** Dec 22–Jan 20
Leo July 23–Aug 23	**Aquarius** Jan 21–Feb 18
Virgo Aug 24–Sept 22	**Pisces** Feb 19–Mar 20

THE BASIC
FACTORS

Sun-, Rising- and Moon-sign

Introduction

The three most important elements in the fully-calculated birth-chart are the Rising-sign, Sun-sign and Moon-sign—in that order. We all know our Sun-sign, because we know the date on which we were born. This is, in the opinion of many astrologers, second in importance to our Rising-sign, which relies implicitly on the precise time and geographical location of our birth. Generally speaking, it is necessary for the layman either to learn how to calculate the Rising-sign by mathematical calculation (not too difficult), or to ask a competent astrologer to calculate it. The tables on pages 225–232 of this book offer a way of discovering your Rising-sign, though necessarily a fallible one.

If you were born at or near sunrise, your Sun- and Rising-sign will be the same. This will double the emphasis of the characteristics of that sign on your personality, but do not forget that those characteristics will still work on two distinct levels of your personality. Similarly, if you were born at the time of the new Moon, your Sun- and Moon-signs will be the same, but again working on two levels. In both cases you will be known as a "double" Aries, Aquarius, or whatever.

> Because the earth's axis is at an angle, some signs take longer to rise than others, and the further away from the equator you live, the greater the difference. Signs are known as of "long" or "short" ascension.

The Sun-sign denotes our self-expression, and its characteristics relate to the way in which we present ourselves to the world. It can also have a very strong bearing on the way we look—our overall image. The sign the Moon was in when we were born is also very individual to us, and like the Rising-sign it is not easy to discover unless one has an ephemeris (a book of tables showing the planets' positions for every day of the year). Once more, however, we have been able to surmount this difficulty, and if you turn to page 234 you will find out how to discover the sign in which the Moon stood when you were born.

This is a beginning. But there are some very important things to remember when building up an interpretation of these three factors. For instance, if your Sun-sign is Gemini, your Rising-sign Capricorn, and you have the Moon in Cancer, you are not just an amorphous combination of the characteristics of these three signs. Certain elements of their characteristics will be present in your personality, but it is vitally important that you learn how the three signs work for you as an individual.

The Sun-sign represents the "you" people experience when they first meet you. Your Rising-sign works at a different level, and represents the "real" you—the "you" known to your lover, or your closest friend. When he or she hears other people talking about you, the chances are they will be describing your Sun-sign characteristics, but your lover will be able to add, "Yes, that is true, but·...." and go on to describe your Rising-sign characteristics.

Put this to the test yourself: read the section on image which relates to your Sun-sign. You will probably agree with a great deal that is said there. Then read the relevant piece on your Rising-sign in the following section of the book, and note the difference. Soon the various levels will be clear to you.

To the Sun- and Rising-signs we can now add the Moon-sign, and its group of characteristics. Traditional astrology asserts that the characteristics of the Moon-sign are those we inherit from our parents, and in many ways modern astrologers agree; but equally, your Moon-sign will show the way in which you instinctively respond to situations in life—your reactions to them. For instance, there is a possessive tendency in all Sun- and Rising-sign Taureans. If you have the Moon in Taurus, you will probably respond to certain situations in a possessive way, but because of other elements in your birth-chart you may loathe that reaction, and do everything you can to fight it. You could be very intuitive indeed if Cancer or Scorpio was a prominent sign in your birth-chart—and if one of those is your Moon-sign, your immediate response to situations will be entirely intuitive and instinctive; logic and reason may play a part later, and this will relate to the prominence of other signs.

These points are crucial as you discover more about your birth-chart and the way to interpret it. It is a subtle business to get all the planetary positions into a coherent perspective, but with care you can certainly learn a great deal about yourself and your motivations, and hopefully this book will start you on a trail which will prove to be an unendingly fascinating study.

Aries

Sun-sign, Rising-sign, Moon-sign

Sun-sign period March 21 – April 20

A sign of short ascension in the northern hemisphere, and long ascension in the southern hemisphere

Aries as Sun-sign

Aries is known as the pioneer of the Zodiac, and Ariens like to be first. Those who have this as their Sun-sign are generally uncomplicated in their attitude to life. They plan straightforwardly, and convince the rest of us that there are no complications in what they suggest. They come straight to the point, and do not allow themselves to be held up by details or by boring or niggling problems. In this way they can achieve a great deal, provided they get plenty of back-up from others, assisting them to fill in the detail of their plans, while they themselves move on to achieve further objectives and become more involved with new and yet more fascinating plans. The basic motivation of an Arien is to push ahead, and while it is not vital to them to be "top dog", they hate to lag behind their opponents. The out-in-front position is the truly rewarding one for them, and theirs is a very individual type of expression of ambition. They have plenty of determination which immediately comes to their aid once they have decided just what they want to do. An Arien who drifts mindlessly from one subject, job or relationship to the next (perhaps attempting to satisfy a need for a lively and varied sex-life) will be unfulfilled, and will feel restless and bored. Ariens have to make a tremendous effort to learn to be patient, and some may have to accept the fact that they will never succeed, and will have to call on other levels of their personality to help counter this failing. (Having Mercury or Venus in Taurus will help, if Aries is the Sun-sign.)

The dominant Arien fault, selfishness, must be recognized as early in life as possible, and it is essential to govern it. Guilt, often coupled with some kind gesture such as a small but attractive present, will be the result when an Arien has behaved selfishly to friend or lover. Ariens are passionate by nature, and their enthusiasm for sex and the sheer enjoyment of it is communicated to their partners, who, if sympathetic to Arien needs, will get a great deal of pleasure from the relationship. Ariens have a considerable reserve of emotion which surfaces readily, and in a very positive way. They make really lively parents, and as their children get older do not generally have too much difficulty in coping with the generation gap. Physical exercise is extremely important to them, and sport, or any activity which makes demands on their physical energy, is excellent for them. Like their emotional level, their physical energy level is high, and needs plenty of positive expression.

Ariens will spare nothing in expressing their natural enthusiasm, and at least once in their lives will take some action which would prove extremely daunting to other less assertive people, hence their reputation for bravery. They are motivated to achieve a great deal. Because Aries is a Fire sign, they have enormous warmth, which is endearing to those who like lively, positive, extravert types.

Ariens cope extremely well with working in a busy and even noisy environment. The solitude and quiet of an office away from easy contact with colleagues is not very satisfactory for them, so even those in superior positions will compromise in order not to become remote or out of touch with what is going on in their business or at work.

Arien children will often feign laziness at school, because they are bored, and simply will not get involved in any subject that really does not interest them. They will cut out, drift off and think about their real interests, while the teacher fights a losing battle. It is therefore important for the parents of Sun- or Rising-sign Ariens to nurture any interest that the young Arien expresses, and to make a special effort to keep his or her initial enthusiasm stirring, perhaps by gradually encouraging the child to take up ever more daunting challenges. The competitive spirit is powerful in them, even from an early age, and you can appeal to this. If young Aries does not "win"—come out top—he or she will not have an easy time; but any setback will definitely encourage greater concentration next time round. Provided Ariens have plenty of opportunity to burn up energy and keep to a busy, lively schedule, they usually remain healthy. They have good physical resources.

The Arien body-area is the head. Ariens either get an above-average number of headaches, or none at all; and the cause of such headaches is usually either eye-strain or a minor kidney disorder. Their tendency to cut and burn themselves is considerable, because they are often unduly hasty and rather careless when handling sharp tools or hot dishes. Knocks and cuts to the head are often common. The influence of Mars, the ruling planet of Aries, in that sign is of well above-average importance when Aries is the Sun- or Rising-sign, and will colour the basic motivation and have a psychological and personal influence on the individual concerned.

Aries as Rising-sign
Those with Aries rising will make a considerable impact on others. They will instigate large, successful projects, and will devote much of their time and energy to the achievement of horrendously ambitious objectives. Their powerful motivation is not so much downright ambition for success in the usual worldly sense of the word—indeed, it is often the case that such things as a huge house and expensive possessions do not mean a very great deal to them—but they are prompted to ever greater efforts by the steady advancement of opponents or rivals who seem to be overtaking them. The tendency to selfishness can show itself in what seems to be ruthlessness, for if they were to give consideration to others, they would of necessity have to interrupt the flow of their own energy and concentration on main objectives. There is in the Rising-sign Arien an element of their personality which will emerge in their attitude to their partners—kindness, lovingness and the search for a well-balanced, harmonious life. In other words, where the most important man or woman in their life is concerned, they express themselves in the manner of their polar or opposite sign across the Zodiac, which is Libra. This is something that will almost certainly go unnoticed by even close friends; it is reserved for partners. The drive and sense of urgency in life is overwhelmingly powerful when Aries rises; it is of prime importance to them. They need to set themselves objectives which will motivate and reward them. It is only in this way that they will achieve a sense of fulfilment, and burn up all their energy—emotional and physical—in a really rewarding way, quelling restlessness, impatience and negative aggression.

Aries as Moon-sign
The instinctive reaction to all situations when the Moon is in Aries will be a fast one, leading to immediate action. This may or may not be a good thing, and it is very much up to the Moon-in-Aries type to channel this excellent decisive response in such a way that it will work for and not against him. Only experience of life and the making of many mistakes enable him to do this. But quick decisions will in the end prove right for this particular individual. The tendency to succumb to impulsive and premature action will in due course be controlled, usually by the utilization of the characteristics of the Rising- or Sun-sign, when the directness and forthright, uncomplicated

qualities of Aries will come into their own in an extremely positive way.

Because the tendency is to respond to situations in a selfish way, care is needed to ensure that this aspect of the sign does not mar all kinds of relationships; not giving enough consideration to others, for example, could be hurtful. Other than that, the fire and enthusiasm of Moon in Aries does a great deal for them, and they inspire and motivate action in other people in a very special, individual and positive way.

Taurus

Sun-sign, Rising-sign, Moon-sign

Sun-sign period April 21 – May 21

A sign of short ascension in the northern hemisphere, and long ascension in the southern hemisphere

Taurus as Sun-sign

Taureans, to function properly, need to live their lives in the knowledge that they have the security of a regular income and a stable emotional relationship. When this is achieved they are in the right position to achieve a great deal. Their most outstanding virtue is patience, they will plod very steadily onwards, and soon learn that short cuts are usually disastrous for them. Taureans need a steady, predictable routine, but the sort of rut in which they may get themselves will increase their sense of much-needed security and within its confines they will achieve much. But Taureans must also make something of an effort to break new ground, do new and different things and be open to the opinions of others in order to move with the times and to make sure that they are not missing out on life as it is actually being lived by other people.

Visit a Taurean's home and you will relax on comfortable cushions, find the colours used in decoration pleasing and the place not lacking in beautiful things which will have cost the Taurean rather more than he or she can actually afford. This might seem superficial, but these outward expressions form an important part of the whole Taurean motivation. Possessions to the Taurean are very important. In fact, possessiveness is the major Taurean fault. The two go together. Taureans love to own beautiful things, and they really do need to be aware that their partner is not an extension of this basic urge. The realization that no one can actually be possessed by another can be a cause of real heartache to Taureans. The sooner they learn to adopt a self-analytical and critical attitude in their expression of love the better, as this can help them to express themselves in a less claustrophobic way towards their partners.

Most Taureans have a happy knack either of making money or doing a great deal with what they have. They combine this with the ability to build up their own businesses and—often with the aid of a more adventurous partner—will achieve much. They also do extremely well in banking or working for large multinational companies, as their need for financial security is then taken care of, and they can express themselves in the knowledge that the regular pay-cheque will arrive when expected.

The Taurean body-area is the throat; colds often begin here, with a sore throat or loss of voice. Taureans have the reputation of being the best looking people in the Zodiac, due partly to their ruling planet which is Venus. But because most Taureans love rich food, with heavy sweet things being particular favourites, they have a tendency to put on weight. Also, they are often slow movers and so do not burn up their additional calories very quickly, so a conscious and continual check on the amout of food and wine they consume is essential if they are going to keep the good looks they so often have when they are young.

Taureans make kind and loving parents, but tend to spoil their children with too many expensive presents. They can be on the strict side when disciplining their children, which may or may not be a good thing, according to the individual child. Taurean children are delightful, but it is important for their parents not to rush them. Slow, steady progress is their way, and no sudden bursts should be expected. But once a Taurean has learned something, excellent powers of retention come into play. Many Taureans are extremely musical and it can become an important form of self-expression for them if they study singing or a musical instrument. To others the appreciation of music is important. Some will get great satisfaction from embroidery, sewing, pottery and sculpture. Basically artistic and appreciative of the arts they sometimes need encouragement to get round to spending time and energy in this direction. It is good when involvement along these lines occurs since it is one way of preventing any tendency towards being marginally sybaritic at times.

Taurus as Rising-sign

Although the individual with Taurus rising may not give the impression that he or she needs to feel more than usually secure, the underlying need will be very much present, and, as is the case with Sun-sign Taureans, will relate to both financial and emotional security. The tendency will be gradually to build towards their important objectives in life and Taurean patience will see to it that nothing is rushed. There is a strong sense of ambition, and a need for and love of beautiful things is also in evidence. But the main emphasis is on material progress; the individual may well become overconcerned with the amount of money he or she makes, and the amount of property owned, rather than with the development of true aesthetic values. If works of art are bought they will be appreciated, but the excitement of investment potential cannot be denied.

In emotional relationships there is a high level of intensity and passion. This Taurean could make considerable demands on a partner, but in return the partner would know that the relationship is very deep, sincere and meaningful, and the Taurean ability to enjoy life and get a great deal of pleasure from all aspects of it would definitely add a marvellous dimension to the relationship. However, Taurean possessiveness will certainly emerge, as will a strong element of jealousy, which could be totally unfounded. It is simply something that someone sharing the life of a Taurus-rising type will have to come to terms with, trying to get their partner to understand the weakness—not an easy thing to do. It is here that the emphasis of the Taurean polar sign, Scorpio, will be in evidence, but it will only affect the attitude to the partner.

Taurus as Moon-sign
When the Moon is in Taurus its influence is of even greater strength and importance than in most other cases. Immediate reactions to situations will be slow, but once an opinion is formed the individual will speak up with determination and authority, making opinions known in a few impressive sentences. Yet again the need for security is present, but it is an immediate reaction rather than an essential factor. Moon in Taurus could easily take calculated risks for instance, once having thought out the situation with care. Taurean possessiveness will be a very basic reaction when emotional security is challenged, and a tendency towards a rather old-fashioned outlook is characteristic, though—according to other prominent signs in the chart—the individual may well loathe such a reaction and do everything to fight it. This placing gives a lot of basic common sense and determination. Stubbornness may have to be negated, as with Sun- and Rising-sign Taureans, but again it will appear as a first reaction, or when the individual is young and hasn't yet learned that there are other, better ways in which to carve one's progress. This placing lays some excellent sound "foundations" to the personality, but any slowness of response may have to be countered.

Gemini

Sun-sign, Rising-sign, Moon-sign

Sun-sign period May 22 – June 21

A sign of short ascension in the northern hemisphere, and long ascension in the southern hemisphere

Gemini as Sun-sign
Perhaps the most dominant Geminian characteristic is versatility. Gemini will never only be involved in one specialist area of

one subject and will never get stuck in a rut. If of necessity he or she is forced into that position, they will suffer considerably not only from boredom—something which they come near to fearing—but more deeply psychologically, too. The ruling planet of Gemini, Mercury, gives them a powerful need to communicate at all levels and more often than not it will be Gemini who will speak up when something is wrong, will write to the newspapers or contribute to a "phone-in" on radio or television.

At a more personal level the need to communicate works well for Geminians because they have the ability to build up an excellent rapport with their partners, so that brooding and discontent are kept at a minimum. An air of activity surrounds most Geminians—they tend always to be in a hurry—illustrated by their very distinctive, springy, fast walk. It is absolutely vital that from an early age Geminians should be helped to develop consistency of effort, because there is a strong tendency to be always moving on to some new interest or project, leaving a trail of unfinished tasks. While in many cases a little knowledge of a great many subjects can be of advantage to Geminians, it is good for them to have some kind of structured framework in their interests, in order that superficiality does not mar real progress.

Basically, Gemini is rational and logical, and when their emotions surface they sometimes mistrust them. However, the position of Mercury should be considered here. Its influence on Gemini is not entirely intellectual—for this sign it has a personal and psychological significance. If the planet is in Taurus or Cancer a greater balance is achieved, while if in Gemini with the Sun the tendency will be to suppress or at least question the emotions and intuitions, which will be thought of as irrational and illogical.

The worst Geminian fault is superficiality, and if this can be mitigated by the development of deeper understanding and experience the individual will have much to offer.

Many Geminians carve successful careers in all branches of the media: they make excellent interviewers, and the breadth of their interests allows them plenty of scope for expression and satisfaction. Careers in telecommunications and the travel industry are rewarding and suitable, and Geminians also make superb salesmen and women. Advertising is another field in which this lively Zodiac type will find fulfilment and success. They are also excellent in argument and debate, and very often, for sheer pleasure, provoke what they call "discussion" which usually turns into quite a verbal battle, with Gemini swearing that he never ever changes his mind.

Gemini has very special needs in emotional relationships. Intellectual rapport and a high level of lively friendship is vital, and a partner who enjoys a varied sex-life which has scope for experiment. This Zodiac sign is flirtatious by nature, which makes Geminians great fun. They are usually fortunate enough to keep a youthful appearance, and on the whole tend to be slim, which puts them at a considerable advantage in many respects.

An ability to keep up-to-date with new developments and the younger generation makes Geminians splendid parents—no generation-gap problems here, indeed often the reverse is true and some children seem older than their Geminian parents. The Gemini child should be encouraged to develop consistency of effort but never told to do "one thing at a time"—they simply cannot function that way.

The Geminian body-area covers the shoulders, arms and

hands—which are accident-prone. The lungs too are Gemini ruled, so coughs should not be ignored. There is also an accent on the nervous system, and it is up to Gemini to find a satisfactory cut-out to counter tension and restlessness.

Gemini as Rising-sign

Someone with Gemini rising will find that the Geminian characteristics will marry in an interesting way with their Sun-sign characteristics. Should you, for instance, have Gemini rising but a "strong silent" Sun-sign such as Scorpio, there will be a very lively, talkative, perhaps adventurous person, with a liking for everything that is new and different inside you somewhere, "trying to get out". An individual with Gemini rising may be quieter in company than at home or with close friends. In many cases objectives will be clear cut, and there will be singleness of purpose matched with great versatility and variety of interest in any chosen field of study or career. Geminian duality will work in a rather different way, when Gemini rises. It is often the case that while this type is as versatile as someone with a Gemini Sun-sign, they can be more attracted to working through a great variety of projects in turn, rather than having many different jobs on the go at the same time. This is, in essence, a good thing for them, for restlessness can be a more deep-rooted problem than they may care to admit to, or accept.

When Gemini rises, the need for challenge and a tendency to enjoy taking risks can emerge, and the need for freedom of expression within a permanent relationship is something that must not be ignored, and indeed will have to be accepted by a partner.

Gemini as Moon-sign

Reactions to situations will be remarkably quick. Short, relevant answers to questions, witty responses and a straight-to-the-point directness will do much to put the Moon-in-Gemini type way out in front. But it will be left to other planetary placings to help him or her to get the most from this excellent initial advantage. Restlessness and the need for constant change might become a problem, and the instinctive response will in no way be an intuitive or emotional one. On the contrary it will spring straight from the most logical, intellectually orientated reasoning, and in a flash the individual will not only instantly grasp the situation, but be in a very strong position to use knowledge and experience, almost as if that in itself is instinctive rather than any deep-rooted intuition. A tendency to appear lacking in real interest and concern for other people is something that the Moon-in-Gemini type should be aware of and should watch. To do this they should make a conscious effort to get involved in other people's projects and to listen to what they have to say, thereby adopting a more caring and sensitive attitude. They probably have that already, in reality, but could easily give the impression that this is not so, lively and positive though their responses will be. Deep concentration will not come easily or naturally, and this too is something that may need conscious development, using other planetary influences and that of the individual's Rising-sign.

There may be some lack of real depth of feeling, though this may well be countered by other planets' placings. Moon in Gemini contributes a lot that is positive simply because it is such a rational and logical influence.

such an important part of their being. Cancerian tenacity is perhaps even stronger when the Moon is in this sign, and persistence of effort and strength of will will make themselves felt. But Moon-in-Cancer types are not usually stubborn, and because of the need to respond kindly and in a caring way, they will at once attempt to bring other characteristics into play to counter any seemingly harsh initial reactions. This is essentially a placing that augurs well for parenthood; but mothers who have these immensely powerful protective and caring instincts must make an effort not to become like clucking hens with their chicks. Sweeping and very quick changes of mood are often present.

If individuals feel that they are psychic or have a "sixth sense", they should not smother this instinct, but allow it to develop in its own way. Then, if so inclined, they should seek proper training to enable them to get the best from it. However, controlling a near torrent of emotion and not allowing small problems to get out of perspective is also extremely important to their physical and psychological well-being.

Leo

Sun-sign, Rising-sign, Moon-sign

Sun-sign period July 23 – August 23

A sign of long ascension in the northern hemisphere, and short ascension in the southern hemisphere

Leo as Sun-sign

Leo, the lion, the king of the jungle, must of necessity have his or her own individual kingdom—whether it is large or small. The ability of people with this Sun-sign to organize their own lives and the lives of others is paramount, as is their ability to lead. There is no doubt about it, a really flourishing Leo will make the most of this potential, sometimes stretching ability too far. There will be great satisfaction in inspiring others to make more of themselves, too, and in trying to impress upon them that the development of and concentration on talent is the best way to ensure a fulfilled and rewarding life. Leos get as much out of life as possible, and will always do things in as big a way as possible—spending more money than they should—sometimes simply to show off. When the individual is

21

truly developed and has gained more experience of life, money will be spent freely because he or she really appreciates quality. As for those Leos who are not well off, they will much prefer a coffee in a five-star hotel to a meal in a cheap bistro.

There is creative potential in all Leos, and the more it is expressed the better it is for them, psychologically. This does not necessarily mean that they will all be involved in the fine arts in some way, but that creativity, in the broadest sense of the word, must come into their personal scheme of things. They are ambitious—perhaps for a better lifestyle than one suggested by the mere accumulation of money; a good lifestyle, for them, need by no means cost a great deal, though Leo will probably have to achieve quite a good financial backing in order to cope with what he or she finally wants to do.

While magnanimous, Leos are often accused of bossiness—and not without reason. Inwardly they know that they are capable of organizing other people's lives far better than those others themselves, and find it quite difficult not to interfere. While there is a certain enjoyment in being "boss", it is also true to say that Leos will be willing slaves to someone whom they admire and respect. They need to be in a position of prominence themselves, however, if they are really to shine.

There is a natural sense of drama in every Sun-sign Leo, and they revel in it. They should not, however, just go in for making a fuss, creating scenes in public, but should use their dramatic sense to bring inspiration, light and colour into other people's lives. They should use this sense to set an example to those they come into contact with, and if they see that someone has improved their lifestyle, attitude, or any sphere of their life, then this will make Leo very happy, for every Leo believes that life is for the living, and to be enjoyed to the full. And they will work hard to achieve their ambitions, too, whether personal or career orientated.

Enthusiasm and a positive, fiery emotion are very much part of the Leo personality, and are expressed vividly in the attitude towards sex and emotional relationships. Leos can inspire their partners to greater achievement, and will do much to make marriage and permanent relationships work well, but must certainly be careful not to dominate their partners too determinedly. Their real strength lies in positive support and the continuing development of their own and their loved ones' individual interests.

Leos make lively enthusiastic parents, encouraging their children to keep busy both in and out of school. They tend to expect too much from them, and must be very careful indeed to allow them to develop along their own individual lines and not to overinfluence them, especially where the choice of career is concerned.

The Leo body-area is the back. Many Leos have long straight backs and walk very well, but do tend to suffer from backache from time to time. Leo also rules the heart, so the circulation should be watched—especially during cold weather, which most Leos do not like at all. It is quite common for Leos to have a real lion's mane of hair, and, also rather lion-like, they usually have small waists.

Leo as Rising-sign

The well-known British astrologer Margaret Hone (who had Leo rising) used to say that the only thing to do when Leo rises is to keep it down. There does seem to be quite an element of truth in this statement, for Leo rising can, at times, make the individual autocratic—a big fish in a small pond, and sometimes, too, someone who really will show off a great deal. But this usually happens when the person is unfulfilled or perhaps lacking in confidence. The true light of the individual Leo Sun is then not shining properly, and it really needs to if he or she is to function properly and fully, and to feel that life is at all worthwhile. This is also true of someone who has a Leo Sun-sign, but there self-expression seems to come alive rather more easily and readily; when Leo rises, a more complicated process must take place if the individual is to come to terms with his or her potential and personality.

In emotional relationships Leo rising needs a partner who is "different" in some way—someone who has achieved or will achieve something out of the ordinary, someone   whom the Leo rising personality considers really striking. S .netimes they expect too much from their partners, and will o.ten go through some traumatic experiences and maybe an above-average number of broken romances before finally coming to terms with this sphere of their lives.

Leo as Moon-sign
The immediate response of anyone with the Moon in Leo will be to take situations into their own hands, and to cope very well, becoming a good source of inspiration to others. This ability is really a very natural one, and one which cannot usually be quashed. Provided that there is conscious awareness that these extremely powerful responses and instincts should be controlled, those who have the Moon in this sign are capable of achieving a great deal. The taking of action, the immediate release of enthusiasm and emotion are really characteristic, because this placing causes others to "sit up and take notice". There is an above-average number of famous people with the Moon in Leo and most of them are capable, in one way or another, of swaying the masses. Because the immediate response to most situations can be likened to the lyric "Anything you can do, I can do better", the Moon-sign Leo gives the impression that he or she wants to come out on top, and indeed to "top" anybody else's actions or abilities. The bossiness of the sign at once emerges, hence this rather daunting reputation. A tendency to be autocratic and dogmatic must be controlled, as must the use of the big, sweeping statement (or indeed gesture), which other less self-assured and extravert people may find unpleasant, or at the least somewhat embarrassing. Moon-in-Leo people may well have to learn the hard way, for when they are young the need to "make the right impression" has tremendous appeal. In reality, the "right impression" may simply appear as big-headedness, and be quite the wrong impression, lacking humility. But the ability to cope in tricky situations and to do so with determination and immediacy is also a strong characteristic, and will no doubt be a considerable help.

Virgo

Sun-sign, Rising-sign, Moon-sign

Sun-sign period August 24–September 22

*A sign of long ascension in the northern hemisphere,
and short ascension in the southern hemisphere*

Virgo as Sun-sign

Of all 12 signs, Virgo is the busiest. Those who have it as their Sun- or Rising-sign will surround themselves with a great many tasks, so that their day is full of activity. It is very difficult indeed for them to relax totally—putting their feet up and doing nothing has no great appeal, so the best way for them to cut out is to move from work which is intellectually demanding to something that makes greater demands on their physical energy. Virgoan organizing ability is not very strong, and sometimes a fair amount of time and energy is wasted because they do not allow themselves enough time to get tasks sorted out or executed in an orderly way.

Here we have the critic of the Zodiac, and it is usual for Virgoans to work in a very analytical way on small details. They give marvellous support to "front" men and women, making excellent secretaries and personal assistants, and usually enjoying that kind of role rather than one which carries heavy responsibility. It is, alas, far too often the case that Virgoans are imposed upon. They have by nature a very strong sense of duty, and this can sometimes be carried to extremes, so that a young Virgoan woman will sacrifice her career to look after an ageing or sick mother, who will become more and more demanding of her and her time and energy.

If you want something done, ask a busy person to do it, or ask a Virgoan—the chances are that you will get a quick response, and full value. And how difficult it can be to try to repay any good turn that Virgoans do for us.

Because they have such a high level of nervous energy there is always a danger of tension getting the upper hand, and as a result many Virgoans suffer from bad headaches or migraine. While they are basically very logical and tremendously practical people, worry frequently gets the better of them. This will have a negative effect on their digestion (Virgo's body-areas are the stomach and bowels), and very often this symptom emerges before the individual actually realizes that he or she is overconcerned about some tricky problem. But there are marvellous ways in which this Zodiac type can counter worry, and it is by using their practical and analytical approach to life that they will best overcome it. When faced with problems, they should take pencil and paper and make careful notes of every aspect of the situation; this will help clarify in their minds what line of positive action will eventually be necessary.

Because Virgoans like to live active and busy lives, they enjoy filling their out-of-work hours with a great many hobbies and interests. If they are at all artistically inclined, craft-work using natural materials—wool, clay, wood and so on—is particularly rewarding. They often have green fingers, and love tending gardens and potted plants. To ward off tension, demanding physical exercise is excellent for them, with walking, cycling and jogging being especially beneficial.

Many Virgoans are attracted to vegetarianism, and even more enjoy wholefoods; they make good practitioners of fringe medicine, and are often enthusiastic about it. Just as Virgoans are discriminating and critical in other areas of life, so are they in personal relationships. They choose partners very carefully. There is a natural modesty about any Virgo in love: "He/she will never take any notice of me" tends to be the cry when Virgo is attracted to a new partner. They make good parents, and are especially keen to develop their children's intellects. Sometimes they tend to carp or nag their children (and their partners) a little too much, but usually only when they are tense or under strain caused by other problems. Virgoan children are popular at school, willing to help with small tasks which make the teacher's job easier.

Virgo as Rising-sign
The Mercurial need to communicate will be particularly important to people with Virgo rising, and although because of their Sun-sign they may not be especially talkative, once a good relationship has been established a pleasant liveliness will blossom. The practical, logical elements of Virgo are strong, but are only expressed after serious deliberation and constructive thought and always in relation to the characteristics of the Sun-sign. It is particularly good for this group to go in for a little self-analysis from time to time, because in turning these natural qualities towards the self, a great deal can be learned about basic motivation—far more than is usually the case when other signs are rising. There is a lovely, soft kindheartedness and a tender expression of emotion which will emerge in permanent relationships. This is due to the influence of the polar or opposite sign, Pisces, which has a strong bearing on partnership for those with Virgo rising. This is unique, and will bring out traits that the individual may not be aware of until he or she settles into a relationship. It is also totally private to the couple themselves.

Virgo as Moon-sign
The Moon works well from Virgo, since it intensifies the speed at which the individual reacts to all situations. That reaction is practical, helpful and extremely logical. This makes them sharp in debate and argument, and they will accept nothing as fact until they have crosschecked the source of the information or questioned whoever first made it. This placing often encourages an attraction to the medical or caring professions, because the need to help others is strong; but it can cool, or at least over-rationalize the emotions, and it is up to the individual to realize that this may be so, and to make quite sure that the process has no adverse effect on psychological development or well-being. This also makes for an extremely down-to-earth and sensible, reliable person, who will help anyone solve their difficulties but equally will not allow slacking or put up with lackadaisical behaviour.

As is the case with Sun- and Rising-sign Virgoans, there is often literary talent, and writing can become an important and rewarding occupation. There will also be a strong tendency to curb extravagance—a conflict indeed for those whose Sun- or Rising-signs veer towards luxury and expense. Remember, however, that the tendency will, as with all Moon characteristics, be the initial response. While worry will also be something to cope with, the Rising- and Sun-signs will in most cases help the individual to come to terms with that problem. Should they not get enough support from Sun- or Rising-signs, it will be as well for them to follow the advice given under the Sun-sign heading.

Libra

Sun-sign, Rising-sign, Moon-sign

Sun-sign period September 23 – October 23

A sign of long ascension in the northern hemisphere, and short ascension in the southern hemisphere

Libra as Sun-sign

Perhaps more than with any of the other signs of the Zodiac, the symbol for this sign, Libra—the balance—sums up very accurately the basic motivation and needs of the individual who has it emphasized in his or her birth-chart. Balance and harmony are crucial if Libra is going to function at all well, and it is the vital factor if they are going to live a fulfilled and satisfying life. Librans are not loners. They need to relate to other people in a well above average way and in all spheres of their lives, most importantly of course with a permanent partner. They have a great deal of love and affection to give to their lovers and it is only when a stable relationship is cemented that Librans become psychologically whole and function to the full. Sometimes, however, this need is so great that they will commit themselves prematurely, and as a result suffer very considerably when things go wrong.

A peaceful existence is also an important priority and the theme of "anything for a quiet life" is a recurring one. Interestingly, however, Librans need a great deal of reassurance that they are being loved, and it is not uncommon for them to go in for "rocking the boat" tactics to get that particular reassurance. They will sometimes aggravate their partners and provoke a row—because it is so nice when they make up afterwards. They may not care to admit that this happens, but it does and it is all part of Libra's interesting but not uncomplicated set-up. But it is keeping the peace that they care most about, and this leads us to consider the possibility of their inherent indecisiveness. "Wait and see" is a constant cry. They will not commit themselves, and if the possible outcome of a firm decision might be marginally unpleasant or—even more importantly—unpopular with their partners, then the chances are that they will simply wait until the situation does not exist any more. It seems that the reason for this is that they do not want to upset their partners, and the whole thing is rooted in their inherent need for harmony. But Libra has great charm, and can achieve a great deal "all in good time". They are not to be rushed but are seldom late. Some astrologers consider them lazy but I have not found this to be so.

Librans make easy-going parents, but will often pass the buck. A Libran mother will say "See what Daddy says, dear" rather than come up with a straight answer, which can be more than annoying to anxious, enthusiastic children. Libran children will break down even the toughest adult defences and will wind the strictest teachers round their little fingers.

Libra rules the kidneys, and those strongly influenced by this sign could be prone to slight kidney disorders. If they suffer from headaches this could be the cause. But their well-balanced lives—and the balance is so important to them—will usually ensure that they keep healthy.

When it comes to choosing careers, Librans do well as agents or in any role in which they have to negotiate between two people or groups of people. They should aim always to work in partnership, and could do splendidly in the diplomatic corps.

Spare-time interests most likely to appeal are those aligned to beauty, and which have in a sense a relaxing air to them. Music is often important; many Librans make excellent accompanists, for instance. Dress-making and all kinds of sewing are rewarding, while golf and bridge also come high on the list. Social dancing and tennis are also popular.

Libra as Rising-sign

The need for a good, rewarding and permanent relationship is paramount when Libra rises and achieving this becomes an important part of the Libran's psychological motivation. But the need to express affection in an outward and immediate way is less in evidence. Decisiveness—or lack of it—will be modified by the Sun- and Moon-signs, so that someone who has a powerful, rational or very practical Sun-sign will be in a good position to bring those qualities into play at times of decision-making, though it may well be that the individual, once having made up his or her mind, will often have second thoughts. There is a natural kindness and sympathy when Libra rises, but this does not necessarily weaken the individual. However, one interesting and unique factor is worth consideration. Between 1941 and 1957 Neptune made a long, slow journey through Libra. Those born with Libra rising at that time will have this planet very powerfully placed in their individual charts, so due attention must be given to it when assessing the characteristics of their Rising-sign. It could encourage them to take the line of least resistance, or if it works well then these individuals will have considerable resources of inspiration and intuition to draw on. This factor is much stronger when Libra rises, than for those with Libra as their Sun-sign.

There is an additional influence which works in relation to partnerships, when Libra rises. This centres on the Libran polar sign, Aries. There will be a forthright enthusiasm for and energetic and particularly lively attitude towards sex, a keenness to make a go of permanent relationships, and a terrific will to work hard for and with the partner. The fire of Aries will sparkle indeed, and will be a delightful surprise to the subject and his or her partner once the relationship has got off the ground. Resentfulness is less likely to be a problem too.

Libra as Moon-sign
The immediate response could well appear to be lackadaisical. There will be no rushing into sudden action, and the appearance of calm will be notable. People with the Moon in Libra are excellent in a crisis, since they do not panic; they will wait calmly until told what to do, then take action. They can also under such circumstances calm others who are scared or nervous. There is in such cases an element of bravery when the Moon is in Libra—again something which probably relates to the Aries polar sign—and it is useful. Kindness and a sympathetic response are also paramount: here is a good listener, someone who will at once try to make life easier for other people, a peacemaker at a moment's notice. This is the right person to calm two warring factors and to do a great deal indeed to ease any kind of strain. But the most dominant factor is the air of peace that surrounds them. Maybe even more than a Sun-sign Libra, those with the Moon in that sign will speak in rather a drawling fashion and steer a right-down-the-middle course in argument and debate.

Scorpio

Sun-sign, Rising-sign, Moon-sign

Sun-sign period October 24 – November 22

A sign of long ascension in the northern hemisphere, and short ascension in the southern hemisphere

Scorpio as Sun-sign
This, the eighth sign of the Zodiac, is the strongest, offering the greatest resources of both emotional and physical energy. Those born with Scorpio prominently placed in their birthchart must find ways of using these resources positively and in a fulfilling way. This is best achieved by expression in a career.

No mere "job" is good enough for a high-powered Scorpio—they should spend their working hours doing something they consider worthwhile as well as engrossing. It does not matter whether this calls for some highly developed skill or extended study, as long as it is meaningful to the individual. When it is, then all is well, and energy will be directly channelled through this vital involvement. It is to be remembered, then, that Scorpios are capable of a great deal, and the more they have to do the better it is for them. The worst thing possible for them is when their abundant resources stagnate; then, a lot can go wrong—they will be bored, and waste their talents; worse still, Scorpio faults of jealousy and to a certain extent envy—usually of those who are making the grade—will emerge.

Scorpio emotional intensity is terrific and this, too, needs positive direction and expression through a rewarding sex-life. However, the sexy element of this sign is often somewhat overstressed. It is vitally important to most Scorpios and probably in an above-average way, but there are many other ways in which their energy can be directed, and as I have hinted it is very often through the achievement of daunting objectives. It is also true that this drive and determination can sometimes become obsessive, and it is important that the individual realizes that he or she may tend to become too involved. If this happens, other factors in life may be neglected, which might eventually lead to a kind of imbalance which is not healthy either physically or psychologically. However, this in itself is probably preferable to the reverse situation—inactivity caused by unemployment or some other reason not directly connected with the Scorpio himself. Restlessness, stagnation and discontent are the greater evils.

Scorpios are the natural detectives of the Zodiac. They make superb researchers, working scientifically or in libraries. Many engineers are Scorpios, as are prominent members of the armed services. The wine and oil trades are also attractive to Scorpios. From a purely physical point of view this Zodiac type needs a lot of exercise, and many will enjoy demanding sports. Boxing, the martial arts in general, diving and underwater swimming are all rewarding and popular.

The Scorpio body-area is the genitals, and it may well be this connection that has given Scorpio the sexiest image of all the 12 signs. There is a vulnerability to throat infections due to the influence of the Scorpio polar sign, Taurus. Scorpios make demanding but exciting partners. They have a great love of life and never do things by half. They need partners with a similar attitude to life. Although many are of a wiry build, more tend to put on weight, usually due to good living, and this is something that needs conscious controlling. Alas, Scorpios do not find it easy to cut down—in any way. Scorpios want their children to be as energetic and as fulfilled as they are themselves and will be demanding but inspiring parents. If the Scorpio child is the eldest, great care must be taken and attention paid so that when a younger brother or sister is born there is no cause for jealousy—the worst Scorpio fault. But the children of this sign will achieve a great deal once they have become dedicated to some specific interest or subject, and such interests must be allowed to blossom.

Scorpio as Rising-sign
When Scorpio rises, drive, energy and dedication are still very much present and energy resources will give terrific force to the individual's mode of expression, whatever that might be.

Someone with, for example, a Leo Sun-sign and Scorpio rising will express their creativity with force and energy. Someone with a Gemini Sun might well become an investigative journalist. Scorpio, then, will provide the all-important backup, and the need to be emotionally involved with the chosen profession will be strengthened. The intensity of Scorpio will be present, while Scorpio rising may not necessarily show it. It will do a great deal to help strengthen powers of concentration. No matter what Sun-sign this person may have, the Scorpio characteristics will perhaps tend to overlay other characteristics, rather than to work at the deepest level of the personality. This is partly due to the very nature of the sign itself. These characteristics might show in the person's eyes—which would be penetrating—although he or she may well fight hard not to give the appearance of "looking right through people", which they are almost bound to do.

Someone with Scorpio rising will be an even more demanding partner than those with a Scorpio Sun-sign. Passion and intensity of feeling will almost pour out, and those on the receiving end will need considerable inner strength if they are going to get as much out of the relationship as Scorpio rising hopes they will. It is important for their joint well-being that each partner plays a part in building up a good rapport. It is only in this way that the energetic, demanding but exciting qualities of Scorpio rising will be positively expressed, recognized and reciprocated.

When Scorpio rises possessiveness towards the partner is something which needs to be controlled, otherwise jealous scenes are likely to occur. The sooner the individual realizes that jealousy is a negative emotion the better.

Scorpio as Moon-sign
Sudden outbursts of emotion and the expression of powerful feelings occur when the Moon is in Scorpio. Certainly this creates an immediate impression but it is one that can be very different indeed from the real person, who may have another set of characteristics totally different to the intensity and strength of Scorpio. Nevertheless such people will achieve a great deal, and if making others sit up and take notice has anything to do with it they score very high indeed. Here we have people of action who will respond with all their strength and energy. They can also inspire others to take action and get things moving, but they will do this by degrees in many circumstances, gradually adding the weight of their opinions and taking time to influence others or to get the better of opponents. Emotions will be powerful, and those close to them will soon learn when and under what kind of circumstances they will surface. Any situation which might provoke jealousy will certainly provide an opportunity for an emotional outburst. However, if these powerful sources of energy are controlled and positively directed, here is real inner strength indeed.

Sagittarius

Sun-sign, Rising-sign, Moon-sign

Sun-sign period November 23 – December 21

*A sign of long ascension in the northern hemisphere,
and short ascension in the southern hemisphere*

Sagittarius as Sun-sign

Challenge and a need to feel free to express themselves in their own individual way are the two most important requisites for those who have this sign emphasized in their birth-charts. They cannot function satisfactorily without either. Put a lively Sagittarian in a situation where he or she has work that is repetitive or makes no demands on them and they will crumble. But many, of course, have to cope with such dreary circumstances, and then it is important that they should work out ways to divert their attention from what is basically an unrewarding set-up. Usually Sagittarius is resilient enough to find interesting alternatives, and it is vital that they do so, otherwise the psychological suffering they will have to endure will be nearly intolerable.

Sagittarius is a Fire sign, and this element makes its presence felt through a high level of enthusiasm for life and individual interests. To this it is possible to add that Sagittarians are keen to enjoy all aspects of life in a very positive way, and as they do so they will also inspire others to get as much out of life and their abilities as they do themselves. But challenge must be there; if it is not then Sagittarians must create it by presenting ideas to those who matter, and by showing others precisely what they are made of. It is important though that in the pursuit of many varied and diverse interests they do not lose out on the full development of what they can do best. It is also a good thing for those of this sign to express their versatility in a controlled way—by doing many different things, but making quite sure that one project is completed before another is started, so that when a year's work is assessed there will be a feeling that a great deal has been achieved in a variety of fields.

A lot is said about sport and the Sagittarian. I tend to think this is overstressed, having found no greater number of sportspeople born under this sign than any other. They do most certainly need exercise, and often enjoy it more than many Zodiac types, and it is true that a young Sagittarian will be "coltish"; hopefully, however, as time passes they will develop fine, somewhat philosophically orientated qualities which will be a source of inspiration to others. Restlessness is a major fault, but can be overcome once the individual has sorted out his or her real objectives and decided that the grass is not always greener on the other side of the hedge.

There is plenty of scope where careers are concerned. The intellectual Sagittarian will enjoy publishing or may work well in the fields of higher education, and working abroad often appeals, since many of this sign have a fine flair for languages. The veterinary profession can also be rewarding. Tradition suggests that the Law and the Church are quintessentially Sagittarian.

Claustrophobic conditions of any kind cannot be tolerated by this Zodiac group, especially when it comes to emotional relationships, chiefly because of their need for freedom of expression. Obviously if they want a meaningful relationship to last they have to compromise to a certain extent, but it is important that they are not constrained by a partner who is jealous, or does not fully understand the way they function. Rather less importantly, Sagittarians hate a room with no view—it makes them feel closed in. Their sense of fun is infectious and their positive, extravert enthusiasm second to none. This is the sign of the hunter, but that does not mean that they enjoy the pursuit of wild animals; interestingly they do enjoy hunting for bargains in junk shops.

Sagittarians make exhilarating partners in spite of their need for freedom, and will always encourage their lovers to develop their individual interests. They need an energetic, lively sex-life and will get very bored indeed with a partner who has no sense of fun or who is too pessimistic in outlook. If they keep busy and active they are usually very healthy, but the hips and thighs—the Sagittarian body-areas—are vulnerable, and it is here that most Sagittarians (Sun- and Rising-sign types) put on weight very easily. The liver is also Sagittarian ruled, hence slight "liverishness" and hangovers can be a problem.

Sagittarians also make extremely lively and somewhat demanding parents—no bad thing, as they will certainly get a great deal out of their children because of their ability to encourage them in just the right way. Children of this sign must be given a lot of positive encouragement, but may need controlling in a gentle but firm way so that their exuberance does not become too overwhelmingly boisterous.

Sagittarius as Rising-sign
Many Sagittarian qualities complement and enhance the characteristics of the individual's Sun-sign. They will, for instance, counter the somewhat heavier, practical side of the Earth signs, and give a longer-lasting enthusiasm and strength of will to those who have an Air Sun-sign. Those who have Aries or Leo as their Sun-signs fare particularly well, since here we have a sympathy which is automatically present when two Fire signs come together, and provided there is enough to "anchor" the personality there should be little reason for serious conflict.

But as always the tendency to spread time and energy over too wide a field must be controlled. Care should be taken, too, that the inherent need for freedom does not get out of hand. Love of challenge, which may not be taken up immediately but which will after due consideration be met with excitement and even joy, is very common, and it's as necessary for those with Sagittarius rising to have to stretch themselves intellectually and often physically—through making their bodies function well, and keeping fit—as it is for someone with a Sagittarian Sun-sign.

Basically, then, there is usually good potential when Sagittarius rises, and a keenness constantly to move forward in all spheres of life. If the individual feels thwarted, he or she has the ability to work out precisely why, and determination and the expenditure of excellent resources of emotion and energy will stand them in good stead.

The attitude towards partners and relationships is a lively, rather light one. Sagittarius rising will not allow themselves to be constrained by marriage or family commitments, and young mothers who have this placing must be sure to set aside some time for interests totally unconnected with the children.

Sagittarius as Moon-sign
There will be a quick, enthusiastic response to all situations; here is someone who will never "beat about the bush", and will come up with a ready and understandable answer. If suggestions are needed the chances are that they will be practical and sensible, and backed up by wisdom. There are considerable resources of emotion, but the way in which these will be channelled will be very much related to other dominating factors of the chart, and to how the planets work for the individual concerned. Hopefully these resources will flourish and help the Moon-in-Sagittarius type to flourish too; but if that is not the case, astrology could be of enormous help to the person concerned, since he or she may be able to use other strengths and areas of their personalities to achieve a more positive expression. A lot will depend on how other people react to them; youngsters in this group who come up with some lively imaginative scheme which is either ignored or overcriticized by parents will feel deflated. As a result when grown up they may well display a tendency to express an extremely off-hand manner—"see if I care" or "so what, what does it matter anyway"—a clear signal that Moon in Sagittarius is not responding well to present situations, and is also far from fully integrated into the personality as a whole. But here too is splendid potential, and the will to make much of what talent is present.

Capricorn

Sun-sign, Rising-sign, Moon-sign

Sun-sign period December 22–January 20

A sign of long ascension in the northern hemisphere, and short ascension in the southern hemisphere

Capricorn as Sun-sign
Capricorn is the sign of the Goat. Here we have someone who is sure-footed and negotiates every obstacle with care but with

a lively step. Only getting to the top will do, and a great deal of determination will be present in the character to help Capricorns every step of the way. But people with this Sun-sign will not stride upwards without reflection; we must not forget that here is an Earth sign, and the influence of that element is ever-present. Every decision will be carefully taken, every challenge and opportunity carefully assessed, so that risks are minimal. The free-ranging mountain goat will then be able to use every bit of potential to the full, and feel that life is worth living.

But what of the other half of Capricorn? Remember that the creature of the sign is only half goat. It has a fish's tail. Is this the "wet fish" side of Capricorn? Or the poor domestic goat, forever tethered to a post in the valley, and in no position to scale the mountain top? Both, I think, for in essence they are similar. A negative, hopeless attitude can make its presence felt with those of this sign. Many feel that they will never "get on" in life because there is so much against them. When this is the case, their friends and lovers must do their best to reasssure them. As I have said, there are two distinct types of Capricorn. Our lively "giddy" mountain goat, and our "wet fish", or if you prefer it, our "domestic animal". Basically it is not difficult to decide which category our Capricorn friends fall into, but what is interesting is the fact that they will from time to time reverse their roles, so that unexpectedly we will find the lively, positive, aspiring mountain goat making its presence felt in someone who tends in general to be negative in outlook, and we can get more than the odd grumble and moan from our sure-footed, ambitious Capricorn friends.

One of this sign's most endearing qualities is its off-beat sense of humour. We find the most dour, serious-minded Capricorn suddenly making the most unusual and witty remark—natural to them and a delight to others. Very often at such times they themselves will smile a grimacing kind of smile—the corners of their mouths turned down rather than up—an instantly recognizable characteristic.

It is often the case that those born under this sign do not have a ready gushing flow of emotion. There is a tendency to coolness in love, for instance, and enthusiasm for new ideas may be somewhat muted by their typical matter-of-fact attitude. However, once committed in love they have tremendous loyalty, and while most young Capricorns will to a certain extent "play the field", on a more serious level they are usually discriminating. They have on the whole very good powers of concentration, and long arduous study will pay off. Short cuts do not. There is, too, a considerable sense of pride, and their inherent ambition will encourage them to aspire to move up the social scale. A desire to impress other people is also characteristic.

The Capricorn body-areas are the knees and shins; these are vulnerable, as are the teeth, skin and bones. Capricorns make good athletes, and long-distance running and rock-climbing are sports that could well appeal. Individual effort can be more fulfilling than participation in team games; Capricorns do well on their own and can cope with loneliness far better than many Zodiac types.

Capricorn parents are eager for their children's progress and so will make considerable demands on them. Sometimes they can become somewhat remote from their children; they are very keen to carve a better life for them than they themselves had, and as a result they may become preoccupied with their own careers and have less fun with their children than they might. Parents of Capricorn children should help them to develop warmth and sensitivity.

Capricorn as Rising-sign

Capricorn rising gives considerable stability, and practical common sense second to none. According to the Sun-sign, however, there is often conflict between the positive expression of emotion and its suppression. If other planets' placings indicate a high emotional intensity it is up to the individual to learn to channel and control it, using Capricornian elements, and not simply to stop its flow at source, otherwise there will be quite serious complications. But here is someone who will almost inevitably be in a superb position to shape his or her life and to plan it in an extremely careful and practical way, so that self-expression, through the utilization of potential from the individual's Sun-sign, will really blossom.

Capricorn rising must not underestimate himself. This can all too often occur and it is usually due to lack of self-confidence, or to genuine shyness, which can be somewhat style-cramping. Anyone with Capricorn rising should develop an interest in music. If they are creative this might well be their individual art form, for in many latitudes when Capricorn rises the sign Taurus is "on the Midheaven" (see page 223), and both these signs have affinity with music. (Sculpture and architecture may also be of interest.)

In emotional relationships, Capricorn rising will develop an extremely tender, sensitive and caring quality once committed to a long-term emotional relationship, picking up here the influence of its polar or opposite sign in the Zodiac, Cancer. Thus the loyalty of Capricorn is enhanced, and the emotional level increased in the best possible way.

Capricorn as Moon-sign

Those with the Moon in Capricorn will react to situations and people very coolly and calmly indeed, perhaps to the point where an element of remoteness surrounds them. But in addition they will want to come out on top, and may at times have a tendency to look down their noses at other people's suggestions. Here, however, the Capricornian off-beat sense of humour will assert itself, with a shrewd degree of truth and an amusing turn of phrase. But there will also be the Capricorn tendency to grumble about anything that goes unexpectedly wrong: the lateness of the bus, the lack of certain items in the supermarket, and so on. Then, having had their moan, Moon in Capricorn will give way to their Sun- and Rising-sign characteristics, and will probably hate themselves for their instant, impatient reaction. It is important for those with this placing to understand fully all the characteristics of Capricorn, and to discover just how these work for them on the instinctive level. Because so many are strong and powerful they can get a great deal that is really practical and helpful from their Moon-sign, since here, as in the case when Capricorn rises, is a good foundation to the personality. Their immediate reaction, for instance, will be an ambitious one. They will want to think and plan big. Let them go on from there. But if Moon in Capricorn is making them fearful and apprehensive when someone puts an idea to them, then they should consciously try to overcome their lack of self-confidence, and to help them do so they must really convince themselves of the truth—that they have many fine, aspiring qualities.

Aquarius

Sun-sign, Rising-sign, Moon-sign

Sun-sign period January 21 – February 18

*A sign of short ascension in the northern hemisphere,
and long ascension in the southern hemisphere*

Aquarius as Sun-sign

Aquarius is the individualist of the Zodiac. Show two people
with this sign prominent in their birth-charts a list of characteristics of the sign, and the only thing they will agree on is the
fact that they share none of them. This sign bestows a great
need for independence, which very often emerges in the
building of a rather special and somewhat different lifestyle.
Here, too, are some of the kindest, most helpful and friendly
people of the Zodiac. They have a happy knack of knowing
when help is needed and will give it freely without ulterior
motives. However, although we may know them extremely
well, if we think seriously about it they are in many ways
extremely private people. This could well be because of their
need to be independent, and while having the capacity to give
much of themselves to others they do not want to get too
emotionally involved or find themselves in a situation which is
at all cloying or heavy.

Unfortunately it is often the case that a great many people
with this sign stressed in their birth-charts have considerable
psychological difficulty in relating intensely and in depth to
other people. The reason for this is very complex, and does of
course vary considerably from individual to individual, but
basically it may well come back to the very powerful inherent
need for independence. To live with someone or to marry them
must of necessity mean that considerable independence is
relinquished, and when it comes to a total commitment many
Aquarians do not feel they can make what to them is a
considerable sacrifice. But let it be stressed that there are
obviously a great many who have Aquarius as Sun-, Rising-, or
Moon-sign yet are settled and fulfilled in their permanent
relationship. These will understand my comments, but other
planets will have given them support where it is most needed,
and the problem has been solved.

Aquarians have great originality and real flair, which can be
used in a variety of fields, and should be allowed full expression. They often do well in the so-called glamour
professions—theatre, television, the beauty trades, or any-
where where their originality can be expressed freely and
rewardingly. Many carve successful careers in science, and
interestingly it is very often the case that Aquarians are
fascinated by the remote past and the equally remote and

distant future—archaeology and geology at one end of the scale and space fact and fiction at the other. This too can colour the choice of spare-time interests.

Aquarians make excellent forward-looking parents, and will sympathize with their children when they become involved with the concerns and crazes of their generation. But, surprisingly, Aquarians can be very stubborn and extremely unpredictable, and it is their children, as much as their friends and partners, who will become aware of these particular, and to all intents and purposes somewhat unexpected, traits. Parents of Aquarian children must respect their tremendous need for independence, and learn to accept it and the fact that while they may appear somewhat zany there is probably more common sense in their personalities than may appear on the surface. Interests that are way out or wild must not be discouraged—here is young Aquarius expressing his or her originality.

The Aquarian body-area is the ankles. These are vulnerable. The circulation is also ruled by Aquarius, and it is necessary to keep it moving well. Skiing is often enjoyed, and is good exercise. Dance, aerobics and athletics are all excellent.

Aquarius as Rising-sign
The inherent need for independence and the Aquarius flair and originality will be present but may not be immediately apparent, so that as far as general impressions are concerned the qualities that make the Sun-sign Aquarian "different" and individual may not strike those who only know people with Aquarius rising, and only know them somewhat superficially. There is less likely to be the unpredictability that occurs when Aquarius is the Sun-sign. There can also be a tendency to be dogmatic, and a dislike of admitting that one is wrong. But liveliness will not be lacking, and there will be a great willingness to try new and interesting things. There will also be a sympathy with the younger generation and much less huffy disapproval than is often the case when other signs rise. Organizational abilities will be very good, and the powerful humanitarian qualities of Aquarius will emerge, especially when others need help. Here is someone who will take over and cope extremely well under difficult conditions.

Reactions to emotional relationships are particularly interesting. This is anyway a somewhat complex area for the Aquarius type, but it takes on interesting and different dimensions when Aquarius rises, because of the influence of the polar or opposite sign, Leo. Here we have someone who at best will give terrific encouragement and support to their partners, while at the same time making sure there is time for them to continue to develop their own individual interests. But here too is a tendency to be bossy, and to "take over" rather than share. Care is needed that this possibly negative trait is controlled. When Aquarius is rising the emotional and sex-life should be extremely rewarding and fulfilling, though we must not forget that this too needs to be spiced with plenty of variety and originality, as is the case with the Sun-sign Aquarian, whether he or she is independent or committed to a permanent relationship.

Aquarius as Moon-sign
Here the Moon shines with a clear brilliance, as on a frosty winter's night. There is real glamour and dynamic power of attraction, and those coming into contact with a Moon-in-Aquarius type will at once get the impression of someone who

is different in some way that they probably cannot quite pin down. This gives such people an intriguing appeal. The expression of emotion is filtered, in the first instance, and it may take quite a while, according to the sort of situation being encountered, for the full expression of the individual's Sun-sign to emerge. The immediate response will be quick, certainly, and there will be absolutely no lack of kindness and help (given very freely if it is needed). Likewise, Moon in Aquarius will also be moved by human suffering, and will do everything possible to help eliminate it; the true Aquarian spirit will emerge here just as much as when Aquarius is the Sun- or Rising-sign.

The unpredictability of the sign will make its presence felt in the need to take immediate action, so we must be ready for the unexpected from those with this placing, especially at times of decision-making. With experience it will work well for them, but they may have had to learn from a whole cluster of stupid mistakes along the way. There is no doubt that the Moon in Aquarius gives some splendid potential, and as back-up for the development of talent instilled by the Sun- and Rising-signs, it is excellent. This is because of the unique originality which is so much a part of the whole Aquarian principle.

Warmth, passion, and the expression of true feelings will have to be taken care of by other planets. They are not, on the whole, strong features of the Moon in Aquarius; though those of this sign can be surprisingly romantic and sentimental in an interesting way when they let their hair down.

Pisces

Sun-sign, Rising-sign, Moon-sign

Sun-sign period February 19–March 20

A sign of short ascension in the northern hemisphere, and long ascension in the southern hemisphere

Pisces as Sun-sign
Pisces is the poet of the Zodiac. With signs of the Water element emotion is plentifully expressed at a moment's notice: the dilating pupils of the Piscean eyes will at once tell us when the individual is moved. Pisces is, of course, the sign of the fishes. But look at the symbol—two fishes swimming in oppo-

site directions, with a cord in their mouths connecting them. This sums up Pisces beautifully, for along with Gemini and Sagittarius this is the third of the "dual" signs of the Zodiac, giving the usual versatility, but also in this case a tendency to oppose the self. Though Pisceans know what they want to do, for reasons best known or possibly unknown to themselves, they often tend to take a totally different line of action, and in doing so can cause chaos and confusion for themselves. This kind of action seems a psychological necessity for many Pisceans, and it may have its roots in their highly developed sensitivity to other people's feelings, for they put their own feelings very low on their list of priorities. This can certainly make life extremely complicated. But there are other reasons, too, for in their Piscean confusion they often deceive themselves (tending to drift up on to cloud nine) and will also tell the odd white lie to get themselves out of any mildly tricky situation. However, it does not end there for they then have to go in for ever-increasing cover-ups, and all too soon the situation has got out of hand and Pisces is in dead trouble—either at work, or with their parents or lovers. It is hard for them to learn that this is not the way to a truly rewarding and fulfilling life; but once they realize this crucial fact they develop in a very positive and rewarding way.

Here we have the kindest and most charitable of all the signs. Pisceans will make many sacrifices for other people, a trait they share with their polar or opposite sign, Virgo. Sometimes this tendency will get out of hand, and the marvellous potential present in most Pisceans is frittered away or comes to nothing because Pisces is otherwise occupied. But it might just be that Pisces will divert time and energy in some "sacrificial" way because of an inherent lack of self-confidence. If they are busy caring for others or fulfilling a supportive role, then they do not have to fight to keep up with opponents in their field or cope with the rat race. Opting out, they find that a cloistered life gives them a sense of security, and this in a subtle way is a modern expression of the religious aspects of this sign, the "monk-like" or "nun-like" aspirations of the past, in essence very Piscean. They do particularly well in the caring or medical professions.

But what of the Pisces poet? Of course not all Pisceans go dreamily around with notebook in hand composing verses, though when they do, they do it very well. There is, however, creative ability in most Pisceans. It needs tremendous support and encouragement from partners, as do all practical aspects of their lives. When this is available, their talent emerges strongly. They make excellent dancers and ice-skaters and enjoy swimming, and all these activities are physically good for them. But above all it is involvement in the fine arts that is particularly satisfying on all levels.

Pisceans make excellent, warm lovers and their abundant emotion is expressed well and positively in this sphere of their lives. They should be careful not to allow their feelings to get out of perspective or their ample imaginations to run away with them. They need a sound, sensible but sensitive partner. They tend as parents to be too kind, and may perhaps let their children get away with "murder". This is something their partners should look out for, and if necessary intervene if children seem to be getting out of hand.

The Pisces body-area is the feet, Pisceans either have marvellously neat ones, and no trouble, or are in constant difficulty. Shoes will either be a perennial problem or a continual source of delight. There is a tendency to worry, which may cause stomach upsets. When troubled in this way, Pisceans should fall back on their ample intuition and natural instincts.

Pisces as Rising-sign

When Pisces rises, there seems to be no question that the characteristics of the sign will work at the deepest level of the personality. Here, perhaps more than in any other case, the Sun-sign will dominate, but underlying that particular set of characteristics will be the sensitivity and emotion, and every other quality that is quintessentially Piscean, working both positively and negatively. Those who get to know well someone with Pisces rising will develop their astrological technique considerably, because of the very clear-cut way in which the two elements of the chart emerge in this particular combination, irrespective of the Sun-sign. But Pisces rising does not make for a wishy-washy kind of person, for there is a powerfully critical edge which will chiefly surface in the individual's reaction to a partner, and will hardly ever be expressed to colleagues or friends. They do not suffer fools gladly, even if they seem to when in argument or in direct personal contact. Their critical attitudes and complaints about other people's stupidity will emerge in conversation with the wife or husband at the end of the day, and encouragement will have to be given them to take defensive action as and where necessary. This placing will take the harsh edge off most Sun-sign types and add a delightful gentle quality; but Piscean faults must be recognized and countered.

Pisces as Moon-sign

Because the Moon has a powerful effect on our emotions and intuitions, and because Pisces is a sign denoting a high level of both, the sign and the planet complement each other very well. Anyone with Pisces as Moon-sign will have a high level of emotion and intuition, and both qualities will surface readily, especially when the individual comes into contact with suffering, cruelty or poor living conditions. He or she will want to help, but to do so in a constructive and practical way will need to call upon the characteristics of the Sun- and Rising-sign. Yet again the Moon can be seen to be the source of immediate response. When Pisces is the Moon-sign the tendency to deceive—to take the easy way out of difficult situations—will be a constant temptation. The quick answer which is not precisely true, or a total untruth in some small, insignificant circumstance will be easiest, or so Moon in Pisces will think. This is a "Moon fault" other levels of the personality will probably dislike. Conscious awareness of it is the way to grow out of it, as is of course the knowledge that it can lead to endless confusion in the long run—but that has to be learned the hard way. The imagination should be recognized and used creatively in some way, and the individual will then get a great deal that is truly positive from it.

THE INNER
PLANETS

The Mercury and Venus factors

*Before reading, turn to the tables
on pages 238–245 to discover which
signs Mercury and Venus occupied
when you were born*

Because Mercury and Venus have their orbits nearer the Sun than the Earth, their positions in the Zodiac are always in the signs near that of the Sun. Each sign is divided into 30 degrees, and Mercury can only be 28° either side of the Sun, as seen from the Earth, while Venus must be within 48°.

If, for instance, your Sun-sign is Gemini, you can only have Mercury in Taurus, Gemini (with the Sun) or Cancer. Venus can only be in Aries, Taurus, Gemini (with the Sun), Cancer or Leo. If your Sun-sign is Aries, Mercury can only be in Pisces, Aries (with the Sun) or Taurus, while Venus can only be in Aquarius, Pisces, Aries (with the Sun), Taurus or Gemini.

The influence of Mercury and Venus is also strongly relevant to the question of people "born on the cusp", that is, on the borderline between two Sun-signs. There is a variety of opinion about this factor among astrologers, but I think that people who claim to have, for instance, a "Libran influence" in their birth-charts, because the Sun was just in Scorpio at the time of their birth, are actually interpreting the position of Mercury and/or Venus, for while they really are Sun-sign Scorpios, they may well think in the manner of Libra (because Mercury was in that sign), or love in a Libran way (if Venus was in Libra). I believe that the first few degrees of a sign (ie, those days early in a Sun-sign period) endow by far the strongest characteristics of that sign, and people are *never* a mixture of one sign and another as far as the Sun is concerned.

The Mercury factor

Mercury in Aries
This is a positive and progressive placing for Mercury. It will help the individual considerably at times of decision-making, and will colour the mental attitude, encouraging a forthright, uncomplicated approach to all problems—other people may even get the impression that there are no problems to be solved. Little attention is paid to detail, and those with this placing should rely on others to cope with tidying up and finalizing overall plans. Here is someone who is provocative and lively in argument, but can become rather too easily annoyed. While quick decisions are usually right, the tendency to impulsiveness and a lack of patience with other slower-thinking people must be countered. When Aries is the Sun-sign, the impulsiveness and quick decisiveness of Mercury is enhanced, and the thinking processes will work like lightning. When Pisces is the Sun-sign, Mercury will counter the tendency to dither at times of decision-making, will help the individual to a positive outlook and give them greater self-assurance and confidence. When the Sun-sign is Taurus, we get someone who is assertive, punchy in argument and always ready with a straight-to-the-point answer. Mercury will help mitigate the general slowness of response in most of this Zodiac group.

Mercury in Taurus
While this is a good steadying placing for Mercury, it will help the individual to think carefully and c...
times slow down the...
Usually, how...

bornness and the impression that opinions once formed are unchangeable. This is in no way always the case, though many people with Mercury in Taurus positively enjoy pretending to others that they are less flexible than they really are. This is particularly so when the Sun-sign is either Aries or Gemini; but for them Mercury really does act as a good counter to the hastiness present in both these signs, and will encourage much-needed patience. Those with a Taurus Sun-sign will be slow, steady, deliberate and very careful about their utterances and opinions.

Mercury in Gemini

Mercury rules Gemini, and so when it is placed in this sign its influence is increased considerably. Many people with this placing will be described by their friends as "mercurial". They will think very quickly and have a certain brightness which will help them through tricky situations. They will change their attitudes and opinions at a moment's notice, and will be able to cope with a great variety of problems at the same time. They will also be extremely talkative; the communicative side of Mercury will be noticeably present. Here, too, are people who love to move around, spending an above-average amount of time travelling. They will also have considerable versatility, but may tend to be superficial. These qualities will be very powerfully stressed if Gemini is the Sun-sign, and the quick-change tendency of Mercury will be more noticeable in those who have a Cancer Sun-sign: here Mercury will help quell the Cancerian emotional forces and give the individual a more rational and logical outlook. If Taurus is the Sun-sign the acceleration of the mental processes will do a great deal to get the slow, steady Taurean individual moving, and help him or her to be less stubborn.

Mercury in Cancer

Mercury in Cancer does a great deal to enhance the imagination and give the individual a superb memory. While there is a te_____this placing to be somewhat sentimen-
_____od old days" (no matter how
_____ the placing is

having masses of enthusiasm and mental energy to pour into whatever fascinates them most. They often have good powers of concentration, and will be thorough in study. Sometimes the creative urge of Leo makes its presence felt, and if this emerges the individual should develop it to the full. The Leo sense of drama is also not far away, and may be expressed in speech, argument and discussion. Those with this placing will make a dramatic impact when lecturing or speaking in public. However they must make an effort to develop flexibility, and give consideration to other people's opinions. When Leo is the Sun-sign, the thinking processes will be expansive—big ideas will come thick and fast, and there may be a tendency to brag to others who achieve less, or who, in the individual's opinion, could learn from their example and make more of themselves. If Cancer is the Sun-sign, this placing will give a more positive outlook and will help diminish the worrying tendency of the sign. If Virgo is the Sun-sign, the individual will show markedly Leonine qualities, because Mercury rules Virgo, and its effect will be a very personal one.

Mercury in Virgo
Mercury is in lively mood when in Virgo, the second sign it rules. It is at its most practical and constructive and those with this placing are capable of a great deal of demanding intellectual work. Their approach is careful and thorough, but they may not always have the confidence to make the most of their abilities, because of a tendency to think themselves less competent than they really are. There is, however, an abundance of nervous energy, and a keenness to be fully occupied all the time. Generally, the imaginative forces are not much increased by Mercury in Virgo, but common sense and practical ability are, and the result is someone who likes to know precisely what they have to do and when they have to do it. The critical acumen is heightened enormously; here too is someone who is highly communicative and enjoys conversation with all sorts of people because of a very enquiring mind. When Virgo is the Sun-sign, Mercury will increase the emphasis of the characteristics of the sign considerably, and the result will be someone who is very critical, logical and rational. If Leo is the Sun-sign, it will scale down the individual's big ideas and give a more practical outlook. If Libra is the Sun-sign, Mercury will aid decisiveness.

Mercury in Libra
Although Mercury in this sign enhances sympathy, kindness and consideration, this placing can cause indecision, and a tendency to want to achieve a great deal with the minimum of mental effort. There may be little inclination to take on projects which involve deep concentration, and the individual may well express himself or herself in rather a slow, languid way, taking an above-average amount of time to answer questions, and doing as much as possible to keep away from controversial subjects, or anything which might disturb the cherished pleasant atmosphere. Those with this placing may have a rather romantic outlook on life and a tendency to be over-optimistic. "Everything will be alright in the end", they say—and interestingly enough, it usually is. More seriously, while this placing contributes a great deal to make the individual a delightful person, it is not likely to instigate quick, incisive thinking. This is spectacularly the case if Libra is the Sun-sign. It will, however, add a kinder and gentler quality to incisive, determined Sun-sign Scorpios, and those who have

a Virgo Sun-sign will find it easier to relax with other people, and will be able to develop their emotional relationships in a satisfactory way—sometimes a problem for Virgo types.

Mercury in Scorpio
Here we have the intensity and intuition of Scorpio combined with the logic, the rational approach and the inquisitiveness of Mercury. A formidable combination, and one which will give the individual a terrific sense of purpose and some very strong investigatory qualities. There will be a deep desire to find out facts and to know the precise reason for things. A need to solve problems and to get down to the most minute detail of every aspect of life will be in evidence, so there is real potential here for a career as a researcher, analyst or perhaps psychiatrist. It may be that the individual will be a "strong silent type", saying little but missing not a thing—the powers of observation are extremely high with this placing. The communicativeness of Mercury is not at its most powerful when the planet is in this sign, but it will certainly complement the Scorpio's sense of purpose and determination. There may be a tendency towards obsessiveness, which will need to be controlled, and a fascination with mysteries and perhaps with the occult. When Scorpio is the Sun-sign, Mercury's influence will be intense and the source of highly intellectual and imaginative potential. If there is a Libran Sun-sign, resentfulness and jealousy will have to be consciously controlled, but decisiveness will be increased. When there is a Sagittarian Sun-sign, enthusiasm and optimism will be steadied.

Mercury in Sagittarius
Here we have an individual who needs to be constantly studying something of compelling interest, but it is important that initial enthusiasm is maintained, and that restlessness does not come between the constant and positive direction of some really excellent intellectual potential. There will be versatility and perhaps a natural flair for languages. The outlook will be enormously optimistic, and the need for challenge almost insatiable. Travel will be important, and any kind of stuffy attitude in other people will in no way be tolerated. There will be considerable breadth of vision, and the ability to grasp instantly even the most complicated ideas. It may be necessary for this group consciously to develop persistence of effort, since there may be a tendency to turn to new, attractive and less complicated or boring projects when difficulties arise. When there is a Sagittarian Sun-sign, Mercury can get a little out of hand, but enthusiasm and a positive outlook will be likeable qualities. When there is a Scorpio Sun-sign, this planet will add a breadth to the whole outlook, complementing the Scorpio's intensity and deep emotion. When the Sun-sign is Capricorn, Mercury will help stave off pessimism, which is common to many of this Sun-sign. It will also add another dimension to the Capricorn sense of humour.

Mercury in Capricorn
Here, Mercury is in a cool, clear, steady mood, and will give the ability to calculate all situations in a very clever and careful way. There could well be a flair for figures—maths will probably be enjoyed. Here is the sort of mind that thrives on problems, and enjoys working out plans in a very matter-of-fact way, both for the long-term and the short-term. There will be efficiency and a practical outlook, with perhaps a tendency to take oneself rather too seriously; the whole approach to life

is usually cautious. Much thought will be given to progress and the attainment of objectives, and while there are many successful people with Mercury in Capricorn there is a tendency to underestimate what has been achieved. When Capricorn is the Sun-sign it is usually the influence of Mercury in that sign which enlivens the individual, making him or her an aspiring and ambitious "mountain-goat", and doing a great deal to increase optimism and lessen pessimism. If Sagittarius is the Sun-sign, Mercury will steady the tendency for the individual to be blindly optimistic, and also increase practicality and common sense. If the Sun falls in Aquarius, we have someone of originality, but whose liking for the unconventional will conflict with a love of tradition and doing the "right" thing at the "right" time.

Mercury in Aquarius

While this placing gives the individual originality and a quick mind, it can also add an element of stubbornness. There is, too, a hint of eccentricity accompanied by a touch of brilliance and the potential for taking a "different" line of approach when dealing with difficult problems. Mercury in Aquarius will only really come into its own if the individual consciously develops persistence of effort to get the most out of the lively individual qualities that are an inherent part of his or her mental processes. There will be no lack of really bright ideas—whether the individual is creative or scientific—and there will be a delightful ability to communicate in a friendly way with all kinds of people. If Aquarius is the Sun-sign, Mercury will intensify the originality and independence of outlook of that sign, and the ability to rationalize and take a detached view of every situation. If the Sun is in Capricorn, Mercury will enliven the serious attitude which can be part of that particular Zodiac type's outlook, but will not increase flexibility. Someone with a Piscean Sun-sign will be helped enormously by this placing, because the emotions—so powerful in this sign—will be steadied, and the ability to become detached from daunting and confusing situations and to look at them objectively will be increased—as will logic.

Mercury in Pisces

Mercury in Pisces is in a dizzy mood. The individual will be kind and considerate and will have a willing attitude, but will often not be terribly practical when it comes to planning or the day-to-day organization of their life. They will have a pleasant, gentle quality and a high level of emotion, but forgetfulness will often be something of a problem. This tendency may lead the individual into all sorts of complicated situations, and—because of a dislike of hurting other people—he or she may then resort to mild deceitfulness as a cover-up. This can cause even greater problems, and the sooner the Mercury-in-Pisces type realizes this is so, the better. Concentration must be consciously developed, for there is a tendency for those with this placing to "drift", especially when they are being given instructions. Rather differently, here is a placing that gives considerable ability to take and hold on to vivid impressions, so that the mind is camera-like. If the Sun-sign is Pisces, Mercury will strengthen all Piscean characteristics, and the individual could be interested in the occult, and even have occult abilities. If Aquarius is the Sun-sign, originality and individuality will be powerfully marked. When Aries is the Sun-sign, Arien assertiveness is softened and there is greater consideration of other people.

The Venus factor

Venus in Aries
Venus is in lively, passionate mood when in Aries. There will be a strong tendency for those with this placing to fall in love very quickly, and they will do everything in their power to win the affection of those to whom they are attracted. Their enthusiasm for love and sex is delightful, and a real sense of fun and pleasure will colour their attitude. This will in most cases be in their favour, since their charm is in the straightforwardness of their approach, and if they are reasonably careful not to sweep their loved ones totally off their feet, they have much to offer. It is, however, important for them to be aware that they tend to put their own needs and ideas about how the relationship should develop rather too forcibly, and they must try to counter this somewhat selfish attitude. It will not be difficult for them to become fully aware of this if their Sun-sign is Pisces, for here the tender sensitivity of that sign will act as a superb counterbalance. If the Sun-sign is Aquarius or Gemini, this placing will warm the emotions and make the individual less detached in their attitude. In Taurus we have someone who is passionate indeed, while if the Sun-sign is Aries, "Faint heart never won fair lady" (or gentleman) could well be a theme song.

Venus in Taurus
Venus is powerfully placed in this sign, which she rules. Here we have someone who is truly loving and affectionate, who will do a great deal for loved ones, but who could at times tend to become rather possessive towards them. But there is considerable generosity present, and the individual will express his or her feelings in a beautiful and romantic way. There will be a considerable need to enjoy life together, and expensive outings and presents will enhance the relationship. But Venus in Taurus is not without a certain caution, and while sensuous in the expression of love and sex, there is no great desire to rush into a relationship, because every step of its progress is there to be enjoyed. This is particularly the case if the Sun-sign is Taurus, when possessiveness must be countered. This placing will steady the feelings of those who have a Pisces or Cancer Sun-sign, but at the same time will enhance their positive expression. If Aries is the Sun-sign, there will be a steady, rather more mellow expression of love than sometimes occurs with Sun-sign Ariens, and if the Sun-sign is Gemini the lively flirtatious attitude of this sign will be given greater depth and sincerity.

Venus in Gemini
Here is Venus in lively, lighthearted and flirtatious mood. Those who have this placing get considerable pleasure and sheer fun from their emotional relationships, and need, as well as a varied sex-life, plenty of friendship and good intellectual rapport with their partner. Sometimes the duality of Gemini

will make its presence felt, with the individual having more than one relationship at a time. Usually they cope with this potentially tricky situation very well, and eventually decide—before confusion catches up with them—which is the most rewarding partner. When Aries or Leo is the Sun-sign, the natural passionate and high emotional level of these signs has a lighthearted quality that prevents the individual from getting too bogged down in relationships, and adds additional colour. This placing will also help a Sun-sign Taurus not to become possessive, since a detached and rational attitude will emerge in an interesting way. The sensitivity of Cancer is also lessened, though if young the individual could become nervously talkative. All Gemini characteristics will be strengthened and expressed in relationships if Venus is in Gemini with the Sun.

Venus in Cancer
There is something intrinsically beautiful about Venus in Cancer, perhaps because it brings together the caring qualities of that sign, and the love and affection of the planetary influence. There will, however, be a tendency for those with this placing to become unduly worried and concerned over their partners. But here too is kindness personified, and the ability to tune in to the partner's real needs and feelings. There is also a very high level of emotion which needs to be expressed through a deep and sincere form of love, and this will emerge to a certain extent whatever the Sun-sign might be. It will have an element of smouldering intensity if Taurus is the Sun-sign, but the Taurean tendency towards possessiveness could become a problem. This placing will do a great deal for those who have Gemini or Virgo as their Sun-sign, because here the lighthearted, flirtatious side of Gemini and the modest retiring element in Virgo will be countered. When Leo is the Sun-sign, there will be less inclination to dominate the relationship, but considerable passion and a sense of drama will certainly be present, and in no small way.

Venus in Leo
Here Venus moves into the big time. Those with this placing will want to do everything possible for their partners; they will often spend a fortune on the sheer enjoyment of their relationship, and will not hesitate to live it up. They will be generous with money, and with the expression of emotion. Venus in this

sign makes for passion, and while this tendency will be modified by the Sun-sign and Rising-sign nevertheless there will be considerable potential for the expression of love to be positive, passionate and meaningful. Here, too, is a need for excitement, glamour and an exciting partner, always present in one way or another when Leo is marked; this will most certainly emerge in relation to love when Venus is in this sign. It can get a little out of hand when Venus is in Leo with the Sun, and the tendency to dominate the relationship will then be considerable. The placing adds colour and warmth to the expression of feeling when Gemini and Virgo are the Sun-signs, and the tenderness of Cancer is less tense. When the Sun is in Libra, a tendency to gush and overdramatize needs to be controlled.

Venus in Virgo
Venus is not terribly well placed in Virgo, which is discriminating, rational and modest. It is also emotionally fairly low-powered, and very critical. So those with Venus in Virgo will probably find that they get more help in their relationships from their Rising-sign and their Sun-sign, whatever they might be. There is a tendency with this placing to underestimate the powers of attraction, and the inherent modesty of the sign will be expressed in a genuine shyness when it comes to developing a relationship. This is a pity because those with this placing have a lot to offer, especially in the way of sharing good communication with their partners. They need, too, plenty of friendship, but their attitude towards sex could be somewhat cool, as could the emotional level. However, for someone who has Cancer or Leo as their Sun-sign there should be little or no problem in this respect, and the placing could help them to be selective in the best possible way. It will also steady the terrific emotional force of Scorpio, while sometimes adding a marginally harsh edge to the verbal expression of feeling. It is a tricky placing for Sun-sign Librans, for they are true romantics who have to come to terms with an element of shyness and modesty that they find hard to understand in themselves. Those with a Virgo Sun-sign must consciously learn to relax into their relationships.

Venus in Libra
The effect of Venus is strengthened when it is in Libra, because the planet rules this sign. Here is Venus in tender, romantic, considerate mood, and those with this placing will be extremely kind and diplomatic. The need to relate is considerably heightened, and individuals may tend to commit themselves early in life to a permanent relationship. This can sometimes work adversely for them, because they are not always ready to cope psychologically; sadly, as is often the case with Sun-sign Librans, lessons are learned the hard way. There is a great appreciation of beauty and the fine arts and when there is creative ability this is expressed with refinement and will have real quality, with music and fashion design being particularly rewarding. A great deal of the psychological motivation will centre around the partner if Libra is the Sun-sign, and this placing will be of enormous help to Sun-sign Virgoans, since it helps them overcome shyness and any lack of self-confidence they may feel in relationships. It takes a lot of the heavy passion away from the Sun-sign Scorpio, and adds much that is gentler and more sensitive. It can certainly make the extravagant Leo even freer with both feelings and money, and makes an enthusiastic fiery Sagittarian Sun-sign type more understanding and loving.

Venus in Scorpio
By tradition Venus is not supposed to be very well placed in this sign, and certainly the effect of the planet can be somewhat heavy and overpassionate at times. Here is a deep intensity of feeling which needs full expression and a very understanding partner. The individual will work enormously hard at his or her permanent relationship, to make it work for both partners, but sometimes the intensity is too great, and the partner can feel a little claustrophobic and need a less cloying and freer lifestyle. This is something that the Venus-in-Scorpio type must be constantly aware of; they must also remember that the inclination towards jealousy and possessiveness can be a real threat to their happiness. If they can learn to express the depth of their feelings in a truly meaningful way, they will get a great deal that is positive from this interesting but demanding Venus sign. Coming to terms with it and a Virgo or Capricorn Sun-sign may not be easy, but the respective characteristics must be accepted and recognized. The Scorpio way of loving will be very apparent when Libra is the Sun-sign, and will add a passionate dimension to the attitude and expression of love, while those with a Scorpio or Sagittarius Sun-sign will be passionate and highly sexed.

Venus in Sagittarius
Here Venus adds some lively if somewhat boisterous qualities to the expression of love. The attitude will be breezy and very casual. There will be a need for a partner with a matching intellectual level, but the individuals will in no way be undemonstrative in expressing their feelings, and their sexual appetite will be considerable. Most importantly this sphere of life must be lively; here is someone who will not tolerate an iota of boredom in a relationship, and the duality and versatility of Sagittarius will have a rather special kind of expression through Venus and will affect the attitude. Restlessness could be a problem, so it is advisable for those with this placing to recognize the possibility, and to remember that partners should not suffer as a result of this—indeed, they should make sure they do not. This placing works well for those with a Libra Sun-sign, since it helps them to focus less rigidly on the partner. It increases the emotional level of the rather cool Capricorn and Aquarius Sun-sign types. Those with a Sagittarius Sun-sign should be careful that they do not take their partners for granted, while a Sun-sign Scorpio will have a sense of sheer fun and enjoyment, with less "steamy" passion.

Venus in Capricorn
The expression of love is refined, and while there is an element of coolness there is usually tremendous fidelity, and a caring quality. Those with a Capricorn Venus sign will want to do a great deal for their partners, and will work particularly hard to make more money to provide everything possible for them. A terrific sense of pride will also emerge, and the individual will want to show off their loved one in an impressive way. The degree of warmth and the true emotional level must be assessed from other planets' positions, because Venus, although caring in this sign, is not very expressive here. When Scorpio is the Sun-sign, the emotions will be channelled and controlled. They will be present, but there could be a tendency to hold back at times. There will be a surprising air of formality in the early stage of love for those who have the Sun in Sagittarius, though this will probably melt as time goes on. Nevertheless the need to do the right thing will emerge from time to time.

Those with a Capricorn Sun-sign will cope with being alone better than most; they may have very few partners, and this may also apply to the Sun-sign Aquarian, though there the dynamic powers of attraction could work in the individual's favour. This placing will help steady and guide the wealth of Piscean emotion.

Venus in Aquarius

This is, *par excellence*, a glamorous placing for Venus. Here is someone who has in their own individual way a kind of star quality and dynamic powers of attraction. But there is a distinct tendency to distance themselves from partners, so that deep and meaningful emotional relationships are not always fully attained. Of course the emotional content of Rising-sign and Sun-sign have an important part to play here, as always, but Venus in Aquarius, while giving some intriguing qualities, is not high on affection and warmth. It works well in ties of friendship, however, for there is no lack of kindness, which in itself can contribute a lot in deeper relationships. It will have a cooling influence, and add an interesting dimension where love and sex are concerned, for those who have Sagittarius or Aries as their Sun-signs, and will contribute a modern, somewhat unconventional attitude and outlook for the Capricorn Sun-sign type. Those with an Aquarius Sun-sign will have some delightful qualities and characteristics, but may well have to get their needs very carefully sorted out in their own minds before committing themselves to a permanent relationship. When there is a Pisces Sun-sign, Venus will contribute a useful ability to detach the self from the emotions, and add a positive, cool objectivity.

Venus in Pisces

There is in this placing a wealth of feeling and a warm sensitivity which will be directed towards the partner in a kind, loving way. A tendency to worry unduly over the lover is common, as are feelings of inadequacy and a constant need to do even more for them. Those with this placing should not allow their attitude to become smothering; but if they can steady their feelings and realize that they have much that is truly worthwhile to give in a relationship, and that in doing so they will still be contributing substantially, Venus will work extremely well for them, irrespective of Sun-sign. This is an excellent placing for those with a Capricorn Sun-sign, for here the emotional level is increased by Venus and there is a less "up-tight" attitude than is sometimes the case. The cool, distant quality of Aquarius is also warmed by Venus but those of this Sun-sign must recognize that their way of loving is not totally in line with their Sun-sign characteristics, which makes for interest as well as possible conflict. A tendency to gush and to want to do too much is present when the Sun is in Pisces with Venus, and the brashness of Aries is toned down and a greater sensitivity is present. Venus works well for Sun-sign Taureans, since it helps counter possessiveness.

THE OUTER
PLANETS

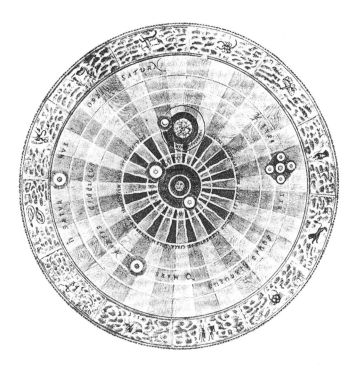

The Mars factor

Mars can fall in any of the 12 signs of the Zodiac, irrespective of Sun-sign. This is because the orbit of Mars lies outside the orbit of Earth. Mars and the sign it falls in represent our energy and the way we use it, and also our sex-drive. It has an influence on the red blood corpuscles and the adrenal glands, and can sometimes provoke minor cuts and burns (usually acquired through hastiness). It represents the masculine element in both sexes and is also related to aggression and heat—both physical heat and the heat of anger. People whom astrologers would describe as having "a strong Mars" usually have the qualities of pioneers and leaders, and an urge to defend the weak.

Mars in Aries
Mars is at its most powerful when in Aries, because this is the sign it rules. Here we have someone whose very high level of physical energy needs plenty of outlets. They should be aware that in their need to push forward they may tend not to listen to other people's opinions as carefully as they might. It is vitally important for those with this placing to have some physically demanding interest, because their energy must not be allowed to stagnate; sport of any kind, or perhaps work for youth clubs in their spare time, would be excellent for them. There will be no lack of enthusiasm—a considerable help to many who perhaps have a somewhat unassertive Sun-, Moon- or Rising-sign. It is possible that patience will not be a strong feature, though again the three dominating signs will have a strong influence. There is also a tendency to be accident-prone—especially when young, when knocks on the head, minor cuts and burns will be very common.

Mars in Taurus
The energy-flow is usually controlled and steady, but when the individual is roused to anger there will be a considerable show of temper. Although this will not emerge very often, when it does the individual will certainly make an impact. There will be no lack of steady persistence of effort, and generally there is the ability to plod steadily towards the achievement of objectives. The pace will not be rushed, because the chances are that those with Mars in Taurus will know that forcing issues or working in fits and starts does not suit them. Considerable stubbornness is often present, and the liking for routine can become almost obsessional. Physical activities requiring control of the body and a careful assessment of each movement will be rewarding, and the powers of endurance should be excellent. Speed of action is not a strong point, and the body's metabolism might be slow.

Mars in Gemini
Here Mars is in lively but somewhat restless mood. There is often a tendency to fritter away energy, and a conscious

54

awareness that this can happen is an advantage. If the individual has a good sense of purpose and is ambitious there should be few problems. There will also be an emphasis on intellectual energy, so interests will need to incorporate this kind of challenge. Sporting and physical activities that also require mental alertness will suit those with this placing. A lively, assertive attitude will be taken in argument and debate, and there will be no lack of things to say on any occasion. Here, too, there is often more than a hint of Geminian duality, and it should be accepted and developed as versatility. Those with Mars in this sign are not terribly patient, unless the Sun-, Moon- and Rising-sign contribute this quality in force. Boredom can therefore catch up with them very easily. Obviously the expression of versatility and a change of scene and occupation will be a superb counterbalance to this.

Mars in Cancer
Here, Mars picks up the tenacity of Cancer so that a terrific effort is made to achieve whatever is important to the individual. There is also a strong combination of the forces of emotional and physical energy once the initial motivation is sparked off. There is, however, a tendency to burn energy unevenly, and while periods of laziness are unlikely, there is a temptation to overdo things when the individual feels that he or she is under any kind of pressure. Tension can result, leading to an inability to relax. This is a marvellously sensuous placing for Mars, and the expression and enjoyment of sex is usually extremely colourful; also, a sensitive and intuitive quality gives an instinctive realization of the partner's needs. The accident-prone side of Mars is only likely to emerge when the individual is overconcerned with other people, and not giving enough attention to personal safety.

Mars in Leo
The showing-off tendencies of Leo will be energetically expressed when Mars is in this sign. The individual will spend a great deal of enthusiasm and energy on making his or her presence felt, but will also have the happy knack of getting other people to do things. Here we have a team leader, someone who has abundant energy. They will work hard—very hard—and the creative side of Leo will probably emerge, so spare-time activities may be directed towards amateur theatricals. This is a good placing for Mars as far as the

career is concerned, for here is an energy-force second to none, and—irrespective of Sun-, Moon- and Rising-sign —awareness that a great deal can be achieved through the strength of this planet will be of enormous help to even the most self-effacing person. Extraverts with this Mars sign must be aware that they can be somewhat bombastic and dogmatic at times. Here too is sexual exuberance.

Mars in Virgo

There is a high level of intense nervous energy when Mars is in this sign. It can cause considerable inner tension, and can be the root of bad headaches or migraine. Therefore while it will not be easy, it is essential that the individual, if he or she suffers in this way, should learn relaxation techniques. Yoga is particularly beneficial, as the exercises can be both calming and restorative, but are physically demanding as well. Fresh air, long country walks and cycling are also excellent for all those with this placing, and because the level of intellectual energy is very high, there should always be time for them to indulge in demanding and fascinating mental tasks. Mars in this sign adds a critical and discriminating tendency to the expression and fulfilment of sex.

Mars in Libra

Mars is in a terribly languid mood when in Libra so from the point of view of injecting the individual with energy it is not at its most exuberant. The mind might be willing, but the flesh is weak. There could be a certain amount of procrastination, although the strength and determination of the Sun-, Moon- and Rising-sign will do a great deal to counter the relaxing influence of Mars in Libra. However, the enjoyment of sex is much in evidence, and once motivated those who have this placing can achieve a great deal, especially if they find they are gaining praise and the appreciation of their efforts from other people, which is important to them. Here the aggression of Mars is toned down a little, too, but conversely there is a side to this Zodiac group which will provoke a good row and enjoy every minute of it. The need for a permanent relationship is strong, and Mars in this sign will work hard to achieve a meaningful one.

Mars in Scorpio

By tradition, Mars rules Scorpio, so the planet's influence when placed in this sign is extremely powerful. Here we have someone with a very high level of emotional and physical energy which needs careful consideration and direction. These forces need to be expressed powerfully and positively in the career or the daily work, whatever it might be, and equally need less complicated but essential channelling through some sporting or physically orientated activity after the day's work is finished. There is a terrific sense of purpose and determination in those who have this as their Mars-sign, and Scorpio's intensity and intuition are also present to a certain extent. The forces of Mars in this sign need a rewarding and fulfilling sex-life, and considerable demands may be made on partners. They should be aware that this is so, and should use other planets' influences to help counter a tendency to jealousy.

Mars in Sagittarius

There will be a need for challenge, especially the sort of challenge that makes demands on physical energy. Here is an ideal placing for ambitious sportsmen and women who will forever want to improve their personal best records. They do need, however, to be careful not to try to be too versatile; in the desire to experiment in new and different fields they might miss out on becoming as perfect as they could be in some rather smaller area of interest. The intellectual energy level is high, too, and again challenge is important. In both cases there will be plenty of will to succeed, and an equal desire to enjoy all aspects of life. There is a natural infectious enthusiasm and a somewhat bright and breezy attitude. While the sexual appetite is considerable, this sphere of life must be great fun.

Mars in Capricorn

Mars is by tradition well placed in this sign. Its energy is controlled and disciplined, and it denotes considerable ambition and the will to achieve a great deal. But Mars is in a somewhat chilly mood; this placing, for instance, does not do much to enhance the sex-life or warm the emotions. But a driving force is present, and those with Mars in this sign have some formidable resources to fall back on, especially when they experience difficult conditions. He or she will cope well with a lonely and powerful position, since inwardly they will know that they are in such a position because of their determination to get to the top. Here too is someone who will have what it takes to build up a business, if the motivation coming from the Sun- and Rising-sign is sympathetic to that kind of self-expression. Demanding exercise is important for the physical well-being of a Mars-in-Capricorn type.

Mars in Aquarius

Here the Mars influence works in rather a zany way. Eccentricity is often present, and the energy level is somewhat erratic. Mars in this sign increases originality, and there is a natural keenness to explore new ideas and possibilities, so that a fascination with experiment, both with subjects well-known to the individual and in totally different areas, is never far from the surface. Perversity, too, is in evidence. The level of physical energy may not be terribly high, but a kind of tense excitability and nervous energy is present, and that can be expressed physically from time to time when the individual will do daft things, perhaps to raise money for charity. This is rewarding for those with this placing, as there is a will to help anyone in need (even when Aquarius is the Mars-sign the humanitarian qualities of the sign make their presence felt). Sexually, the Mars-in-Aquarius type will want to experiment, and an element of restlessness may also be in evidence.

Mars in Pisces

Here Mars increases the emotional energy and contributes a rather lower level of physical energy than when placed in most other signs. But if the emotions can be channelled positively those with Mars in Pisces will achieve much. It is a marvellous placing for those who enjoy physical activity which is essentially creative—such as skating or dancing—and indeed it is advisable for those with a Piscean Mars to consider taking up something along these lines, since it is the best possible way for them to enjoy exercise. Mars in Pisces works well from the sexual point of view, as here there is a kind sensitivity and a sensuous quality that combine well in warm and attractive expression. Understanding of the partner's needs will be instinctive. Consistency of effort should be developed, and perhaps, too, greater determination, though this will depend to a greater extent on the Sun-, Moon- and Rising-sign.

The Jupiter factor

Jupiter has an influence on our outlook on life and on the way we approach challenge. The planet also influences our intellectual capacity and potential. Expansion is a Jupiter key-word, and so the sign in which it falls at the moment of our birth will reflect the way in which we cope with demanding situations and with new possibilities that are likely to lead to an improved status in the future. The planet also influences the expansion of the mind through travel and study. Higher education is also a Jupiter concern.

Jupiter takes some 12 years to complete a journey through all the signs of the Zodiac, and so every 12 years returns to the precise position it was in when we were born. Astrologically this is known as the Jupiter Return. At such a time we usually take important steps forward and improve our income, and must be on the look-out for opportunities to put our ideas to those who can help us. Refer to the Jupiter tables on pages 250–253 to see when you last had a Jupiter Return. Count 12 years on from then to discover when your next one will be. It should be a memorable and rewarding year for you.

Jupiter in Aries
The straightforward, uncomplicated approach of Aries will be in evidence, and the love of challenge will be considerable. Here is an individual who may not be terribly good at coping with details—unless other planets give support in that direction—but whose grasp of an overall plan will be terrific. There will be considerable breadth of vision, and a fiery enthusiasm usually maintained until the end of a project. Here is someone who will be optimistic and very positive in outlook, and who will enjoy taking adventurous risks.

Jupiter in Taurus
Here Jupiter exerts a steady, cautious influence, and there will be a somewhat above-average concentration on financial progress. If the influence of other signs suggests a good business sense, Jupiter will strengthen this considerably, and expansion and growth of capital will be of great interest to the individual. This placing can slow down the ability to study, though what is learned will be remembered. There might not be a great desire to travel very far. But here is a tremendous love of comfort and a true appreciation of good food and wine (there could well be a weight problem as a result of Jupiter's influence).

Jupiter in Gemini
Those with this placing could find it difficult to sort out their priorities and direction in life. Many different subjects will interest them, and they will have a boldly versatile streak which will need full expression. They will have intellectual flair and ability, and need a career with plenty of variety. Work in the travel business or in the media could be successful, and perhaps

there will also be the ability to sell. Restlessness could be a problem at times; but the individual will basically have a happy, optimistic temperament and will get a lot of fun out of the trickiest situations. Bright repartee, a sense of humour, and an enquiring mind will all be in evidence.

Jupiter in Cancer
Traditionally, Jupiter is said to be well and strongly placed in Cancer, where its influence is gentle and caring. There will be a genuine feeling for the well-being of others, and this may be expressed in the choice of profession, since "caring" will combine, for positive and practical expression, with "challenge". Those with this placing should also have an excellent memory and good imagination, which will be used to advantage. Jupiter in this sign will add a certain shrewdness which might emerge as business sense; there is ability to make money, and to make it grow. This placing adds sensitivity and the emotional level is increased.

Jupiter in Leo
Those with this placing will have an exuberant zest for life. There will be a tendency to show off, and perhaps too a certain bossiness (which often emerges when there is an emphasis on Leo). There will be good powers of leadership, love of challenge and possibly creative talent. Those with Jupiter in this sign will think big and get through a great deal of work, which they will love. They will make and probably spend a lot of money, since they need to do things in a big way and are also very generous. There will be the ability to enjoy things enormously and the quality of life will be important. The intellectual powers are usually good, provided an open mind is maintained and the tendency to be dogmatic is avoided.

Jupiter in Virgo
Here Jupiter will exert a discriminating critical influence. There could well be literary ability, and the ability to study carefully. Challenges will only be accepted after careful consideration of all the aspects involved. So, while there will be excellent judgement, this placing is not conducive to adventure or risk-taking. The outlook on life will be very practical and there will be no lack of common sense. This placing will be of considerable help to anyone in the teaching profession. There could be problems with the bowels and digestive system, so

some care should be given to diet and to the amount of rich food that is eaten.

Jupiter in Libra

Kindness, generosity and a warm, loving quality will emerge in those who have this placing, but Jupiter is not at its strongest where direction in life and the acceptance of challenge are concerned. Here is a desire for pleasure and fun, for a relaxed lifestyle. This in itself could promote considerable effort if other planets' placings show energetic determination. There could well be a tendency to take life sitting down, and perhaps too an element of blind optimism. All the finer elements of life will be keenly appreciated, and comfort, elegance and the quality of life will be important.

Jupiter in Scorpio

The depth and intensity of Scorpio will be given a breadth of vision, so that determination, the love of challenge and the ability to achieve much will combine to add an important dimension to the individual's personality. Here is considerable potential, and an enquiring mind which will be of considerable use. Jupiter will encourage enjoyment of life; moderation will not come into the general scheme of things, and a tendency to go the whole hog will be extremely noticeable in all spheres of life. There will be an inherent need for challenge and an ability to face up to horrendous tasks, and while there will in no way be a lack of seriousness in the individual's attitude towards problems, the desire and ability to make the most of all their potential will be characteristic.

Jupiter in Sagittarius

Jupiter rules Sagittarius, so its influence is increased when placed in this sign. Here Jupiter works well and strongly, and the best philosophical side of the planet's influence will emerge. This placing will be of considerable help to the individual, who will have good intellectual powers—though these may not emerge very early in life. A liking for sport and risk-taking and a sort of coltish quality will be present, but the potential for greater things will develop from a youthful, carefree spirit. Jupiter in this sign can promote an interest in religion, philosophy or the law, and many writers and publishers have this placing. Here too is a potential facility for languages and an above-average love of travel.

Jupiter in Capricorn

Here Jupiter's influence is rather sober, but it will help those with this placing to achieve their objectives, and denotes considerable ambition. The need for challenge will be strong, and will be directed towards the career or improvement of the lifestyle. Although the individual's outlook will be somewhat serious the sense of humour will be especially interesting and off-beat, with a jovial sense of fun combined with Capricorn dourness. Those with this placing will have methodical minds, and the ability to calculate every move will be an asset. It is possible, however, that a certain conflict between Jupiterian optimism and Capricorn pessimism will have to be overcome, and if a balance can be maintained it will work in the individual's favour.

Jupiter in Aquarius

Aquarian originality will be positively expressed when Jupiter is in this sign. Here the intellectual capacity could be excellent, and evidence of an inventive mind will soon emerge. It is important that those with this placing are allowed scope to develop this. Here too is an extremely independent spirit who will very much want to express himself or herself in an individual way, which could be very different indeed from the norm. An element of eccentricity may be present, but there will be sound back-up for ideas which may seem extreme. There will be a need to break new ground in the chosen field, and a determination to stick to beliefs and opinions.

Jupiter in Pisces

Here is Jupiter at its most philosophical. There may well be a firm dedication to beliefs; this may emerge in an adherence to a religious faith, but equally could relate to some compelling interest, or perhaps an art-form. The charitable, sacrificial side of Pisces will also be present in the best possible way, for here may well be someone who will do a great deal to improve the lot of less fortunate people. Here too, however, will be a good capacity to enjoy life, and a tendency to put on weight. These individuals can be artful and somewhat deceptive, and they will be excellent mimics.

The Saturn factor

The sign in which Saturn falls has a bearing on our sense of purpose and direction in life. Its influence is basically a very serious one, and it is, in many ways, linked to one's destiny, although we must never forget that there is nothing fatalistic in modern Western astrology. We all have some inhibitions and hang-ups, and from a psychological point of view Saturn indicates how we come to terms with them. An astrologer, when assessing a fully calculated birth-chart, will give serious consideration to this planet, and especially to the way in which it relates to others, through the aspects (see glossary) it receives. In this book we can only deal with its sign placing, but some clarification as to its influence is given below, and the reader must—as is the case with all the planets—consider the sign interpretation in relation to the all-important Sun-, Moon- and Rising-sign.

Saturn takes some two and a half years to travel through one sign of the Zodiac, and so is in the same sign for all people born during that length of time. It takes some 29½ to 30 years to complete a journey through all 12 signs, and for this reason as we approach 30, and again as we near the age of 60, we get the important Saturn Return. Many people with no knowledge of astrology, including some analysts and psychiatrists, recognize these periods of life as extremely important times of change and reassessment. Astrologers put this down to the serious dominating influence of Saturn.

Saturn in Aries
There may be feelings of conflict when the individual is faced with challenging situations. The urge to accept them and to move forward may be held back somewhat by a certain amount of inhibition. If negative feelings can be overcome and caution is allowed to take the place of any lack of self-confidence, the individual will get a great deal that is constructive and helpful from the influence of Saturn. There will be no lack of ambition and desire to get on in life—just a complicated "stop-go" attitude in the manner of achieving goals. The influence of Mars will be particularly important in this case.

Saturn in Taurus
This is a good placing for Saturn because the planet is in many ways sympathetic to much that is characteristic of Taurus. Here we have someone who is ambitious for material progress, but who will be patient and ready to build slowly and carefully to achieve ambitions. They will soon learn that progressing in leaps and bounds is not their way, and the acquisition of property and a sound bank balance will do more to build their self-confidence than anything else. They need that kind of security; it is psychologically important to them. They may tend to be overcommitted to routine, and a hint of complacency may emerge from time to time.

Saturn in Gemini
Here the logical and rational approach of Gemini is very controlled, and at its best the mind is steady and capable of profound thought and reasoned decision-making. Sometimes there is scientific ability, but from a psychological point of view there can be an element of restlessness present, since the lighthearted Geminian principle and the serious Saturnian attitude can conflict. At times the youthfulness of Gemini will emerge, while on other occasions the maturity of Saturn will clamp down on what could be adventurous and exciting. The individual must find ways of keeping a balance between the two, especially when it comes to the formation and expression of opinions.

Saturn in Cancer
Tradition, the past and the individual's family background will be important and will influence those with this placing far more than they may realize, and what has been learned in early life will undoubtedly be less modified than in most cases. There may be somewhat above-average inhibition or shyness when young, and the self-defensive tendencies of Cancer will be brought into play when the individual is challenged. While anyone with this placing will be brave, the self-preserving instinct will be strong, so risk-taking will be minimal. If other planets' positions show a high emotional level it may be that Saturn will inhibit this.

Saturn in Leo
While the fire, exuberance and enthusiasm of Leo is totally opposite to the serious, practical and constructive elements of Saturn, the two together do not entirely conflict. Here, for instance, we have a need for everything that is of high quality, and a perfectionist attitude. Here too is a liking for ceremony. Thoroughness in work, ambition and determination are pres-

ent in considerable force, and a kind of noble regality will colour the opinions and attitude towards life. This placing makes for conventionality; those who have it will conform to the standards of their own generation. The ability to carry responsibility and powers of leadership will emerge if other planets support this placing; so will a hint of pomposity.

Saturn in Virgo

A serious attitude towards life, discriminatingly expressed, is likely, as is a tendency to worry; there is also the possibility of pessimism at times. But here is someone who is extremely practical, and will take a clinical approach to the shaping of their life and ambitions. It may well be that the individual will tend to underestimate himself or herself, and self-confidence is often not a strong point; it should be slowly and carefully developed, relying on the assertive and extravert qualities of the Sun-, Moon- and Rising-sign. But Saturn in Virgo can have a somewhat steadying influence, since it adds a constructive element to the personality and denotes plenty of common sense.

Saturn in Libra

Saturn is traditionally well placed in Libra, and it is often the case that those with it in this sign have a well-balanced attitude towards life, and are able to recognize their own psychological problems and make the adjustments necessary to resolve or counter them. Here too is a need to be fair to other people, and while there is no lack of ambition the individual will usually consider other people's feelings and opinions. There will be a serious attitude in emotional relationships, and an element of loyalty and faithfulness is also likely to emerge. Sometimes the individual with this placing will be committed to a rather older partner.

Saturn in Scorpio

The emotional intensity of Scorpio is present, but it may well be difficult for the individual to express his or her feelings. A tendency not to discuss problems is very common, and often compensation must be made for inhibition. But some extremely powerful resources attend this placing—toughness and determination, ambition and the will to succeed. These resources need positive expression, perhaps through the acceptance of challenge. At all events, the traits must be recognized, or

stagnation and discontent will dog the individual's progress and attitude to life. A preoccupation with the unknown—generally or in the form of introspection—is also a strong possibility.

Saturn in Sagittarius
Ideally, here is a combination of breadth of vision and singleness of purpose, but it might well take quite a long time for those with this placing to come to terms with these excellent qualities. Perhaps while they are young the temptation to sway from a set determined path in order to experience new and challenging situations will be too great for them, though inwardly they will instinctively know the right road. Alternating moods of optimism and pessimism will occur, sometimes to the point that the individual will feel ecstatically happy about one aspect of life, but desperately miserable over another. They must remember that Saturn is a great source of practical common sense, and that life need not be a series of dramatic changes of feeling and mood.

Saturn in Capricorn
Saturn rules Capricorn and therefore its influence from this sign is particularly powerful. It is almost bound to enhance the individual's ambition and determination to succeed. There will also be the ability to carry responsibility, and it should not be difficult to cope with a lonely top job. It may well be, indeed, that here is someone who is better working alone, although this will largely depend on the placings of the Sun-, Moon- and Rising-sign. A certain preoccupation with business, career, or material concerns can occur, so that others may get the impression that the individual is distant and perhaps somewhat unapproachable. Psychological problems will be solved through self-analysis. The Capricorn sense of humour is likely to be present.

Saturn in Aquarius
Here the influence of Saturn works in a rational, logical and positive manner. The individual is usually able to take a detached view of his or her psychological problems, and while there may not be a great deal of flexibility in the attitude of mind, there will be the ability gradually to learn what is wrong and to do everything possible to counter it by using stronger and more positive characteristics and traits. There will be an element of individuality, and no great attraction to over-conventional or well-established ideas or outmoded concepts. Saturn's mood in Aquarius is positive and hopeful; there is always faith in the future, and an attraction to the best that the individual's generation, and the next, has to offer.

Saturn in Pisces
Control of emotional forces should be relatively easy when Saturn is in Pisces—useful if the individual has a high emotional level arising from the Sun-, Moon- and Rising-sign. This can help to steady and anchor the personality in a constructive way. But it is sometimes the case that inhibition and shyness is present, and this must gradually be overcome. If the individual is creative, he or she should be encouraged since Saturn in Pisces can make people rather quiet and lacking in any ability to show off. There could be a very genuine religious faith, and a marvellously charitable disposition; sacrifices will be made, but the individual must learn not to underestimate himself or herself.

THE MODERN
PLANETS

The Uranus factor

Uranus is the first of the three "modern" planets. It was first discovered in 1781 by William Herschel. Because of its distance from the Sun, it takes around 84 years to complete a journey through all 12 signs of the Zodiac. It therefore takes about seven years to travel through each sign, and it is in that sign in the birth-charts of all people born within the seven-year period. Unless that sign is also occupied by the Sun or Moon, or is the Rising-sign of the individual, the characteristics of the Uranus sign are merely supportive factors. For instance, if eccentricity emerges as a strong characteristic (due to other planets' influences), then it is possible to look to the placing of Uranus to see how this trait is strengthened or to a certain extent how it emerges in the individual concerned. Uranus will also increase originality, if this is indicated elsewhere. The planet also has the capacity to provoke changes in life; but otherwise astrologers think of it as influencing a whole generation rather than a particular individual.

However, as the planet moves around the sky and makes specific angles to the position it was in at the moment of birth, it activates the "natal" planets in a lively, tense and interesting way. Perhaps its most important influence occurs when it has travelled halfway round the Zodiac, and is in a position exactly 180° away from the point in the sky it was in when one was born. This happens when we are about 40, when Uranus is travelling through its opposite or "polar" sign. For instance, if Uranus was in Gemini when you were born, you will experience what we call your Uranus "half-return" when the planet is travelling through Sagittarius. The occasion is an important one for all of us. We may feel old, and sometimes rather tense, but it is up to us to use the influence of Uranus at this time to take on a new lease of life, improve our image and develop new interests—in this way Uranus will be of enormous help to all of us. The full Uranus Return occurs when we reach 84 years of age. Elderly people often have a new lease of life, and they are capable of doing many new, different and interesting things as Uranus "returns" to the precise position it was in at birth.

Uranus in Aries
A pioneering spirit will emerge, and there will be no lack of energy and drive. The individual will thrive in a position of power if this and the quality of leadership emerges from other planetary influences. This placing will be an enlivening influence for a sensitive person, and will generally increase the emotional level. Tension is a strong possibility for those who have Cancer, Libra or Capricorn strongly emphasized.

Uranus in Taurus
This could cause the individual to work unevenly, and there might be a conflict between expressing originality and behaving in a totally predictable and conventional manner. It will, however, add a certain spicy liveliness to those who have

Taurus emphasized by Sun-, Moon- or Rising-sign, and should work well for Virgos and Capricorns. It will stabilize those who work creatively or scientifically, since it will control the outflow of ideas and help them consider them carefully and in detail.

Uranus in Gemini
Here the influence of Uranus is excellent. It will add a spark of versatility and additional originality to all those who have it, and it can be used positively—especially if the dominating signs are Gemini itself, Libra or Aquarius. While the influence will often bring an element of tension, particularly to Sagittarians or Virgos, the planet works well from Gemini, since it is in many ways sympathetic to this sign, making people alert and outspoken in the liveliest way.

Uranus in Cancer
Those with Cancer emphasized by Sun- or Moon-sign will tend to be ultra prone to worry, and the ability to relax totally will probably be very slim. But all who have this placing will at best benefit from a good imagination and they must seek their own individual ways of expressing it. There could be a conflict between wanting to express their own personalities and concern for family opinion, and this might become a source of difficulty. The planet should work well for Scorpio and Piscean types.

Uranus in Leo
There are very strong connections between Uranus and power, and when the planet is in Leo the liking and need for power can emerge, especially with those who have Leo dominant in their charts. An interest in politics is likely in this case, and here too the creative forces of Uranus will emerge. Stubbornness will be increased, especially if Taurus, Scorpio or Aquarius are emphasized. The planet will enliven Ariens and Sagittarians.

Uranus in Virgo
The discriminating ability of Virgo can be used, but if the individual is prone to worry and tension this can build up very quickly and easily. Erratic, premature action may also occur, especially if Virgo is emphasized. Taureans and Capricorns can make Uranus work for them, since it increases originality and will help them to be less conventional. There may be above-average interest in ecology, and the conservation of the Earth's resources.

Uranus in Libra
Uranus is well placed in Libra, and a sense of justice will be present for those who have it in this sign. A need to see fair play will emerge quite strongly if Libra is accentuated. The tension of Uranus is somewhat mitigated from Libra, though it will probably catch up with those who have Aries, Cancer or Capricorn dominating their charts. It is an excellent placing for Aquarians and Geminians, who will be more than usually ready to listen to other people's opinions and to act on them in their own way.

Uranus in Scorpio
The power-seeking tendencies of Uranus are likely to emerge and it is possible that those who have Scorpio dominating will in many ways be generation leaders. They will want to move mountains, and some will be able to do so. More generally the

influence will add intensity and a sense of purpose. This will emerge most strongly in Cancerians and Pisceans, and can do a great deal for them, since here is an additional energy force which can be tapped. It will also add a measure of confidence for those who are generally rather shy.

Uranus in Sagittarius

The fire, enthusiasm and challenging needs of this sign are present to a certain extent, and if the individual is intellectually inclined the planet will add the ability to evolve new concepts. The humanitarian aspects of Uranus are likely to emerge, as is additional originality—especially if Sagittarius is a dominating sign. The planet will also be of considerable help to Ariens and Leos in particular, but all those born with it in this sign can make good use of its positive, enthusiastic, forward-thinking traits.

Uranus in Capricorn

There could well be changes of opinion on important issues. Sometimes the individual will veer towards what is new and unconventional, while at other times there may well be a surprising tendency to cling to what is traditional and well tried. It is possible to get the best of both extremes, but a balance must be sought. The tendency is likely to emerge most strongly in dominantly Capricorn or Aquarian types, and could be a potential source of tension for Ariens, Cancerians and Librans, while Taureans and Virgos should benefit from this placing.

Uranus in Aquarius

Here the influence of Uranus is at its most powerful, since the planet rules Aquarius. So Aquarians who have it in this sign will express an above-average number of the basic characteristics of their sign. Eccentricity and unpredictability will emerge, but on the positive side, so will true friendliness and a humanitarian spirit. For all other types an element of Aquarius will be present in their personalities, and it is interesting for students of astrology to study anyone they happen to know of this generation (born 1912–1920), to see how this planet works. (See also *The Basic Factors: Aquarius.*)

Uranus in Pisces

Because Pisces is a sign noted for kindness and charity, those who have Uranus in Pisces will bring the humanitarian elements of Uranus to the fore. While these tendencies will not, of course, be a dominating factor, there will be a basic sympathy for those who are working to improve the lot of less fortunate people. The tension of Uranus will come into contact with the emotional forces of Pisces—not an easy mix, but if they are recognized and channelled in constructive ways they can work well. Pisceans and Virgos will feel this influence most strongly, while Cancerians and Scorpios will benefit most.

The Neptune factor

Neptune was discovered in 1846. Because of its distance from the Sun it takes about 168 years to travel round the Zodiac, through all 12 signs, spending about 14 years in each. This planet, then, has a distinct "generation influence", which emerges in a marked and interesting way. It will, of course, work on a personal level for every individual, but the overall influence is worth serious attention as well. This will be evident in the interpretations set out below. You will see that there are no interpretations for Neptune in Aries, Taurus, Aquarius or Pisces. This is because there is no one alive with this sign placing. Neptune travelled through Aries and Taurus between the 1860s and the 1880s, and it will not enter Aquarius until 1998. Dates listed below are approximate—see tables for greater accuracy (page 255).

Neptune in Gemini (1888–1901/2)
The overall influence of Neptune in this sign seems to accentuate the communicative elements of Gemini. The telephone became more widely available, and travel by rail and by car developed considerably during these years. Some very elderly people who are alive today were born when Neptune was in this sign, and there seems always to be an element of curiosity present in their personalities. They are inquisitive, but confused over the rapid changes that have occurred in their lifetime; they may not entirely trust new developments. While this is a tendency in the older generation generally, it does not always go hand in glove with suspicion and scepticism, which will be a marked facet of the personality—especially of those who have Gemini, Virgo, Sagittarius or Pisces as a dominant sign.

Neptune in Cancer (1901/2–1915)
While Neptune was travelling through this sign World War I broke out, causing disruption and a great deal of suffering and sorrow within family life. Those born during these years later repeated their parents' experience as they themselves brought up young children during World War II. Cancer being the sign of home, family and motherhood, it is not difficult to see its sad sacrificial influence over this generation. From a personal point of view there is an increased imagination and sensitivity. Many of this generation are more prone to worry than others, especially if their dominant sign is Cancer, Capricorn or Libra.

Neptune in Leo (1915–1928/29)
Here Neptune takes on a far more glamorous and exciting mood. It was during these years that the cinema really came into its own. Millions escaped from dreary reality every week into a world of illusion, glamour and drama—combining the influence of Neptune with the creativity and panache of Leo. Those with this placing seem to have Neptune working for them in a marvellous way. Of course it will not be powerfully

69

placed for all, but if the individual is at all creative here is a boost to that creativity and to their imagination. It will work extremely well for those who have Leo accentuated, and interestingly will give enormous help to Pisceans, because Neptune rules that sign and will help them mould their ideas—they will have rather more confidence in their own efforts than they usually have. It could cause deceitfulness in those with a powerful Aquarian or Taurean emphasis.

Neptune in Virgo (1928/29 – 1942/43)

The critical aspect of Virgo is accentuated here, for those born during this period seem to take a far more critical view of social conditions and religion than their predecessors. They always seem to be ready to ask "why?" and to develop some fine idealistic attitudes from which a more caring general attitude emerges. There is an ever-increasing concern for conservation with those of this generation which motivates action in this direction. On a personal level the planet works badly for those with Gemini or Pisces dominating their charts, though it can be marvellously creative for them; they must try to use their imagination in a positive way, and not allow escapist, negative tendencies to cause confusion. It will tend to soften Virgoan types and increase their emotional level. Others can generally express a critical attitude in a kind way.

Neptune in Libra (1942/43 – 1956/57)

Those born during these years grew up to become the "flower power" peace-loving generation. Here we have a perfect example of the Neptune generation influence; the peace of Neptune, and the opting out (taking the line of least resistance is essentially Neptunian), plus the beauty-loving relaxed attitude of Libra. The planet has had a marked personal influence on those with Libra dominant. At worst it encouraged many to take to drugs, but at best it gives considerable inspiration, though other influences must to be powerful enough to allow that initial inspiration concrete expression. It may tend to make some Ariens rather forgetful and vague at times—an interesting and different characteristic for this assertive group—and can be tricky for Cancerians and Capricorns since it may have a weakening effect on their personalities.

Neptune in Scorpio (1956/57 – 1970/71)

Here Neptune's influence is exciting but harsh. There is an element of mystery and a somewhat weird feeling to this placing. The image of this generation has a rather cruel edge, and those with a powerful Neptune influence (because Scorpio is their Sun-, Moon- or Rising sign) have been known to put safety pins through their noses—the punk rocker image is very evocative of Neptune in Scorpio, as is the whole rock music scene. Neptune in Scorpio adds to the imagination and the result can be very intense and powerful. Those with this placing will certainly leave their mark on the world and should be aware that they must use their power, which could have a sinister side, for good. The planet may cause conflict for those with Taurus, Leo or Aquarius strongly marked in their birth-charts.

Neptune in Sagittarius (1970/71 – 1984/85)

There is a sympathy between Neptune and Sagittarius, so the planet should work extremely well for this generation. Here is Neptune at its most inspirational. Many will develop a truly philosophical attitude and outlook. There should be the ability to express a very natural sense of social justice, and those who lead this particular generation should be able to do much for mankind. Their image and overall "feel" will be very different indeed from those who have Neptune in Scorpio. The planet will work very well for those with Sagittarius dominating their charts, and could also do a lot for Ariens and Leos, making them as enthusiastic as ever, but adding an element of humility and sensitivity. Geminis and Virgos born during this period may tend to be deceitful or take the easy way out, but the placing should strengthen Pisceans.

The Pluto factor

Pluto is the most distant planet to have been integrated into the astrological structure. It was discovered in 1930, and takes some 248 years to travel round the Sun and through all 12 signs of the Zodiac. It stays in some signs for as long as 30 years, but because its orbit is very eccentric it travels through others in less than half that time. When Pluto was discovered there was depression in most western countries, Prohibition in the United States and the rise of the Nazi movement in Europe. Pluto is, then, connected with violence, extreme action and reaction. It is now the accepted ruler of Scorpio (up to 1930 this was the prerogative of Mars), and while it stays in a sign for a very long period, and consequently is in that sign for all people born during that period, its generation influence is less clear-cut than Neptune's. However, it does have a dynamic influence on individuals, as will be seen below.

Note that there is no interpretation for Pluto in Aries, Taurus, Sagittarius, Capricorn, Aquarius or Pisces. This is because there is no one alive or about to be born with Pluto in any of these signs.

Pluto in Gemini (1883/84–1912/13)
This placing can cause a certain amount of mental restlessness if other more personal planets also indicate this. The generation as a whole had the ability to make drastic changes. In Britain this period covered the whole of the reign of Edward VII, whose influence helped the new century to move forward in interesting and less repressive directions.

Pluto in Cancer (1913/14–1937/38)
As Neptune ended its journey through Cancer so Pluto entered that sign. The disruptive factors of Pluto have been emphasized very powerfully indeed through its effect on family life. Considerable periods of upheaval have tended to occur in the lives of those with Cancer, Capricorn, Aries or Libra

accentuated by Sun-, Moon-, or Rising-sign. It is important that Cancerian types with this placing do not keep problems to themselves; a tendency to do so is a strong possibility.

Pluto in Leo (1937/38 – 1956/57)

Perhaps the best thing to emerge from the overall effect of the transit of Pluto through Leo has been the development of the United Nations. The protection of mass interests is a concern of this transit, too, to a certain extent. The regal connotations of Leo and the force of Pluto combine to give power, but perhaps we really need more time to assess what may have been motivated during this period. A lot of positive good could come as a result of what was triggered off at this time, but unrest and the more domineering elements of Leo are, alas, present. Those Leo types who were born during this period may well have a tremendous power complex, and must use and direct it positively. There will be a marginally fanatical tendency in Taureans, Scorpios, and Aquarians born at this time, which could emerge as some kind of obsession or psychological problem. If well directed, this force can be most advantageous, motivating action in the individual and in others.

Pluto in Virgo (1956/57 – 1971)

Many people born with Pluto in Virgo also have Uranus in that sign (check in the tables). Here is a generation influence working on Virgo. Those with a Virgoan Sun-, Moon-, or Rising-sign are in a very powerful position to lead their generation and make really dynamic changes which will not only affect their personal lives but could have world-wide connotations. There is a need to uncover facts and to bring injustice into the open. All those with Pluto in Virgo have a rather special kind of power to use in their own individual way.

Pluto in Libra (1971 – 1983/84)

It is of course impossible to assess how Pluto in Libra will work for those born during the Seventies and early Eighties; nor is it possible to sum up what the planet's overall influence will be. It seems logical to assume that its action will be more gentle and subtle in its effect on individual and mass opinion and action—a kind of "iron hand in a velvet glove". If this is so, action will hopefully be taken on various world difficulties and injustices. The sense of justice, harmony and balance of Libra may have to be seriously shaken before it is allowed to settle again. A final resolution of the international nuclear situation must, of necessity, rest with those of this generation.

Pluto in Scorpio (1983/84 – 1995)

Pluto rules Scorpio. Vital changes are very likely to occur as the century ends, and these will be of world-shattering importance. If they are well directed our planet will survive for generations, if they are not we may not survive to care.

SELF-EXPRESSION

General characteristics
of the signs

The following pages form a compact, self-contained guide to the Zodiac, including for convenience a résumé of the characteristics of your own sign. This section will tell you about your friends and relations around the Zodiac and help you to understand some of the other signs, apart from your Sun-sign, that may feature strongly in your own birth-chart.

The signs of the Zodiac can be compared to lenses through which the forces of the planets pass. Each one colours the planetary influences in a special way and focuses them towards the area of life with which the sign is associated. In human beings the signs correspond to the 12 types of person familiar to readers of Sun-sign astrology in the newspapers. They also correspond to areas of the body, so that each one emphasizes a particular part, causing that part to be made either stronger or weaker just as a muscle is either strengthened or damaged when it is subjected to strain. Hence the apparently puzzling fact that Ariens, for example, whose sign rules the head, will either be prone to headaches or else will have none at all.

In addition to their human attributions the signs have a whole set of correspondences with other things. Places, herbs, flowers, animals and so on are said to be "ruled" by particular signs. This means that the object has some of the characteristics of its ruling sign or has some traditional link with it. These correspondences have been arrived at in various ways and passed down from one generation to the next, though they are constantly developing. Usually there is a reason that explains a correspondence. For example, London is thought to be ruled by Gemini because of the city's long history as a mercantile trading centre, Gemini being ruled by Mercury, the planet of trade and commerce. But there is often a difference of opinion about an attribution, especially where gemstones are concerned. In the lists of correspondences I have taken into consideration several alternatives and have listed the attributions I think most appropriate. Herbs are traditionally listed under the planets, but some are given zodiacal associations as well in the old herbals.

Your Sun-sign dates
Are you puzzled about which sign the Sun was in when you were born? Someone born on April 20 may sometimes find themselves listed as an Arien, sometimes as a Taurean; a person born on October 23 may appear in one Sun-sign column under Libra, and in another under Scorpio. This is because the Sun does not always leave one sign and enter another on the same date every year—and if you are in doubt you may need to find out not only the exact time you were born, but the precise time at which the Sun left one sign for the next one. Unfortunately there is no easy way of discovering the truth; you will either have to consult an astrologer or look up a table of the Sun's movements in an ephemeris, a list of the planetary positions for each day of your year of birth.

The three most recently discovered planets, Uranus, Neptune and Pluto have been gradually taken into the astrological system and given their own signs to rule. These rulerships are listed as well as the ancient ones.

Each sign is traditionally "positive" or "negative". The positive signs are masculine in a non-literal sense and tend to be extravert, whereas the negative and feminine signs tend to be introvert.

The signs are also divided up into four groups of three (triplicities), which correspond to the four traditional elements of Fire, Earth, Air and Water, and into three groups of four (quadruplicities), which are given the names "cardinal", "fixed" and "mutable". These groups and their characteristics are as follows:

Triplicities or elements
Fire (Aries, Leo, Sagittarius) = enthusiasm
Earth (Taurus, Virgo, Capricorn) = practical ability, stability
Air (Gemini, Libra, Aquarius) = intellectual ability
Water (Cancer, Scorpio, Pisces) = intuition

Quadruplicities or qualities
Cardinal (Aries, Libra, Cancer, Capricorn) = outgoing by nature
Fixed (Taurus, Scorpio, Leo, Aquarius) = rigid in opinions
Mutable (Gemini, Sagittarius, Virgo, Pisces) = flexible by nature

Polarities
Another important factor is the complementary relationship between "polar" signs, that is to say those that are opposite each other across the Zodiac. Here are the six pairs of polarities:

Aries—Libra
Taurus—Scorpio
Gemini—Sagittarius
Cancer—Capricorn
Leo—Aquarius
Virgo—Pisces

Aries

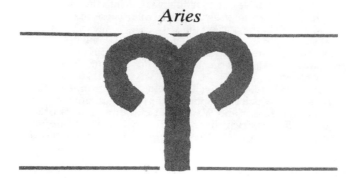

Positive
Ruling planet: Mars
Triplicity or element: fire
Quadruplicity or quality: cardinal
Colour: red
Gemstone: diamond
Metal: iron
Flowers: honeysuckle, thistle
Trees: all thorn-bearing trees
Herbs and spices: capers, mustard, cayenne pepper
Foodstuffs: onions, leeks, hops
Animals: sheep and rams
Countries: England, France, Germany
Cities: Naples, Florence, Krakow, Birmingham (U.K.)

The Aries personality is straightforward and basically uncomplicated. Ariens have a rare clarity of mind which helps them simplify issues which to most of us would be endlessly tricky and complex. Ariens are highly competitive, but any close friend of an Arien will know that, while the theme of the sign is "me first", this is not based entirely on selfishness but on a desire to win and to be out in front. It is a natural expression of the Arien energy and drive.

At school and in early life Aries will very often want to win at sport or be top of the form (though conversely, many are easily bored and couldn't care less about studies). In later life that winning characteristic gets positive expression through the career or the achievement of ambitions for their own advancement and the good of their families. This is the Arien need to be first at its best, since they are great supporters of their families. Arien mothers, for instance, will champion their children's causes to the hilt and stick up for their rights at school. In every Aries there is also an element of the pioneer, which will emerge in a variety of ways.

Ariens are highly sexed and enjoy their sex-life to the full. They make excellent partners provided they can control their selfish tendencies. Their lively enthusiasm for sex is, however, a great asset if they consider their partners.

The Aries body-area is the head, and Ariens are apt to suffer from headaches. Children of the sign tend to hit their heads when they fall, or prematurely knock out baby teeth. Because Ariens are often rushing about they are sometimes careless and will cut and burn themselves more than most people; so they need to be careful when handling sharp tools or working with metals—as they often do.

Aries in friendship, love and marriage

Astrologers are very often asked "which sign goes with which?" This is a difficult question and one that should be taken seriously. But general indications can be misleading, and it is impossible to be specific unless the astrologer has a fully calculated birth-chart to study. I remember a few years ago, on a radio phone-in programme, being asked by a young Arien girl whether she should go out with a Piscean boy. She rather liked him, but she thought she shouldn't encourage him, because Aries and Pisces "weren't any good for each other". I was upset to think that the poor girl had been so misled, and tried to reassure her—and indeed all the listeners—that we should never prevent the development of a friendship because we think our Sun-signs are incompatible.

Of course some Sun-signs are easier to get on with than others, but it is not fair to yourself or a prospective partner to let a superficial knowledge of Sun-sign astrology come between you and them.

If you learn about the characteristics of the Sun-signs, you can to a certain extent know what to expect of a person, and be on the look-out for those characteristics. This is interesting and fun. But it is only when you get into astrology in depth that you can use it fully to assess a personality.

Because we have quite a lot of scope in this book we can develop this area, and coming back to some generalizations and traditions, the *overall tendency* in friendships and in love is for you to get on best with other Sun-sign people who have the same "triplicity" or "element" as yourself. Ariens, on this criterion, will tend to be more in harmony with the other two Fire signs—that is, Leo and Sagittarius. Next down the scale, another element which would be sympathetic is Air, and the Air signs are Gemini, Libra and Aquarius. Earth signs

(Taurus, Virgo and Capricorn) and Water signs (Cancer, Scorpio and Pisces) are by tradition less good. But we must never dismiss them, since there could well be other links to help cancel out the traditional Sun-sign indications. You could, for instance, have Venus in Pisces, which is good for friendship and rapport with Sun-sign Pisceans. Similarly if you had Venus in Taurus you would relate well to Sun-sign Taureans. Mars, too, could have been in any of the signs at your birth, so its position might well help you towards a lively and sexually rewarding relationship with someone of your own Mars sign. And so on. The moral about all this is: don't ever just think of Sun-signs when forming friendships. It could spoil a lot of fun.

Relating this to marriage: those who know their birth-time and hence their Rising-sign (see pages 225–232) can take into account another important dimension, relating to the interesting theory of the polarity of the signs. The Aries polar sign (ie, the one directly opposite across the Zodiac) is Libra. On the Sun-sign level, then, it is possible you may well find some attractive Libran partner. But you also might well find someone who will become of above-average importance to you, whose Sun-sign will be the polar sign to your Rising-sign or vice versa. The polarity influence can also work between your two Rising-signs—rather like the possibility I mentioned above for Sun-sign Ariens and Librans. (For the list of polarities see page 75).

In astrology we often find that the best permanent relationships are between couples with these important polarities working for them. I have certainly found it to be so in the many birth-charts I have compared of couples with very successful and long-term relationships. This may have something to do with the proverbial attraction of opposites. There is always a rapport and, while the partners do not always agree or necessarily have the same interests, they always seem to say: "I understand you—I can see what you're getting at." This of course gives considerable depth and tenacity to a long-term relationship. As you will gather, polarity is not the only factor that makes for such relationships; the other more general ones work extremely well, but a good polarity makes for an excellent basis.

Arien friendships

If you are enthusiastic about some interest and want to encourage your friend to share your enthusiasm, this will not be difficult. You will yank them off to your favourite sporting event, show them the right books and magazines, and generally stir up their enthusiasm. Your own natural and lively enthusiasm is infectious to others, who will like you for it. There is, however, something you must remember: you are, alas, naturally rather selfish. It is all too easy for you, having accepted an invitation to dinner or to some outing, to find that something else—more important or perhaps just more fun—crops up. Your selfish trait will urge you to cancel your original arrangement with your friends, and take the "better" offer. Fine for you, but extremely hurtful to your friends if they find out about it. Now you may be very good indeed at ringing up with the prettiest, soundest, cleverest excuse, which they will no doubt accept; but when the same thing happens again—and again—they will see through you however much you exert your considerable charm. And of course the nearer the event, the weaker the excuse will sound and the more hurtful the result will be. You can cause more offence this way than you may realize. So do be aware that people are not all that thick-skinned, or even all that dim!

Try to give as much as possible within your friendships, and be patient when you have friends in need. Others may well want a shoulder to cry on—well, yours is strong enough. And remember, you may be a bit down in the dumps yourself some time, and they may well be very willing to give up their time and energy to help you through.

Aries in love

When Ariens fall in love, they fall quickly and very passionately. Sometimes it is all too easy for them to rush ahead and expect a relationship to develop very quickly. This can of course happen, and the result is fun for all. But Ariens should be just a little cautious, for they could spoil things by being just too pushy. A really charming trait, which is very Arien and which you might like to develop if it hasn't occurred to you, is to give the object of your affections a small, unexpected gift from time to time, for no apparent reason. This is always fun for the recipient, and its sheer unexpectedness will certainly get the evening off to a good start.

Because you are passionate, you may not be too concerned about your partner's comfort. You are less likely to grow out of the stage of making love in the back seat of the car, or on a rather damp rug in the bracken, than many other types. This is something of which you should be aware. Others may be less eager to embrace discomfort along with you, and for instance if you have your heart set on a Leo they may flinch a bit. So do consider your partner's comfort when going in for the kill.

It is fair to say that, whatever the position of Venus and Mars with their strong influence on one's love-life, Ariens are passionate and, unless there is some serious problem, highly sexed. Theirs is usually a very beautiful and positive sex force, and they will instinctively know the right way to express it. They should have as few problems as guilt after the event. Because of their basic, straightforward, uncomplicated personalities, they have the ability to get this sphere of their life sorted out at an early age, which is excellent. It is important, however, to remember that because Ariens have possibly above-average needs in this area, they need enthusiastic partners, and if there are difficulties for Ariens in a love relationship it is usually because their sex drives and those of their partners are unbalanced. It is at this level that care is needed in assessing your partners. You should make sure you keep your love-making active, amusing, engrossing and new. And your partners in turn will have to realize, and soon will realize, that their sex-life with you will be demanding—for even if you have one of your Arien blinding headaches it is unlikely to diminish your lively libido.

Aries in marriage

Ariens make good husbands and wives. Again, we get the enthusiastic need to get on in life and, in a rather child-like way, the desire and need for support from a partner who will be "nice to come home to". Ariens will be keen to decorate the house, make space for the workbench, sewing or hobbies room or an area for a favourite game. Homebuilding and expansion will present a lively challenge and will usually be greeted with pleasure—the pure Arien type is supposed to dislike do-it-yourself, but most Ariens seem to enjoy it. Of course if the Arien is rich and busy the same enthusiasm will be given to getting a local firm round to do the work!

As parents, Ariens will not mind too much the noise of the baby crying or get overanxious or worried about their children. If their offspring are slow to read or if progress at school isn't as fast as they would really like, they will do all they can to put this right. But they could rather too easily run out of patience. If they do they should try to remember their own childhood and ask their parents how good *they* were at school, and if *they* got bored with lessons, as young Martin or Miranda are tending to do. Like as not, there will be a groan from a grandparent, and some muttering about telling them the old, old story.

The cliché about there being give and take in marriage is one that Ariens should bear in mind. It is important that they reassess themselves from time to time. In all marriages, there are "taking" periods—times when we rely on our partners more than normally, times when restlessness may cause us to take lines of action that under other circumstances we might not think totally desirable. But likewise, there must be times when we *give* more than average, when the other partner has a particularly demanding work-load, when examinations are imminent, or when a baby is about to be born or has just arrived. During these periods Ariens must hold back, and really ask themselves if they are burning enough of their abundant energy in making everything as easy as possible for their partner.

It is also vitally important to remember that the major Arien fault, selfishness, is likely to emerge from time to time. When it does the individual Arien type is the least likely to recognize it, and when confronted with it by his or her partner the reaction will be one of total surprise. Perhaps thoughtlessness has been the root cause of the difficulty, and it is this, as well as any downright putting of the self first, that needs correction. Ariens by nature are uncomplicated, and, as ever, it is their straightforward attitude to life that can be appealed to at such times.

To sum up, then: if you are a committed Arien you have a lot to offer and a lot to give in marriage. Your marvellous zest for life will merge with your partner's positive traits, creating something special and well worth guarding with great care.

Arien careers and money matters

When assessing the Arien potential in careers and financial ability we must consider not only the psychological motivation and mode of expression attributed to Aries but also the thinking processes of Mercury, and how these two factors combined can be best used in both areas. Then there is the influence of Venus, a planet as strongly related to finance and possessions as to relationships. The latter aspect is also important in this sphere as it will affect how a person will get on with colleagues, in business partnerships, and so on. Mars may well give some hint as to the direction of energy and will most certainly influence the physical element—the drive and energy put into the day's work. As we shall see, the influence of the combined Sun and Rising-sign is interesting and very personal; but if your birth time is not available and you cannot find out your Rising-sign, do not be too disappointed; you should be able to glean plenty of information about this sphere of your life from the more general paragraphs.

The basic Arien characteristics will need as much positive expression in the career as in any other sphere of life. So at the simplest level, it is fair to say that in their working life Ariens need a job that is demanding, that will use up a great deal of their abundant energy, that keeps them on the go, is challenging, competitive and in general rather tough. The toughness can of course be physical, but it can also mean mental challenges: intellectual battles to be fought, competitors to be out-thought and out-manoeuvred, and so on. The Arien "me first" motivation must have plenty of expression, so it is a good thing for Ariens to have to force themselves in their working lives to be out in the field, to get in first with a new product, to make some breakthrough with a new and untried foreign customer, and so on. In other words, to *explore*, to *pioneer*, and most importantly to *win*. The greater the competition the better, and that competition can be stimulating to people as different as the factory-floor worker and the energetic youth worker urging his troop to even greater achievements or injecting some enthusiasm into a couldn't-care-less group of delinquents!

81

What would not be a happy situation for pretty well any Arien would be work in a very repetitive and boring job, with little or no chance of promotion or the possibility of any kind of progress. There are exceptions to this rule, but generally there must be a good incentive to work, so that something can actually be seen to have been achieved. The achievement need not necessarily be a fatter pay packet, though obviously this is very important and is always helpful and encouraging. Ariens are not totally financially oriented as a rule, and despite the very great need for money they will not be satisfied by a good salary if interest and enthusiasm in the daily work is lacking.

Generally a quiet, tense atmosphere will not be agreeable and most Ariens would be happier in a noisy workshop, typing pool, factory, garage or busy department store than in some office in which a small group of people arrive every morning on the dot of nine, hang up their coats, make the same comments about the weather, and sit down at their desks not to raise their eyes until coffee time. All much too dull. If Ariens make a career in such professions as the law or real estate they should see to it that they are the ones doing battle in court, showing and persuading people to buy new property, and so on, leaving as much of the contract-writing and routine jobs to others as possible. Ariens represent action, not, generally speaking, stodgy detail, in which they may tend rather dangerously to cut corners.

While it is possible to draw up a list of "Arien jobs and professions", if we look around us we find, of course, that Ariens are working (together with people of all the other Sun-signs) in every area of life we come across; so it will be more useful to be a little more precise, and come to some definite conclusions by relating the other planetary positions to Aries Sun-sign types. Before getting down to detail, however, remember to bear in mind the position of Mars (see pages 246–249) and the sign it was in when you were born. That sign will help you assess the degree of your drive and energy and whether they are emotionally or physically oriented. Remember, too, that Mars is very important to you, as it is your Sun ruler. You may even have some of the characteristics of the sign it was in when you were born. You can discover this if you look up the brief descriptions of the other signs. You may at least feel some identification with those characteristics, because the planet's influence is a very personal one for you.

Mercury at work

Check position of Mercury on pages 238–241

Mercury in Pisces
If Mercury was in Pisces when you were born it will have given you a higher level of sympathy and a kinder attitude to others than many other Ariens. Remembering that perhaps you might be forgetful and possibly rather less assertive than other Ariens, you could perhaps cope best with a job that doesn't rely too much on your having to cope with heavy organizing. You might be very good, for instance, in the caring professions such as social work, because in addition to feeling sympathy you will also have the Arien urge to get things done and to stamp out social injustice. Personnel work might also be a possibility—in fact anything which requires sensitive sympathy and understanding would be suitable. Possibly you will work better from behind the scenes. You may well have

consciously to train your memory, which otherwise could let you down.

If you are about to study, try to keep the various aspects of your subject carefully filed and in good order. This won't be easy, but it will help you to develop your memory and organizational ability. At examination time, work at learning any vital groups of facts as an actor learns lines. This will help put your mind at rest. Put in all the possible time you can, which will alleviate worry about the final result. Don't leave study to the last minute.

Mercury in Aries

If Mercury was in Aries with the Sun you will be able to use your assertive forethought in your work. Advance planning should be a strong point provided that you keep your mind in check and that your natural drive doesn't leap over too many problems and details. You should be very quick at decision-making, so if your work has an element of danger you should be exactly the sort to cope with situations as they arise in an extremely direct and correct way. If you are a driver, pilot, or motor-cyclist, you will know precisely what to do, and when. You are less likely to make mistakes provided you take time and trouble to develop your technique and a really high degree of professional skill. Then your quick mind will direct a sure physical response and you can rest assured that you know the job in hand backwards as well as forwards.

If you are about to study remember that you assimilate facts quickly and probably forget them equally quickly. It is good for you to work particularly hard immediately before your examinations, and concentrate your energy on the development of technique earlier in your course.

Mercury in Taurus

This placing of Mercury at the time of your birth will probably steady and slow down your thinking process. You will have greater patience than most Ariens and more ability to slog away at routine work. You are also more likely to be disciplined. You could take up some work that has financial overtones—perhaps working on challenging financial schemes or areas of insurance in which you are not stuck in an office—assessing claims, for instance. You might do well in your own business since you have the ability to cope with tax, profits and so on. In fact you have a genuinely financial turn of mind. As for the sort of business, garaging, engineering or anything else connected with metals would be excellent.

If you are about to study, remember that someone with Mercury in Taurus, in spite of having an Arien Sun-sign, needs time to assimilate details; so don't leave all your revision (or indeed all your preparation) to the night before you are to sit an important examination. Make a careful scheme at the beginning of the course and stick to it.

Venus: money and rapport

Check position of Venus on pages 242–245

Venus in Aquarius

If Venus was in Aquarius at the time of your birth it would indicate that you are probably not overconcerned about money. But any emphasis on the sign Aquarius has glamorous overtones, so you may well have quite a strong liking for beautiful and original things, and your Arien enthusiasm will cause you to spend money on the latest, best and possibly most expensive items, whether they be clothes, unusual things for the home, or hi-fi equipment. I don't think you will let yourself get bogged down by finance, but as with most Ariens it is extravagance that could cause problems for you. You'll work hard to get money, but not worry too much about where it goes. This is fine in many ways, but remember that credit-card companies send out their accounts with great regularity! Air lines, space, television and uranium might be possible areas of investment for you to follow up.

As far as colleagues are concerned you come off very well—you relate to them in a friendly, cool but understanding way. You'd make an approachable boss and do the right thing at the right time.

Venus in Pisces

With Venus in Pisces at the time of your birth you will have excellent earning potential, but you may not be very good at coping with and planning your financial affairs. It is very important for you always to take professional advice about money, and rely on someone of experience to help you. The further you progress in your career, the more important this is. I would advise you to have an accountant if you have any financial scheme outside your everyday work. If not, at least get on good terms with your bank manager; convince him of your talents and abilities, and trust his advice. You might with his approval like to invest in, say, a shipping line, fisheries, deep-sea oil or the footwear trade. You will find these interesting from a financial point of view.

You make a marvellous colleague and may find that you'll be a shoulder to cry on, since as well as having sympathy you can get things done. If you are in charge, almost too much of your time could be given over to the welfare of your staff. If you instruct or teach you will do well at it, but don't let your Arien assertiveness be swamped by others' misfortunes. You may sometimes have to be cruel to be kind. However, your Arien warmth will see you through on such occasions.

Venus in Aries

If Venus was in Aries at your birth money will burn a hole in your pocket! This is your nature and the way you enjoy life. I'm not saying you are stupid about money—merely that you can't hold on to it very long (unless your Rising-sign gives you really practical and cautious qualities: see pages 225–232). Mercury in Taurus (see pages 238–241) would give you a bit of thoughtful restraint. All this being the case, you will have to work hard for promotion and a bigger pay packet. Why not turn your enthusiasm to the future? Take out a long-term insurance bond, or something that will make a demand on your pocket. Then you'll be able to buy that large, comfortable car of your dreams when you retire and the company stops supplying you with the type you're used to. You might invest in engineering firms, the motor industry or heavy industrial plant.

Where your colleagues are concerned, you may have to be a bit careful, because you could at times annoy them more than you realize. Try consciously to have a little more time for them and their problems, however boring you find them. You may well be able to urge them into actions they may not otherwise feel confident to take. Remember that others, especially subordinates, are less assertive and ambitious than you; so do make allowances for them, difficult though this may be.

Venus in Taurus

Of all Ariens, those born with Venus in Taurus are most likely to want to make money in order to enjoy the creature comforts of life. You will want to get on in your career not just to be out in front but to earn a high income. You will manage your money well and may have an energetic and lively flair for investment—perhaps expressed in your career. You will work with an eye to the future, take out good insurance policies, and make sound investments. All the same you'll like your luxuries and comforts, and have the ability to budget for them. Perhaps you need more financial security than most Ariens. If this is the case, it is up to you to see that you get it! You could do extremely well and even make a fortune, since you have sound financial good sense and at the same time are not afraid to take risks. You would give daring but not unsound advice to others. You might enjoy investing in the cosmetic trade, fashion, agriculture or horticulture, and most importantly in big business.

You work well with other people, and perhaps need partnerships more than many. If you have a secretary you will guard her jealously and will not like changing her—"temps" are not for you. As a boss you are nice and steady. Subordinates know where they stand with you.

Venus in Gemini

If you are an Arien with Venus in Gemini you may well have learned the hard way about money and have a penchant for spending rather too much on things like books and records—though Mercury in Taurus would help towards a sounder attitude (see pages 238–241). So be careful. You need to take informed advice, for your quick, lively mind could get very bored with the tedium of financial matters. It might be a good idea for your partner to do your budgeting for you. You have the ability to sell, but you yourself could also fall for a "sell" rather easily. Watch out: you might, perhaps in your enthusiasm to help a friend, fall for an unsound scheme. Make a conscious effort to slow down and think through any scheme put to you. You might like to invest in department stores, the media or magazine companies.

You will make an excellent, friendly colleague and an informal and approachable boss. You don't suffer fools gladly, and you'll want super-speed and super-efficiency from all staff, but you may well have to compromise. The best way for you to get efficiency is to encourage it in your nice, friendly, unpompous manner, rather than getting too worked up about it.

Rising-signs and your career

First check your Rising-sign on pages 225–232

Note: Careers and the Midheaven

If you develop your interest in astrology one of the first things that you will learn about, but which is outside the scope of this book, is the Midheaven. Roughly speaking, this is the sign immediately over your head when you were born. It is as important in your career, outward expression and identification with objectives in life as your Rising-sign is in your personality. To combine it with your Rising-sign is complicated and would be impossible in a book of this length: but, while I cannot help you to discover yours in this book, rest assured that I have borne the various possibilities in mind when writing the following paragraphs in relation to your choice of profession or job.

Aries with Aries rising

Your huge drive and enthusiasm will make you a natural in building up your own business and doing things in your own individual way. You need to press on regardless. You are likely to be very ambitious and an individualist, and might be a bit of a loner. You have excellent powers of survival, and can cope with having the buck passed to you. You might be attracted to architecture or the construction industry, politics or humanitarian causes.

Aries with Taurus rising

You might want to work behind the scenes in an executive capacity, but make sure that you have plenty of challenges. You have a good business sense and potential and an individual flair and approach. You are ambitious and need security more than most Ariens. The chances are you'll need a somewhat conventional career, and would progress well in any large organization, eventually reaching a high position. Any business career, agriculture or work involving financial investment would be suitable. You may well be very musical; don't neglect this talent if you feel you possess it.

Aries with Gemini rising

You have great powers of persuasion and the ability to sell. You could well be quite a strong influence on other people, so if you have a cause you'll be able to make your point and get your ideas over to other people extremely well. You will do well in work that takes you out and about. Travelling suits you. You might like to work for an airline or a cruise line (perhaps as a cruise co-ordinator) or in the travel industry generally. Science and chemistry may attract you. If you are artistic you might like to write.

Aries with Cancer rising

You should not find it difficult to achieve your objectives and will do extremely well. Your instinctive protective urge may well emerge in your career; you would do well working with children, perhaps as a teacher. You might also be attracted towards the hotel trade and catering as you have the makings of a chef. If you like to work for yourself you might do well as a restaurateur or in the antiques trade. You could have a love of history, archaeology and astronomy. You need to be psychologically involved with your work.

Aries with Leo rising

Your enthusiasm and dramatic flair will be best expressed in a career that allows you to show off. You might be a commissionaire, or better still at the reception desk telling others what to do. You should reach the top of your profession, which might be in the services, the theatre, a large department store, a computer firm or perhaps the media. Don't neglect creative ability, and always encourage others to make the best of themselves. You're a natural boss, generous to your employees and able to command loyalty.

Aries with Virgo rising

You have well-developed powers of observation and the ability to work very hard. You would make an excellent teacher or lecturer, secretary or personal assistant. Working outdoors is excellent for you, perhaps in horticulture. You could well be a born reporter or journalist, and if you want to write do not underestimate your ability—there might well be a novel in you. Do not take on too much responsibility: you need security and to be kept fully occupied.

Aries with Libra rising

It is not good for you to work alone. You need to be with others, perhaps in partnership. You have drive plus tact (though less tact if Mercury was in Aries when you were born—check on pages 238–241). You might enjoy the hotel trade. You would be good at liaison work or in any organizational job. You would enjoy looking after others' creature comforts, as airline hostess, barman or hairdresser. Or, since you may have a creative flair, you could do well as an interior decorator.

Aries with Scorpio rising

You need a job that makes heavy demands on your physical and emotional energy. In choosing your career you must let your instinct be your guide, and it may well be that you made the decision when you were little. Perhaps you wanted to be a general or admiral, another Helena Rubinstein or 007. Whatever you do you need excitement. You will probably do well provided you never allow yourself to stagnate.

Aries with Sagittarius rising

You must have challenge in your work, and may be better working with other people or in partnership than alone. You would make an excellent lecturer, but working with older students rather than schoolchildren. You would be a good courier, tour organizer or translator, and would find working for a publishing firm very interesting. If you love sport and the outdoors, working at a riding stable or stud could well attract you. You could also find a niche as a physical education instructor.

Aries with Capricorn rising

You could cope with really difficult conditions—perhaps working in a cold climate or in field work of some kind. Surveying, mining, engineering or the Army are all possible areas. You might be attracted to dentistry or osteopathy, and would make an excellent masseur or masseuse. You are a very independent type of Arien and would do well working for yourself—possibly building up some kind of cottage industry or business that fires your imagination and requires specialist knowledge.

Aries with Aquarius rising

The usual characteristics of Aquarius might be expressed in your choice of career. You could be attracted to out-of-the-ordinary studies, and later on use them profitably. If you are artistic you might have a flair for ancient or ethnic music or art forms. You might also like to specialize in biology, scientific research, or modern languages. Don't allow yourself to get into a rut, for there is a danger that you might resist change and thus thwart progress in your career. Medical science of an advanced nature could be a suitable area for you, especially if research is involved.

Aries with Pisces rising

You may well have an urge to start your own small business—possibly a publishing enterprise. If so, take it easy and steady. Don't be afraid to specialize. Keep the business under control, and don't force its growth. You might like to run a shoe shop. Or, if you are creative, you could be a writer. You would also make a good teacher, or perhaps you should have a job involving travel over considerable distances. You should study languages and always use your abundant imagination creatively. You would also be good at stimulating this in other people—your students perhaps.

Taurus

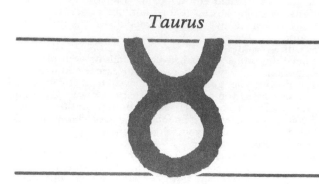

Negative
Ruling planet: Venus
Triplicity or element: earth
Quadruplicity or quality: fixed
Colour: pink
Gemstone: sapphire, sometimes emerald
Metal: copper
Flowers: rose, poppy, foxglove
Trees: ash, cypress, apple, vines
Herbs and spices: cloves, sorrel, spearmint
Foodstuffs: wheat, berry fruits, apples, pears, grapes
Animals: cattle
Countries: Ireland, Switzerland, Iran
Cities: Dublin, Lucerne, Mantua, Leipzig

Of all the 12 signs Taurus is the one that most needs security, routine, and the knowledge that certain things will happen at certain times. This is of extreme importance to them. They tend, for instance, to prefer a solid monthly pay cheque to some more erratic form of income. So generally speaking Taureans will find a niche which gives them that essential security—which can provide a stable background to their individual lifestyle.

It is important to remember that Taureans are patient plodders; children of this sign must be allowed to develop at their own pace, and parents may have to curb impatience if they feel that their offspring are not making as much progress at school as they would like.

It is not only financial security that is important to Taureans; emotional security is of prime importance too, and while Taureans make excellent, stable partners, they must learn that there is a possessive streak in them which can cause companions to feel a certain claustrophobia within the relationship. Taureans are extremely passionate, though sometimes slow to get going—they like to be as sure as possible of the eventual outcome before committing themselves! They make marvellously sensual and kind lovers and have the reputation of being the most good-looking of the 12 signs, though because they like good, rich, often sweet food, a weight problem can develop and they may tend to put off starting a diet, which might be a great mistake. A handsome Taurean face isn't improved by a heavy double chin.

The Taurean body-area is the neck, and for many a Taurean sore throats can be a problem. Taureans are often musical and many of them sing extremely well.

Taurus in friendship, love and marriage

Perhaps one of the commonest generalizations you hear when you talk in overall terms about astrology is that particular signs "go with" each other. But I cannot stress too strongly that it is very silly indeed to claim that because two people have apparently incompatible Sun-signs, they will not be able to develop a rewarding relationship. Not only is it wrong to suggest this, but it can lead to the destruction of a potentially happy and fulfilling partnership, and thus to considerable unhappiness.

So it is very important to remember that we should never, ever judge compatibility on the basis of the Sun-sign alone. And that applies to ties of friendship and to business partnerships just as much as to emotional and sexual relationships.

It is true to say that people of particular Sun-signs do tend to get on better with each other than with those of some other Sun-signs, and there is an overall tendency in love and friendship to feel initially more at ease with someone whose Sun-sign is of the same *element* as your own. As a Sun-sign Taurean, you are likely to feel more at ease with people who have elements of the two other Earth signs—Virgoans and Capricorns. People who have elements of the Water signs (Cancerians, Scorpios and Pisceans) will also be sympathetic—and just to complete the picture, you may find it less easy, on a very basic level, to strike up a rapport with Ariens, Leos and Sagittarians (Fire signs) and with Geminians, Librans and Aquarians (Air signs).

But please remember that it is *only* when the complete birth-charts of any two people are calculated and interpreted that anybody can reach any positive (or negative!) conclusions about a partnership between them. And even when an astrologer has done this, you will find that—if he or she is a really good astrologer—there will never be any question of your being told that you should or should not share a relationship with someone of any other sign. That is always a matter just for you, yourself—and it is always worth remembering that apart from astrology there are your relative environments, backgrounds, education—all sorts of other things—to be considered. What an astrologer can do is assess areas of compatibility or incompatibility, and point these out, so that you can make the necessary allowances and adjustments. For instance you, as a Sun-sign Taurean, will probably like your creature comforts, and your attitude to love will be tinged with a need for permanence and security; you could be possessive, too. If you were framing a relationship with a Sagittarian, you would have to accept the fact that he or she might well be less concerned with comfort and financial security, needing a certain amount of freedom of expression within an emotional relationship.

In some Sun-sign books or magazines you may find it said that Taurus and Sagittarius should "never go together". But when the full charts are calculated, there could well be some extremely powerful astrological links between them: your Sagittarian friend's Rising-sign, for instance, could be highly compatible with your Taurean Sun.

Using this book, you can make some calculations for yourself. If you meet an Arien or a Geminian to whom you feel attracted, look to see if you have Venus or Mercury in the relevant Sun-sign; that would be a marvellous starting-point, and would certainly help mitigate the apparent incompatibility of your Sun-signs.

Where marriage or a permanent relationship are concerned, I have always found that the most important element to look for in chart comparisons (*synastry*, as astrologers call it) is a strong element on the polar or opposite sign. If you know the time of your birth you should by now know your Rising-sign (see page 225). It may be that your partner's Sun-sign is the polar or opposite sign across the Zodiac. (For a list of polar signs, see page 75). If so, this is excellent; there will be a special rapport between you. And while of course you won't always agree about everything, at least real understanding will be possible. Polarity can also work equally well between two Sun- or Rising-signs. The Moon, too, can play an important part: for instance someone whose Moon-sign is compatible with your own will respond well to your suggestions, understand your moods. And if the link is a pair of shared Moon-signs, the way in which you will pick up each other's changing moods will be positively uncanny!

Taurean friendships

You are a very steadfast and constant friend, and if you are asked to do something for someone you will not let them down. If you are asked at a busy time you will be honest enough to say right away that you can't help out at that particular moment, but you will go on to make some practical suggestions as to how they can get help elsewhere.

It may be that you are a little reluctant to make new friends, liking old and well-tried ones best. There may be periods in your life when you have to make a conscious effort to be a bit more adventurous in that direction, for instance if you have to move to another area away from those whose companionship you enjoy and trust. Should this happen the best thing you can do is get to know new people on your own ground. Once you have settled into a new apartment or house you would do well to give a small party for your prospective friends. You can then begin to assess them within your own new environment.

There is one thing you may need to consider rather carefully in regard to friendship, and that is the pace at which other people live their lives. This varies of course according to the individual, but it could well be that your pace is slower than that of a great many people with whom you come into contact. While you are not likely to be the sort to keep friends waiting for hours at a rendezvous, you could seem a little slow to them. If you recognize this fact, you will be able to adjust more easily.

Most people, of course, find friendship among those with common interests, but for you, common ground is very important. You will probably develop life-long interests when you are young, and if you are an older reader you will at once think of two or three subjects that have fascinated you for years. Your enthusiasm grows slowly and very steadily, and you need people of similar tastes to be with and to get to know well, so that you can have long, carefully considered discussions about your common interest.

You must try hard not to feel as if your nose had been put out of joint when a firm friend finds a new interest that doesn't attract you. Obviously this will bring them into contact with a new group of people and you might be a little resentful.

Your strong point in friendship is that you are always ready to give support and practical help—doing the shopping if someone is ill, relieving people of mundane cares at times of stress or sorrow, and generally being a tower of strength.

Taurus in love

When you, as a Taurean, are attracted to someone you will initially weigh up the situation with great care and patience. Then, when your passion is aroused, you feel like going into a bull-like charge. But in the long run you will probably learn that steady caution and charm is a better way of getting what you want. You will not be reluctant to state your case, but you are far more likely to be successful simply by being your charming self than by forcing any issue or attempting to overwhelm someone. It might be as well for you, when the situation is reversed and you get an inkling that someone is attracted to you, simply to go along with them at their pace; you could well find the experience very rewarding. It is some-times said that Taureans are slow to arouse sexually, but that having been aroused they are very passionate indeed. There is a great deal of truth in this statement and if you examine yourself you might find some restraining factor in your psychological make-up. It may be that a conventional streak holds you back or—more likely—you want to be really sure that you are not going to be hurt by being rejected.

The worst Taurean fault, possessiveness, can emerge quite early in a love affair; and should a partner want to end a relationship, without your quite understanding why, your own possessiveness could be the reason, even though you might think you haven't been possessive at all. The fonder you are of your lover the more likely you are to behave in this way. Recognizing this tendency will help you to overcome it. Also, be careful not to smother your partner with too much affection.

You may well need to be with your partner rather more than they need to be with you. If you try too hard to enlarge your part in the other person's life, you could well be in for trouble.

There is also a danger that, once you are past the developing stages of your relationship, your deep and passionate feelings could make you need more permanence than your partner is ready to allow. So, while you may feel ready to marry or live together, your loved one may stall a bit before making such a commitment, perhaps on the excuse that they need more time, but probably in fact because they feel that their freedom is threatened.

To sum up: you make a really marvellous lover, and have a natural ability to attract those you find attractive, but don't try to monopolize your partner's life too much or you may find that he or she is frightened.

Taurus in marriage

Bearing in mind the importance that you probably attach to the creature comforts of life you may well be sympathetic to the idea of saving up to get married, so that you have a proper home to move into after the honeymoon. This may sound a bit old-fashioned, but there's nothing wrong with that if you want to make sure that the scene is set exactly as you would wish from the beginning.

This is not to say that you won't live roughly when you are young, perhaps with a partner or a series of partners. But having passed through that stage and settled on a career you will do more than your fair share of home-making, with a view to marriage and the eventual building of a family. You want a sound, stable life not only for yourself but your partner and children—the right environment to support them so that they can blossom and develop in the way which is exactly right for them. Being Taurean, you will work hard to make money in order to achieve this. Having done so, you will rest assured that you have done your bit.

Again, however, I must stress the possibility of possessiveness. It could creep into your marriage. Do be careful that your husband or wife is not just another favourite possession, and remember that one can never own another person. Watch yourself so that you never think of your partner as literally "*my* man" or "*my* woman". When the children are young, remember if you are a man that your wife will have to give a lot of attention to them so that she has less time and may seem to have less love for you. Counter this by, for example, taking on more of the household tasks than your busy career commitments may previously have allowed.

Taureans make good parents, but may err on the side of spoiling their children, perhaps with too many expensive toys that are not necessarily of the kind to stretch and involve their imaginations. Some expensive toys are actually limiting. Plain building bricks can make a palace or a filling station, but one can't convert an elaborate plastic model.

When children reach the teenage years it could be a little difficult for you to cope with the generation gap. Though this happens to most parents, your children may seem particularly unconventional to you. Try not to overdiscipline them if you think their behaviour not up to your standard. Times, after all, change very rapidly. Your lifestyle when you were 16 was probably equally unendearing to your parents. Bearing this firmly in mind will make for an easier, calmer and more relaxed life all round.

Taurean careers and money matters

When assessing the Taurean potential in careers and financial ability we must consider not only the psychological motivation and mode of expression attributed to Taurus but also the thinking processes of Mercury, and how these two factors can best be used in both areas. Then there is the influence of Venus, a planet as strongly related to finance and possessions as to relationships. The latter aspect is also important in this sphere as it will affect how a person will get on with colleagues, in business partnerships, and so on. And as Venus is the ruling planet of Taurus its influence will be particularly significant in the careers of Sun-sign Taureans.

Mars may well give some hint as to the direction of energy and will most certainly influence the physical element—the drive and energy put into the day's work. As we shall see, the influence of the combined Sun and Rising-sign is interesting and very personal; but if your birth-time is not available, and you cannot find out your Rising-sign, do not be too disappointed; you should be able to glean plenty of information about this sphere of your life from the more general paragraphs.

Financial stability and a secure job are essential for Taureans, who need to be assured that the pay-cheque or pay-packet will arrive regularly and on time, so that they are able to plan their finances well ahead, budgeting for purchases, holidays and the education of their children with care, forethought and precision. Of course many Taureans find themselves in less financially stable professions, but when this happens they have the sense to plan as carefully as possible, making investments as and when they can in order to give themselves a sense of security.

One finds Taureans in all walks of life, as with all the Zodiac types. However, certain careers do predominate for Sun-sign Taureans. Most certainly, many really have a flair for business and the ability to make money for themselves and others. The security factor often plays a part in the actual choice of work: Taureans, for instance, often find themselves working in large and impressive companies or consortiums.

93

Taureans are plodders and hate to be rushed in any way. They also like to tread familiar paths, and the unknown can be rather frightening to them. They like to work out a very definite routine, one that will take them along the same roads to the same station to catch the same train every morning, to sit in the compartment with the same group of people (doing the same crossword or reading the business pages of the same newspaper), getting out of the train and going along the same route to the office, starting work quietly and getting through the same amount of reading, dictation or meetings before the coffee break, and so on.

It is important that the Taurean has the right atmosphere in which to work. A large, noisy open-plan office may well have to be tolerated, but the Taurean will work very hard to get out of that office and into a quiet corner in which to work alone, away from everyone else's chatter and rushing about. Whatever the chosen profession, these are the sort of conditions that are right for the rather slow but very sound and steady Taurean temperament.

Taureans will work hard and will get through the work allocated to them, though they could well slow down in the afternoons after they have taken a client to lunch and had perhaps a little too much to eat to make for a productive afternoon's work.

Because Taureans very often choose a sedentary career they can easily get out of condition physically, and successful Taureans (especially the men) must watch their weight. This will all too easily shoot up, especially if there is usually a good dinner to go home to after a substantial and overrich business lunch. They often simply cannot burn up all the calories they eat. Even those working in more active careers such as farming can also succumb in this way. So some careful weight-watching is necessary.

Because a need for security is such an important factor in the Taurean choice of career, it is sometimes the case that the challenge of innovation is lacking. This in fact suits many Taureans since having to think constantly about the possibilities of blazing new paths or finding new outlets for products could be a considerable source of worry to them, and it might well not be worthwhile in the long run for them to put themselves in a situation where demands of this kind are made on their time and energy. They are better at sorting out the details of contracts which other, more assertive types, have secured. They can best support, give additional strength, advise and consolidate, rather than originate. But planetary placings could modify this and bring a greater need for challenge, so this should be thought about carefully at the outset of a career (see positions of Mercury in the following section).

Taurean patience will be extremely useful in the working life, and any area that makes demands on patience and needs long hours of solid concentration will be very suitable— detailed legal work might be an example.

It is a pity that for many Taureans the choice of career is simply a means of earning a living. While they will see to it that they earn more and more as time passes through the application of their reliable, steadfast qualities, there is sometimes no real psychological involvement in the actual work itself. Young Taureans will choose a training scheme after school or a university subject on the advice of the careers teacher, but often without any love of it. This can unfortunately lead to a career in which their real selves are not involved, and could have a negative effect in the long run.

Mercury at work

Check the position of Mercury on pages 238–241

Mercury in Aries
If Mercury was in Aries when you were born, you will have more ability to argue and a greater need for challenge than many Taureans, so if your work has a pioneering and challenging aspect to it you will find it fulfilling. If, for instance, you have to find new customers from time to time you will be well able to do so and will probably enjoy the strategic planning that will eventually lead to a deal. You can cope with such demands and should not be apprehensive of taking on the sort of work that has this kind of spicy element to it.

With this placing I don't think you will have the usual Taurean need to stick rigorously to a rigid routine in your working life. It is probably good for you to have flexible hours, and you can get through a much more demanding, high-speed life than most Taureans and enjoy it. Quick thinking and decision-making followed up by Taurean resoluteness will stand you in good stead. You don't lack incentive, and if you want to start your own business you should do extremely well, and it should give you the excitement and challenge that you need in your work. You are probably not afraid to take a certain number of financial risks, but your sound Taurean caution will control this tendency. You can learn facts rather more quickly than many Taureans, but don't rely too much on last-minute revision for examinations.

Mercury in Taurus
This placing makes you a bit of a plodder. You must allow yourself plenty of time to assimilate facts, so the work you do must be steady, and you must make quite sure that the "in" tray doesn't pile up more quickly than the "out" tray. At times this may be difficult. If you do occasionally get snowed under try not to get flustered or worried and keep your calm. You should not be in a situation where you have to come to snap decisions, or where the pace of work is uneven. It is bad for you to have stretches of time when there is little or nothing to do, then others when you are rushed off your feet.

Reliability is one of your strong points, and you will find that people will depend on you, for you can inspire great confidence. Accountancy would probably come naturally to you, and you might find it rewarding to cope with tax problems. If you have your own business, there should be no difficulty in coping with the books. This position of Mercury is often very appreciative of music. You may love to sing or play an instrument, but you will also very much enjoy listening to others perform. The record business might appeal to you. As your thinking processes are rather slow you should plan your study time very carefully. Make out a programme and stick to it. Never rely on last-minute revision or study when taking examinations.

Mercury in Gemini
If you are in business you will find this placing very helpful. You will be a good talker, enjoy the company of comparative strangers and like meeting new people. Work involving this kind of activity is very suitable. You can project an idea convincingly and you have the natural ability—the charm and eloquence—to inspire confidence. You are good at winning a person over, whether it is a prospective customer or a bank manager from whom you are trying to get an overdraft. You

have a very lively mind and will want to use it. Work in a department store would suit your abilities and give you security and the prospect of a steady rise towards some responsible position such as head buyer. The enjoyment of working with and talking to people should not be underestimated. Public relations work and consumer surveys are possibilities worth considering. Your mind is very versatile, but your powers of concentration are likely to be shallower than most Taureans. You will learn facts quickly, but forget them equally quickly. So when it comes to examinations you'd better allow a good few weeks beforehand to brush up your facts.

Venus: money and rapport

Check the position of Venus on pages 242–245

Venus in Pisces
With Venus in Pisces it is easy for you to feel sorry for those in need, and so you will be generous. Being Taurean you will have an innate sense of responsibility about finance and a natural ability to plan carefully, but you won't be able to suppress your emotion when you hear, for instance, an appeal for the week's good cause on radio or television. In spite of your Taurean qualities it is quite a good idea for you to take professional advice when coping with money problems—especially early in your career, when you could otherwise have to learn the hard way.

There is some risk of your being overkind to others and it might well be quite difficult for you to take a hard line. If you are an employer you will want to help any employee in difficulty. Whatever your profession, it will probably give you pleasure to organize fund-raising events for charity as well as to dip into your own pocket. Venus in Pisces makes you a very nice person to work with; your natural sympathy is something that will endear you to your colleagues. You really are someone they can always turn to, whether you are the boss or the coffee lady! You might like to invest in fisheries, in the manufacture of liquid products such as paint or in the shoe trade.

Venus in Aries
If you have Venus in Aries, you have the ability to make money. But your natural enthusiasm and your equally natural love of beautiful things will get the better of you far more often than you may care to admit, and when they get together you won't be able to resist: You'll spend! You may tell yourself that your purchases are all good investments, and they may well be, but often your spending sprees will be sheer impulse buying. If you feel that this is true, try to call on your more stable and practical Taurean qualities to control this streak before blindly subscribing to that marvellously attractive set of commemorative medals which the advertisers swear will appreciate tenfold in three months!

Looking at the positive side; you do have considerable ability to enjoy your money—and why not? Your attitude in this is less restrained and cautious than that of some Taureans. But why not use a bit of Taurean foresight and take out some additional bonus-linked insurance policies so that you don't have to lower your living standards when you retire? Or, if you have a mind to invest in stocks and shares, try the motor industry or engineering.

You can spur on those working for you to greater effort. You don't spare yourself and will set a good example. They will like you for your enthusiasm.

Venus in Taurus

With Venus in Taurus you are likely to be even more money-conscious than is usual with Taurus. At its best, this characteristic gives you marvellous flair for coping with finance and investment. But if you allow it to get out of hand you might just find that money becomes too important to you and that too much of your psychological energy goes into making and keeping it. An overmaterialistic outlook on life could result in the exclusion of other important and necessary factors which go to make life richer in other ways. So do try to keep money in its proper perspective. You could also attach too much importance to the acquisition of property and possessions. Indeed, all the things that are said about Taureans and their love of possessions is particularly relevant to you, but so too are all the things about business ability.

You are above all a person who has the straightforward ability to make money. Land, real estate, agriculture and beauty products are good areas for investment. It may well be that you like to mix business with pleasure, so a love-interest could develop with a colleague. You will enjoy beautiful people working around you, and you have the ability to charm any employee or boss into seeing things your way.

Venus in Gemini

It is very likely that with Venus in Gemini you don't think of money and financial security as the be-all and end-all of human existence. You no doubt feel that it's pleasant to have money and be able to pay your bills on time (that will be important to you), but you don't worship money. You like to spend it on fashionable, attractive clothes and sometimes you find that you haven't chosen things that are quite as useful, long-lasting or practical as a part of you would wish. While you have the ability to sell you could in turn be rather easily persuaded by sales people when you are shopping. So be a little careful and realize you're vulnerable. The media—newspapers, magazines and telecommunications—are good areas in which to invest, and you will probably find these services or products interesting. Large groups of department stores might raise good dividends for you. It is particularly good for you to spread your capital around, having fewer eggs in one basket than most investors.

You are an extremely friendly and approachable person to work with and for. This won't be overlooked when promotion is being considered. You would be a marvellous organizer of treats and outings for your colleagues.

Venus in Cancer

This placing gives you great shrewdness, which is most likely to be expressed through financial and business acumen. In fact your ability in this direction is probably second to none, and it will be a pity if you don't at some time in your life turn your attention to developing a business scheme of your own. If ever you have a promising idea, discuss it with sympathetic-minded colleagues or friends. They will probably say that you are on the right lines. Perhaps, for instance, you will buy a wreck of a house, recondition it, live in it for a while and then sell it at a more than handsome profit. You could do the same thing with smaller objects, such as cars or furniture, but using the same principle: buy cheap, restore, sell at a good profit. This would provide interest and pleasure for you and give scope to your craftsmanlike skills and creative ability. You will invest your money wisely, perhaps in property, baby-care products or antiques. You will certainly work hard for your capital and will make sure that it grows.

You are a very sympathetic person, and if you employ people will treat them as members of the family. But don't become too clinging and overfussy with them. If you are a secretary, you will take care of your boss very well, and should you teach you will be much loved by your pupils. In other words you are regarded as something of a parent figure.

Rising-signs and your career

First check your Rising-sign on pages 225–232

Note: Careers and the Midheaven

If you develop your interest in astrology, one of the first things which you will learn about, but which is outside the scope of this book, is the Midheaven. Roughly speaking, this is the sign immediately over your head when you were born. It is as important to your career, outward expression and identification with objectives in life as your Rising-sign is in your personality. To combine it with your Rising-sign is complicated and would be impossible in a book of this length; but, while I cannot help you to discover yours in this book, rest assured that I have borne the various possibilities in mind when writing the following paragraphs in relation to your choice of profession or job.

Taurus with Aries rising

You have a lot of drive, energy and ambition and are independent and individualistic. You may have some rather unusual and original objectives and will usually achieve them. You could end up running your own business. You would do well in heavy industry or perhaps working for an airline or a construction company. Alternatively, you would make a good surveyor or architect.

Taurus with Taurus rising

You need a steady, Taurean career with security and routine. You could do well in science or, if you have a flair for mathematics, accountancy might be your métier. You could also be extremely musical, and if you feel you want to become a professional musician you should not stifle your ambition. You will enjoy working hard to develop any kind of technique.

Taurus with Gemini rising

You may feel you want to work in some form of communication, but behind the scenes, perhaps in broadcasting. You would do better in radio than television. You might also become a journalist with a liking for hard facts. Research could attract you, and your Taurean business sense won't let you down. Stockbroking, banking and investment consultancy are other fields you could do well in.

Taurus with Cancer rising

The caring professions such as nursing and the social services would probably suit you very well. You might also like to teach younger children. If you are attracted to cooking you could have the makings of a chef, and if you want to start a business, try opening a restaurant. Your strong imagination would stand you in good stead in any enterprise of this kind.

Taurus with Leo rising

You will probably be very psychologically involved in your career. Simply earning money will not be enough for you. You need to be able to express your positive, outgoing, enthusiastic qualities. Your job could be something artistic or creative, such as the theatre, and will need to have an element of glamour about it. But you will have the gift of bringing a dash of colour and style to even the most, apparently, mundane tasks, making you an exciting person to work with. Whatever your job you will naturally gravitate to a position of command.

Taurus with Virgo rising

Circumstances might force you into a routine business life, but you would perhaps be happier working out of doors in the country, in agriculture or horticulture. Health foods and unorthodox medicines could attract you, and you are probably very imaginative. You would make an excellent teacher, writer or critic. Don't suppress any literary feeling you may have. Just start writing. Earth is your element, so make things grow from it!

Taurus with Libra rising

You are at your best working with other people. Don't try to go it alone, especially in business. You will make an excellent beautician, hairdresser, masseur or physiotherapist. Most areas of the hotel trade would also suit you.

Taurus with Scorpio rising

You are one of the world's natural hard workers. You would be excellent at research of any kind, and could also make a good doctor or psychiatrist. The police force or even private detective work could also attract you. Whatever you do you will need an outlet for your vigorous energies, so make sure that you choose a career in which you will not vegetate.

Taurus with Sagittarius rising

You need a job to take you out and about, world-wide if possible. It's not good for you to be tied too firmly to an office desk. You are likely to have a flair for languages, which could provide a rewarding area for further education. You would make a good lecturer or publisher, and you could also be attracted to the law, since you have a sensitive intuition for justice.

Taurus with Capricorn rising

You may well be more creative than you realize and could have a flair for pottery, weaving, sculpture or some other manual art or craft. In fact if you develop an interest of this kind it could be profitable as a business. You would also make a good architect, surveyor, geologist or town planner, and local government or politics could attract you.

Taurus with Aquarius rising

You may well be deeply attracted to the distant past or the distant future. Perhaps you are a potential anthropologist, archaeologist or pioneer scientist or astronomer. Your career could break new ground, so don't be afraid to think through unconventional schemes, even if they seem impractical at first sight.

Taurus with Pisces rising

You could be happy working hard for old people in the nursing or medical profession or through some charity, even for a smaller wage than you would really like. Job satisfaction is the important thing to you. Turn any artistic talent to money and never neglect your very individual creativity. Photography is an excellent field for you.

Gemini

Positive
Ruling planet: Mercury
Triplicity or element: air
Quadruplicity or quality: mutable
Colour: most colours appeal; yellow seems a favourite
Gemstone: agate
Metal: mercury
Flowers: lily-of-the-valley
Trees: nut-bearing trees
Herbs and spices: aniseed, marjoram, caraway
Foodstuffs: nuts, vegetables grown above ground, carrots
Animals: small birds, parrots, butterflies, monkeys
Countries: Wales, Belgium, U.S.A.
Cities: London, Plymouth (U.K.), Cardiff, San Francisco, Melbourne

The main fear that lurks in the depths of nearly every Gemini is that of boredom; so Geminians do a very great deal, consciously or unconsciously, to make sure they keep boredom at bay. The sign's duality underlines the fact that it is not natural for a Geminian to do only one thing at a time, and parents of Gemini children should not try to cramp their style by insisting on that kind of behaviour pattern. It is very important for Geminians to have plenty of projects on hand, so that they can change from one to the other as the mood takes them—though it is also terribly important that they should eventually *complete* all their projects, which may not be too easy for them. It is to their advantage to recognize their worst fault: superficiality. But this can be turned to advantage, since many Geminians work in the media, and a little knowledge of many things is excellent for the busy interviewer or journalist, and the need to communicate is all-important to this Zodiac type.

The Geminian duality often extends to their relationships—many of them have more than one relationship at a time, which can be somewhat disconcerting to their partners, should they discover what is going on. However, the Geminian ability to talk their way out of tricky situations will come into its own on such occasions.

The Gemini body-areas are the shoulders, hands and arms, which are vulnerable; but perhaps restlessness and the inability completely to relax is the worst Gemini health-hazard and Geminians should recognize this. Gemini has the reputation of being the most youthful of the 12 signs, both in mind and body. The quick pace of the Gemini lifestyle is greatly responsible for this.

Gemini in friendship, love and marriage

Because you enjoy talking, and you have bought this book, you will be just the right sort of person to spread the good word when you next get involved in a conversation about astrology! The chances are that someone will say to you, "I'm a Taurus—so I'm no good with you, am I?" And if that person is a bore, well let's face it, you certainly won't hit it off with him or her! But that would be the case whatever boring Sun-sign person you met up with. In fact, you can tell them right away that they're very probably quite wrong. There is certainly something in the suggestion that the elements (see page 75) have a minor influence on compatibility, but it is just not true that you should not form a relationship with a Taurean or a Cancerian, or indeed anybody with any Sun-sign at all.

Just for the record, it is those Sun-signs grouped as Air signs which are supposed to be "good" for you: Gemini is an Air sign, and so are Libra and Aquarius. Aries, Leo and Sagittarius—Fire signs—are also quite good; Earth signs (Taurus, Virgo and Capricorn) are less good, and Water signs (Cancer, Scorpio and Pisces) are equally negative.

But it is not as simple as that, and it is very important that we do not deny ourselves a relationship simply on the basis of such superficial knowledge of astrology. It may well be that you have Venus or Mercury in Taurus or Cancer, and, if so, that would help to build a sound relationship between you and someone with either of those signs as a Sun-sign. Your Mars may be in a sign compatible to one strongly emphasized by some other means in their chart. And so on. Always remember that it is only when the fully-calculated birth-chart is examined that we can assess compatibility; astrologers call that kind of work *synastry*.

Even when two charts have been fully examined, an astrologer should never say that a relationship between two people would be impossible or disastrous and should not be started. That is a matter for the two people concerned. But an astrologer can tell you where you and a lover will probably be most compatible, and where clashes might be more likely to occur. For instance, as a Sun-sign Geminian, you will probably have a fairly lighthearted approach to love, and the full expression of your emotions will relate to your Venus-sign rather than your Sun-sign. You will probably be quite flirtatious—and someone who is possessive may take this lively tendency too seriously. So you may have to be very careful if you are not to upset them. Interestingly enough, the old traditional general rule will be broken for you where Virgoans are concerned, because you share Mercury as the ruling planet of your Sun-signs: so there will probably be good links between you, with the practical "earth" element of Virgo making an interesting relationship with your lighter "air" qualities. Not perhaps entirely easy—but certainly not boring, and you wouldn't want a relationship completely lacking in edge, or over-simple. Because your Sun-sign is Gemini, you need a good intellectual rapport between yourself and your partner, and one spiced with a lively level of friendship as well as emotional understanding. This is something that may not be entirely obvious from a study of the Sun-signs (though to be fair, Aquarius traditionally shows many of these qualities).

I have always found in the fully-calculated birth-charts of happily married couples, or those in a settled relationship, a strong emphasis on the polar or opposite signs (see page 75). A man with a Gemini Sun, for instance, will make a good partner for a woman with Sagittarius rising, or a Sagittarian Sun-sign. Someone with the Moon in Sagittarius would also make for an interesting partnership.

Here is the real interest of astrology, for it is an indication that while the partners will by no means always boringly agree about everything, there will be a strong rapport, and plenty of understanding. This is not the only factor in a good relationship, but it is certainly an important one. By now you should know what your Rising-sign or ascendant is (see page 225), and I cannot too strongly encourage you to take this into consideration when you are thinking of starting a friendship, a business partnership or a close personal relationship.

Geminian friendships

Gemini is one of the most friendly signs of the Zodiac, and you will not find it difficult to make new friends, who will be numerous and have a great variety of interests. They will also come from many different ages and social groups. This will be because you need a great deal of variety in your life and like to be able to be with different types of people according to your prevailing mood.

When we are very young we tend to introduce someone we met a few minutes ago as "my friend", and it may be that there is an element of this in your attitude to your friends. Although you are in many ways a natural sceptic you will accept people at face value. You will very quickly feel ready to call people who come into your life your friends. Perhaps you need to give this a little thought, because it may well be that you have an extremely wide variety of acquaintances, but few real friends on whom you can depend when you are in need of help. This is a pity, because you yourself will usually be ready to help others or point them in the right direction.

What this amounts to is that perhaps you should give a little more time to developing deep, meaningful friendships as well as lively and amusing ones. Try, if you can, to put up with other people's foibles a little more charitably and don't get too bored or irritable when you are with someone with a slower mind than your own. Sometimes the well-thought-out sentence or remark or the slow, deliberate reaction can be more worth-while than the quick, clever quip.

You are a great enthusiast, and it is obviously very good for you to have similarly enthusiastic friends. Those who maintain their own enthusiasm for hobbies and interests will help you to do the same. This is a good influence for you and will help you to complete projects and see schemes through to the end.

It is also good for your friends to be of a fairly high calibre as far as education and intelligence are concerned. Someone who has a higher degree or IQ than yourself will present an intellectual challenge and make you think through your arguments in greater depth and detail, so that you won't get away quite so easily with those sweeping, provocative statements you so love to make.

Probably you are happiest with those slightly younger than yourself, because you are youthful both in appearance and outlook, though older people—when they are good talkers, like yourself—will also fascinate you.

Gemini in love

Once you fall in love you will waste no time at all in letting the loved one know about your feelings. If you are a romantic Geminian, you'll not find it difficult to express your feelings in a pleasant, easy, uncomplicated way. And if you are on the wily side, you'll think of plenty of different approaches to get your relationship started or to push it on a stage further. If you are the sort of Geminian who isn't too keen on getting straight to the point, you'll circle round the subject with such verbal dexterity that you will soon have mesmerized your lover to the point where he or she gets the message quite clearly.

But remember that you are not terribly patient and may feel that what they are trying to say could be said by you in less than half the time. Resist any temptation to butt in and put words into their mouths. Be patient for once; listen attentively. Sit still and don't waggle your feet or play with the cutlery if you are out to dinner. Such things will build a barrier.

Remembering your overall need for variety and change, it is up to you and your lover to experiment sexually. To keep your relationship alive it is good for both of you from time to time to arrange some surprises to stimulate your sex-life.

We must also take into account the much discussed Geminian need for more than one relationship. In fairness to yourself and your partner you should consider this possibility with some care. If you get accused of being something of a Don Juan it may simply be that you like different partners for different things. One relationship might be mainly sexual, another more intellectual, yet another with a spiritual emphasis, and so on. Committed Geminians with a strong need for several relationships should certainly square this with their partner, otherwise they may find themselves in some pretty tricky situations. Being Geminians they will be pretty good at talking themselves out of them, but they don't get away with it in the long run. After all, you wouldn't choose a stupid partner—and if you did, they wouldn't last long!

Depending on the position of Venus (see pages 242–245) and to a certain extent on the nature of your Rising-sign (pages 225–232) your emotional level will vary. Basically, Gemini is intellectually oriented, so within a permanent relationship you really need a high intellectual rapport as well as a powerful bond of friendship and sexual compatibility.

Gemini in marriage

It is only when things go drastically wrong that Geminians are likely to be really bogged down and bored by a marriage. Because they are such good and logical communicators, they are well able to thrash out problems in discussion and to let their partners know exactly what their feelings, attitudes and ideas are. In addition, it is not difficult for them to find out what their partners are feeling and to persuade them to confide their feelings. So when the time comes to get right down to the nitty gritty of a problem, they will be able to do so. And they will assess any opposite view to their own very fairly. However, they are very clever in argument and, should your partner accuse you of twisting them round your little finger, they could well be right.

Still, your natural enthusiasm and lightheartedness make you extremely attractive as a partner, and because of your inherent abhorrence of boredom you are able to make time fly by. A great deal will get done and a great many experiences will be lived through. You will always seem to be a lot younger than you are.

You should remember that savouring life in quieter moments is important too, and this is something you may well not always do as often as you ought to. You can be rather like the tourist who is so intent on photographing the view that he gives no time to actually looking at it and savouring the atmosphere. Even in the most poignant moments in life or love you will be so intellectually aware of what's going on that you may not be able to fully absorb the experience emotionally.

Your approach to marriage is that you and your partner have equal rights and responsibilities, which is just as it should be, especially in the present social climate. Remember that your needs in a permanent relationship are special and that equality can apply on many levels: sexual, intellectual and domestic. Gemini girls will not, in the long run, be too happy with a purely housekeeping role. Gemini men won't want a mere housewife for a wife. So in an ideal marriage for Geminians of either sex a certain amount of role-swopping is necessary. The Gemini man will probably enjoy cooking or some other household job. The Gemini woman will want some career interest, even when the children are very young.

As parents, Geminians usually do extremely well. Should you decide to have a family you will be able to keep the children on their toes and will be well informed about the current teaching methods, so that you don't confuse your children when they need a bit of help with their homework. But beware—you may be far more devastatingly critical than you realize. One Geminian father earned himself the nickname "Yes—but" from his children, because every time they showed him a drawing or painting or some other creative effort, he'd look at it and say: "Well, yes—but..." and then go on to criticize. Children need criticism, but they need lots of encouragement too if they are to develop their potential.

Geminian careers and money matters

When assessing the Geminian potential in careers and financial ability we must consider not only the psychological motivation and mode of expression attributed to Gemini but also the thinking processes of Mercury, and how these two factors combined can best be used in both areas. Then there is the influence of Venus, a planet as strongly related to finance and possessions as to relationships. The latter aspect is also important in this sphere as it will affect how a person will get on with colleagues, in business partnerships, and so on. Mars may well give some hint as to the direction of energy and will most certainly influence the physical element — the drive and energy put into the day's work. As we shall see, the influence of the combined Sun and Rising-sign is interesting and very personal; but if your birth-time is not available and you cannot find your Rising-sign, do not be too disappointed; you should be able to glean plenty of information about this sphere of your life from the more general paragraphs.

Mercury, being the ruling planet of Gemini, has an extremely powerful say in the whole psychological motivation of Sun-sign Geminians, and if we look at this in relation to the Sun-sign (irrespective of the sign Mercury was in at the time of birth) it very strongly emphasizes the basic need to communicate. This is often expressed through the career, and a large proportion of Geminians work in the media, where they are found at all levels from top TV interviewers to cub reporters on the local gossip sheet.

But communication is not of course only experienced through newspapers, magazines, television and radio. Many Geminians work in book publishing, in market research or as telephonists. They make excellent receptionists and switchboard operators and are generally happy in areas in which they are in touch with the public in a lively, busy way. They also like working in the outdoor world as tourist guides, couriers, or traffic wardens.

Whatever the chosen career it has to be the kind that keeps the lively Geminian on the go. It must be pretty demanding intellectually, but not so much as to worry them or oppress

105

them. For instance, a Geminian would not enjoy collecting mountains of facts or putting together a lot of fussy detail to make a presentable report, or making a study in depth of one narrow area of a subject. That sort of thing can make Geminians restless, and in such situations they will cut corners—extremely cleverly, no doubt, so that it doesn't show. But should some more patient, painstaking mortal check up on them they might get into hot water. For instance, some Geminians find it surprisingly difficult to learn shorthand and will ingeniously devise their own individual system. This will be perfectly sound and reliable to them but could cause difficulties when someone else has to read it. This is one example of how Geminian ingenuity can create problems for them in the long run.

Geminians can sell and make excellent "reps" or commercial travellers. They are perfectly happy driving around in the company car making regular calls, hearing the latest news on the trade grapevine and often adding to it themselves. They are not particularly fussy about the sort of atmosphere they work in, though a totally formal office where everyone works quietly at the same sort of task day in and day out would be anathema to them. They don't mind having some kind of pattern in their working life, but a dreary and totally predictable routine is not for them. The variety of a career in the law, for example, would probably give them the sort of stimulation that they need. But Geminians, being what they are, will make a great deal out of any job. If they are forced into a dull one they will have the ability to make it far less so, perhaps by creating some amusement for their workmates or by observing their idiosyncrasies and indulging in a little satirical imitation. They can also look at the job in hand and apply useful lateral thinking to throw new light and new ideas on something mundane and basic.

The Geminians' psychological needs in this area boil down to a need to communicate, to be in personal rapport with the people they work with and to have space and the opportunity to voice their opinions. Of course this need can be catered for in various professions, and we find Geminians in all walks of life, as with all other Zodiac types.

Another area in which Geminians flourish is related to their body-area, the hands, which are very nimble and often capable of fine, speedy workmanship (though sometimes totally the reverse is true, and they are hopeless at anything practical). Geminians often make good craftsmen in a variety of fields.

The Geminian needs vis-à-vis the career can be summed up in the word "air", the element of the sign. Geminians need plenty of air, that is to say freedom from restriction and relief from dreariness. Some may tolerate a dreary job for years on end, only escaping in their imaginations, but this can be psychologically harmful in the long run.

Mercury at work

Check position of Mercury on pages 238–241

Mercury in Taurus

If Mercury was in Taurus when you were born you will have the ability to think carefully and in greater depth than many Geminians, and if necessary you can use this ability in business. Indeed, having Mercury in this sign will give you a good business sense, so if you work for yourself or want to start your own business you should do very well. You will probably be attracted to high-quality goods and products, so if you sell things you'll do better at the upper end of the market, rather than with products that are cheaply made. Girls of this group might well be very happy working in the cosmetics trade or as beauticians. Agriculture and horticulture could also be rewarding careers. So could floristry or market gardening, especially if Venus is in Taurus too—see pages 242–245. Accountancy (if you feel you have the patience) would be a possibility as well, as you might have a liking for figures. Computers could also attract you.

You have the ability to work hard and steadily and have better powers of concentration than most Geminians. If you are a student, try to plan a careful study schedule and stick to it. You will then not get flustered during examinations. Don't try too hard to impress the examiners: stick to the facts requested, even if you find your own opinions more exciting and interesting.

Mercury in Gemini

If Mercury was in Gemini with the Sun you would enjoy being a general dogsbody at the local newspaper or radio station and will want to learn everything about the complexities of the profession. Perhaps you have an aspiration to be a disc-jockey or to chair your own phone-in programme. If so, why not get experience at your local hospital on its private radio circuit, in your spare time? Or at a local disco? Working on the buses or for some other form of transport industry would also be satisfying for you, as would driving a taxi around a capital city and chatting to your passengers. Any work that calls for very quick thinking and immediate action is excellent. You would make a skilful interviewer and would be good at briefing yourself beforehand, for example by reading quickly through a book whose author you had to interview an hour or so later. Or you would enjoy working in the street, asking people about their buying habits. The advertising profession seems a natural area in which you could express your lively and original ideas.

If you are a student, you will be able to absorb books and papers very quickly, but it is possible that your ability to retain facts and knowledge isn't too good. Set up some good, firm, intensive study sessions while you are at college, but make absolutely certain that you allow plenty of time for revision towards the end of your course, especially for those parts of the course you covered in the early terms. Don't rely on getting questions on the topics that you read up at the last minute.

Mercury in Cancer

If, when you were born, Mercury was in Cancer, you will have an excellent memory and plenty of imagination, so try to find a positive and demanding use for these qualities in your career. You could well enjoy working with children, especially the younger age groups. You can very easily inspire children, and they will love to hear the fantastic stories you can invent at a moment's notice. Using your skill as a raconteur in this way would give you great satisfaction.

You have a naturally caring instinct and will be an extremely thoughtful person. You might well be attracted to social service work or to helping those in need. Work as an almoner in a hospital could be a very good career for you. Your caring instinct could also be expressed through your hands, in osteopathy or massage. History might well be a subject to attract you, and you could do well in the antiques trade. Sailing and the sea might have a special appeal for you, and you could well enjoy the Navy or working for the good of passengers as a steward on a cruise ship.

You have greater tenacity and a better ability to remember facts than most Geminians. Lists of important dates, for instance, will be committed to memory without too much trouble. Remember, you are also far more prone to worry than most Geminians, and you must try to avoid this tendency, especially when examinations are imminent. A good way to counter it is by combining your logical and intuitive gifts, not letting one smother the other.

Venus: money and rapport

Check position of Venus on pages 242–245

Venus in Aries
With this placing it is likely that you will be enthusiastic to make money and will devise many clever and original schemes to do so. But your enthusiasm could well be equally geared to spending, and it is more than likely that you are extravagant. You could be all too easily seduced by attractive-sounding schemes and might find yourself having to cut your losses when they don't pay off. You should be pretty careful, and if you think you are on to a good thing it is as well for you to get some sound professional advice before committing yourself. You might find railways and engineering good for investment. With Venus in Aries you are an enthusiastic person to work with, and you can inject enthusiasm into others. Should colleagues come to you in difficulties, asking you to help them out with a heavy work schedule, try to do all you can for them; you could rather too often tend to put your own interests first. You are probably an extremely hard-working and busy person, and will work well and quickly: but sometimes you might need a bit of extra help yourself, and if you do, you in turn may be refused.

Venus in Taurus
This position will make you good at business, and you will probably be able to make money and invest wisely. Financial security is perhaps of greater importance to you than to many Geminians, and you may find it worth while to plan purchases well in advance and work out exactly how much each rise in the cost of living is going to affect you personally.

At the same time Venus in Taurus gives you a strong liking for everything luxurious and beautiful. Possessions are just as important as cash, so there are likely to be times in your life when you'll have plenty of goods but perhaps not much cash. If you invest in material things, bear it in mind that you could be forced to sell them if the necessity arose; and you won't like that one bit. If you want to invest, you might find shares in groups of department stores both worth while and interesting. Agriculture, banking and insurance might also be suitable. Your business sense and ability are likely to be high; and because Mercury, your Sun ruler, rules trade in general you will be very good at managing your own business.

You would enjoy a life of meeting people in your own premises, say a bookshop or craft studio, and supplying them would be rewarding and worth while. You would make an excellent and fair employer, but once you are used to working with an employee you could easily get a little possessive and dislike it if they want to move on. Your friendly warmth will make you a very easy person to work with.

Venus in Gemini
If you were born with Venus in Gemini along with the Sun you will be good at selling other people's products and could make

rather a lot of money at it. Perhaps you will be in the sort of job that requires you to sell yourself—modelling, demonstrating or perhaps working in beauty culture or as a make-up artist.

You yourself may well be your best asset. Your personality is very exuberant, you are charming and talkative, and when you place yourself in the public eye in some way, all these natural qualities will come through. You have the ability to make others part with their money. You are probably very conscious of fashion, and this could be a good area for you to work in.

You need to develop consistency of effort and staying-power. Don't give up too easily or be disheartened if you think that perhaps you aren't making as much money as you think you should. It may well seem a natural thing to change direction, but you might do it too easily and too often. If you have a good idea develop it to the full so that you are making the most of your natural potential. Try not to spend too much money on trendy trifles or gimmicks.

You make a lively, friendly colleague and employer; you could never be accused of being a stuffy or aloof boss. As for investments, you might do well putting your money in the car or travel industry.

Venus in Cancer
This placing of Venus will give you the ability to nurture your money and quietly make it grow. If ever you come into an inheritance you will choose very wisely how to use it, so that you will get the best out of it. Perhaps owning your own house or apartment is of above-average importance to you, and earlier than most you will see to it that you are able to buy one. You could do extremely well investing in property; it seems an absolutely natural thing for you. However, should you want to buy some stocks and shares, you could do very well with those in a large group of restaurants or hotels. The dairy trade too might prove worthwhile. If you prefer investing in a collection try to go for some really specialized objects. Coins and medals could attract you. Antiquarian books or old silver would also be possibilities. A shelf of fine first editions or some beautiful pieces of silver would make your heart leap with pleasure.

If things go wrong with your colleagues at work they will be likely to come to you with their troubles; you are kind and understanding, and most likely to come up with some logical suggestion to help them out of their difficulties. If you are an employer, you really care about your employees and take a strong interest in their working conditions.

Venus in Leo
You will certainly know how to enjoy spending money if Venus was in Leo when you were born. You'll be in seventh heaven taking friends out to dinner or to the theatre, or having pleasant, chatty, lively evenings at home helped along by good food and wine. You probably feel money is there to be used, and will be content as long as you have some when you need it. You are a good organizer, so you should be able to manage your financial situation very well. If you earn a regular wage or salary you can plan your expenses thoughtfully and allow for each of your different needs. It is just as well that you are financially well organized. Make sure you stay that way, otherwise your liking for the good life could land you in the red.

Quality is important to you and if you have money to invest this should be your guide. If you are thinking about shares, ask yourself if the firm's products are the best in the field; tradition, quality and perfection should be key-words for you. That's what Venus in Leo is all about. And it also applies when you are making purchases. At work you are the organizer, and colleagues will often ask you to intervene with the boss; they know you'll get what is wanted. If you are an employer you are amusing and warm-hearted in the eyes of your employees or subordinates, but you can be a bit too dogmatic at times.

Rising-signs and your career

First check your Rising-sign on pages 225–232

Note: Careers and the Midheaven
If you develop your interest in astrology one of the first things which you will learn about, but which is outside the scope of this book, is the Midheaven. Roughly speaking, this is the sign immediately over your head when you were born. It is as important in your career, outward expression and identification with objectives in life as your Rising-sign is in your personality. To combine it with your Rising-sign is complicated, and would be impossible in a book of this length; but, while I cannot help you to discover yours in this book, rest assured that I have borne the various possibilities in mind when writing the following paragraphs in relation to your choice of profession or job.

Gemini with Aries rising
You are ambitious and have formidable aspirations. You might be attracted to science and mathematics, and perhaps teach these subjects. The airline industry might provide a suitable career, or perhaps you could work well in the technical side of television. Your way to success is by a gradual, steady climb. Though your progress could seem to take a long time, a slow pace is the right one for you and will get you there in the end.

Gemini with Taurus rising
If you are musical it is worth while working hard at it since you could do well in a musical profession. Surveying and architecture might also be very rewarding. You need security and should consider just how much you are reassured by a regular pay cheque. Your business sense is excellent, but you could be just a little too soft on creditors.

Gemini with Gemini rising
Try not to be Jack of all trades and master of none. You will probably be at your best working for the media or in some form of communication. The air force or civil airlines would be good. Avoid dull, repetitive work; it isn't good for you. You are versatile, but must control this quality and prevent it developing into superficiality, otherwise your progress could be held back.

Gemini with Cancer rising
You will want to express your Gemini urge to communicate, but will be best doing so behind the scenes. You would make a good agent (looking after other people's contracts and negotiating for them). You would be better in radio than television, or working on the editing side of newspapers rather than as an out-and-about reporter. Nursing and the catering trade could also be good careers for you.

Gemini with Leo rising
You may be very creative and artistic. If so, work hard and develop your potential to the full. You have excellent organizing ability and will need a prominent position. A job behind the scenes would not suit you. If you like to show off, find work where this is an asset. You would make an excellent buyer in a

Cancerian careers and money matters

When assessing the Cancerian potential in careers and financial ability we must consider not only the psychological motivation and mode of expression attributed to Cancer but also the thinking processes of Mercury, and how these two factors combined can be best used in both areas. Then there is the influence of Venus, a planet as strongly related to finance and possessions as to relationships. The latter aspect is also important in this sphere as it will affect how a person will get on with colleagues, in business partnerships, and so on. Mars may well give some hint as to the direction of energy and will most certainly influence the physical element—the drive and energy put into the day's work. As we shall see, the influence of the combined Sun- and Rising-sign is interesting and very personal: but if your birth-time is not available and you cannot find out your Rising-sign, do not be too disappointed: you should be able to glean plenty of information about this sphere of your life from the more general paragraphs.

Cancerians have an instinct to protect—an instinct so direct and immediate and deep as to be utterly basic to their nature. So, while Cancerians are of course to be found in every walk of life, together with all other Zodiac types, there is a tendency for them to express this natural instinct in such careers as medicine and the social services. But there are other ways in which their caring nature can find outlets: for instance consider the businessman who takes care of "his" customers, or the insurance man who takes care of "his" clients. The owner of a pleasure steamer takes care not only of "his" ship but also of "his" passengers. There are many such examples. Cancerians, as I mentioned earlier, are also compulsive collectors, and this is a trait that can be put to good use in a career. As a museum curator, for example, a Cancerian can satisfy that collecting urge and at the same time perform a valuable service to the community. And he or she will of course at the same time be fulfilling the Cancerian caring nature by looking after the objects in the museum as well as its visitors.

117

The typical Cancerian finds security in the expression of this caring instinct. For most of us, security means the regular arrival of the pay-cheque every month or week: but this does not usually seem to be of prime importance to Cancerians. Of course it is just as necessary for them, and they like it just as much as other people, but their real security and fulfilment is in seeing others enjoying the fruits of their labours. This makes them feel good, comfortable and satisfied: for they know that the satisfaction and pleasure of others is the result of their own careful efforts.

Cancerians can usually settle into almost any working environment, either because they are adaptable enough not to be stifled by the atmosphere, or because their natural Cancerian protective shell comes to their aid in uncongenial surroundings, enabling them to ward off anything which might distress them too much.

Cancerians should be very careful that their tendency to worry does not become an integral part of their working day. It is as easy for them to worry about their careers as any other important part of their lives. Of course it is not possible to tell them just to "stop worrying": it is up to them to find the right approach to the problem. Most Cancerians, like all of us, have to settle down into some kind of daily routine, which can, of course, grow dreary. But Cancer, a Water sign much influenced by the sea, will very much identify with the ebbing and flowing motion of the tides, and maybe this kind of regularity will be in some way a form of strength to them. Yet they must be able to express their changing moods, and their liking for change. How? Every individual must, of course, work this out for themselves. Many will find themselves able to arrange their working day to reflect changing moods, provided all the work gets done satisfactorily. Those who cannot must simply accommodate themselves to the routine, ignoring passing whims and feelings—as their colleagues must do!

The ideal Cancerian working environment should reflect, if possible, their concern with the good of the community as a whole, or be attuned to the good of the individual. Members of this sign tend to "give out" in some way, not necessarily in an extravert fashion, but by using their energy and skills for the benefit of other people. The well-trained teacher widening the horizons of pupils, the experienced chef making superb dishes for the pleasure of appreciative customers, the ship's captain caring for his passengers—all manifest the protective instinct I've mentioned.

Cancer being the sign of the mother and motherhood suggests that the women of this sign may find their careers interrupted for rather longer than other women, because of the attention they will want to pay to having and bringing up children. They will accept this more happily than many other mothers, for it will represent so much that is basic to their natures—such interruptions are a joy rather than a hindrance. They should bear it in mind that, if they do want to return to work after having a family, they ought to spend some time keeping up with the newest developments in their field. They might find this difficult to do: while they have excellent memories, they could find that when they return to using the techniques they learned before the children were born, they may have failed to keep abreast of the latest thought or theory. If a Cancerian mother knows that she will want to resume a career after a long spell of motherhood, she should keep an eye on how her old job is moving with the times, and how she will respond to new and developing situations.

Mercury at work

Check position of Mercury on pages 238–241

Mercury in Gemini

If Mercury was in Gemini when you were born you will have a quick, logical mind, and be far less ruled by your emotions than many Cancerians. This could help considerably if you want to work in the media. If you enjoy writing, and it comes naturally to you, you could remain impartial when dealing with the "human stories" you so love. You may feel you have a "message" you want to put over; if so, you should do it well. The advertising industry would suit you. You will enjoy hunting out facts, and should be good at any sort of research. You might well be happy in business, selling some product you have faith in. Work in a large department store would suit you very well.

You will be capable of starting at tea-making level and working your way up, ready to take on any task as long as it gives you a boost in the firm. You have the ability to deal with the general public, so working at a reception desk in an hotel or elsewhere is suitable. Your versatile mind can be used to advantage if you are a student, but you could find it a bit difficult to concentrate at times, so will have to make a special effort before examinations. Try to cut out distractions and keep to the job in hand.

Mercury in Cancer

If you are a studious type and you have Mercury in Cancer with the Sun, you could be attracted to history, and perhaps read for a degree in some aspect of that subject. There is a toughness in this combination of planetary influences, and quite a number of people with it enjoy the armed services or engineering.

However, your protective and caring instinct will be very strong, inclining you to typically Cancerian occupations. So you may do very well in medicine as a doctor or nurse, or specializing in geriatric care. If you want to teach, you will be happy with the very youngest children; you may find nursery school work especially rewarding. Catering may also appeal to you; or perhaps working as a pharmacist. Remember you are in many ways very Cancerian, and need very strongly to express your "caring" feelings: work in the probation service, or other social services, could appeal to you.

The placing of Mercury in Cancer could also mean that where mental activities are concerned you feel most effective when you are working at home. Hence being a freelance journalist or typist might suit you.

If you are still a student, don't fall into a lazy routine, with the constant intention to put things off until tomorrow. You must discipline yourself if you are to make the most of your potential. If your friends are planning a party for Saturday, restrain your instinct to offer to make another of your excellent paellas and keep your nose in your textbook. It's not good for you to try to "cram" in the last few minutes before an examination.

Mercury in Leo

This placing will make you one of the good organizers of the Cancerian world! You like order, and while in some respects "ordered chaos" might better describe your own life, you will be reliable, and get things done on time. You can take a lot of responsibility, and will be first-rate at taking care of subordinates—which in the eyes of your superiors will mean that you are good at organizing other people, and getting them to do their work well. If you work in a factory or production team, for instance, you will see to it that everyone pulls together, and well. This is an important ability in you, and one you should try to use to advantage. If you are a nurse, you will make a good ward sister, and would be a good supervisor in any environment. Personnel work would suit you. In some ways you are the typical "head waiter" or "maitre d'" type—rather grandly holding court in his restaurant, and ready to snap at underlings for a finger-mark on the wine-glasses. In any event, you can in some way be the boss or key man or woman.

If you are a student, you may find it difficult to be flexible about new lines of approach to any subject once you have set your own pattern of work. You will present your work well, which will be to your advantage. You will work well and steadily, and take a real pride in your work—but will probably be able to fit in a good bit of extramural activity despite the rigours of your course. You should be able to take examinations in your stride as you express your knowledge well.

Venus: money and rapport

Check position of Venus on pages 242–245

Venus in Taurus
If Venus was in Taurus when you were born, you will be financially aware, and will have an excellent potential for making money. Your business sense is instinctive, and if Cancerian shrewdness is added, you have the makings of the archetypal businessman or woman. You will be able to make your money grow, and have an eye for the right savings or investment scheme which will help you to give yourself and family the good things you want. When you buy a house or apartment, you will choose a good investment, and have the taste to fill it with beautiful possessions, which will increase in value as time goes by.

Banking and insurance are especially good areas of investment for you, though you could find agriculture or agrochemicals interesting too. Somewhat differently, cosmetics and beauty products may be worthwhile. Of the various Cancerian types, you need financial security most keenly, and, while your business sense is good, you should try, if self-employed, to make sure of a regular income.

You are a kind and gentle workmate, and your colleagues will find you a pillar of strength. You will treat them warmly and in a friendly, affectionate manner, which would extend to out-of-work activities.

Venus in Gemini
The latest craze or fashion could attract you if you have Venus in Gemini, and you could have a tendency to go a little mad in your favourite boutique on pay-day. Of course you have worked hard for your cash and should enjoy it, but you could find yourself a little short of money as a consequence—though you may, by now, have learned about this the hard way. All Cancerians, however, have a basic instinct for saving, and, even if you have just started your working life, it shouldn't be too difficult to pop some cash regularly into a savings fund so that you will be able to enjoy a holiday, or be ready with a deposit when you want to buy your own home. Should you want to invest, stock in a large department store would be interesting for you to buy; or shares in newspapers or

magazines—indeed any area of "communications". The car industry is another possibility for profitable investment.

You are a lively colleague and should any of your group need a favour from a superior, you are probably the one who will have to go into the head office to ask! You should get what everyone wants, for you have a charming and convincing turn of phrase which stands you in good stead on such occasions. As a boss you won't find it difficult to get extra work out of employees when the pressure is on.

Venus in Cancer

If Venus is in Cancer with the Sun it suggests that you will work hard for your money, and save it diligently. You are not the type to spread it around very readily—though entertaining your friends at home may be an expensive as well as a rewarding hobby. You don't necessarily pile the cash up in a bank account, just for the enjoyment of the ever-larger figure in the monthly statement; but you will pile up possessions, and, being Cancerian, this means that you will probably invest considerably in some collection, which may eventually overcrowd your house or apartment. To others, your home may seem cluttered, but it will be "you": and Cancerian shrewdness will ensure that it is all good stuff—you're not likely to be deceived into investing in a fake.

If you are not a collector, you might care to invest in fisheries, food manufacture, or silver mining. Should you want to give yourself or a loved one a present, a piece of silver jewellery or a string of pearls will be a particularly pleasing choice.

To your colleagues you could seem to succumb to Cancerian moodiness rather more often than average, even for a Cancerian! Try to be aware of this. But you will be a good helpmeet, and will stick up for your rights, even doing battle for them—whether for or against trades unions! You will make a marvellously caring boss, generous with all the facilities you offer your staff.

Venus in Leo

With this placing you will be the big spender among Cancerians! You enjoy your money, and will put it to good use—which in your case means making life pleasant and comfortable for you and your loved ones. That comfort will be much concerned with good food and wine, and the organization and enjoyment of social events. You could tend to be extravagant—though I don't think your Cancerian shrewdness and instinct to save will ever entirely leave you; so that, while having fun, you will keep your financial balance.

If you are a collector, you may collect colourful paintings or prints. Above all, you will enjoy what you buy, whether it's a bottle of wine or an attractive work of art. You will probably be fairly conventional in your choice of investments: it is best for you to think in terms of investing in companies producing quality goods, well established in their own field. Try not to overcommit yourself; in your enthusiasm for a product or a promising scheme, you tend to do that.

You are a very generous colleague, and the sort to organize a collection when another colleague retires. If you chose the gift, everyone should be pleased. An excellent organizer, you could become a little bossy at times. Whatever your status in your firm, you show enthusiasm and generosity. Praise for colleagues comes naturally from you.

Venus in Virgo

Meticulous planning and care in your budgeting, whatever your own individual needs, will mark you out if you have

Venus in Virgo. You manage money well, and you could be rightly accused of being rather overprudent from time to time; if so you should try to enjoy your money more than you do. Many things give you pleasure, and pleasures can be expensive; but remember that, if you are going to get additional fulfilment and happiness out of spending a little more than usual, it could be worth it. If you see some exotic plant that you know you would enjoy looking after, and your room is warm enough for it—why not buy it? Think of the pleasure its brilliant flowers will bring you!

You may like to invest in construction companies, agriculture, machinery, or in dry-cleaning companies. The health food industry could also be attractive and profitable.

You are among the harder-working Cancerians, and will give excellent value for your salary. You may tend to take on more than your share of work, and could be an overwilling secretary. If a colleague is ill, you will be the one to help out and others could take advantage of this from time to time! If you are in control you will make your staff keep at it, but you will also be the first to arrive at the office, and the last to leave.

Rising-signs and your career

First check your Rising-sign on pages 225–232

Note: Careers and the Midheaven
If you develop your interest in astrology, one of the first things which you will learn about, but which is outside the scope of this book, is the Midheaven. Roughly speaking, this is the sign immediately over your head when you were born. It is as important to your career, outward expression and identification with objectives in life as your Rising-sign is to your personality. To combine it with your Rising-sign is complicated and would be impossible in a book of this length; but, while I cannot help you to discover yours in this book, rest assured that I have borne the various possibilities in mind when writing the following paragraphs in relation to your choice of profession or job.

Cancer with Aries rising
You have tremendous drive and energy to use in your career. You may find it difficult to work away from home. You would do well in local government or political work connected with humanitarian or charitable organizations. Work with children would suit you, so would a career in science.

Cancer with Taurus rising
Your sensitivity and imagination could well be directed towards a career in the arts—you could be musical. You probably have a good business sense, on the other hand, and architecture, surveying or work as an estate agent could attract you. You might like a career as a beautician, or in the dental profession.

Cancer with Gemini rising
You may make several changes of direction in your career; try to avoid restlessness. You have originality, and this is likely to show in your choice of career, especially if you lean to science. You would make a good teacher or lecturer, or work well in the media or any circumstances where you had to speak up or out, for Gemini gives you the gift of the gab.

Cancer with Cancer rising
Think seriously about a niche in one of the "caring" professions—nursing, teaching, counselling, the social ser-

vices. You may like working behind the scenes, and letting the results of your labour speak for you. You are probably a born cook, so you might consider catering with an eventual view to haute cuisine.

Cancer with Leo rising

You need a job in which you can show off, but at the same time like to work quietly and in your own way. You could be creative, in a craftsmanlike way, so develop any artistic interests. Museum work, or work in antiques could suit you—but so could work in the computer industry.

Cancer with Virgo rising

Varied possibilities: you will work hard and are at your best out of doors, so farming, horticulture and floristry would suit you. Unconventional medicine and diet may attract. You would also make a good secretary or personal assistant, especially in broadcasting or newspapers.

Cancer with Libra rising

You need far more than just any old job: emotional involvement with your career is vital, and you like work that gives you plenty of contact with people. The hotel trade or the restaurant business would suit you, and you would organize a holiday camp, or a cruise, admirably. Public relations would attract you, as would its ultimate expression—the diplomatic corps.

Cancer with Scorpio rising

You have the tenacity to cope with a long training, so a career as an analyst or psychiatrist would be a possibility. Banking or high finance could also be your scene. Surgery, the wine trade or mining are other possibilities.

Cancer with Sagittarius rising

You may well have the makings of a good vet, or at any rate would like working with animals. Sport or physical education would be worth considering. But the law, publishing or literature in general would also be attractive. Languages and comparative religion would be fascinating.

Cancer with Capricorn rising

You are probably at your best working in partnership rather than ploughing a lonely furrow. The Army might suit you; but so could work in the construction industry, osteopathy, or physiotherapy. You might like studying geography or geology, using that as a basis for a career.

Cancer with Aquarius rising

Though work in designing or the "glamorous" professions could attract you, humanitarianism is a strong element in your character, and you could work well with the underprivileged, perhaps under trying or difficult conditions. You are original, and need room for self-expression. So you would not be happy in a job where you had to toe the line.

Cancer with Pisces rising

Careers which are concerned with water could suit you: the fishing industry, the Navy, boat-building, or deep-sea diving. If you are athletic you could be a swimming instructor. But wherever there is human suffering and help is needed, you can be counted on—this combination is excellent for work in medicine. The oil industry, or brewing, are possibilities.

Leo

Positive
Ruling planet: the Sun
Triplicity or element: fire
Quadruplicity or quality: fixed
Colour: the colours of the Sun from sunrise to sunset
Gemstone: ruby
Metal: gold
Flowers: sunflowers, marigolds
Trees: palm, bay, orange and lemon, laurel
Herbs and spices: saffron, peppermint, rosemary
Foodstuffs: rice, honey, crops and vines in general
Animals: big game, especially the cat family
Countries: South of France, Italy, Romania, Sicily
Cities: Rome, Prague, Bombay, Madrid, Philadelphia, Chicago, Los Angeles, Bath, Bristol

The Sun is the ruling planet of this sign, and every Leo's individual inner Sun needs to shine out. Usually it does, and friends benefit from its rays, for Leos need to enjoy and get as much out of life as possible, and like to see their loved ones doing the same.

They are well organized. They like to be leader, but to those they respect and admire they are quite willing to be slaves. Less exuberant types may well find them rather overwhelming at times, and indeed their worst faults are showing off and being "bossy". But the bossiness is often the result of their excellent organizing ability getting the better of them. A Leo can often organize other people's lives much better than the individuals themselves and is not reluctant to tell them so! But Leos rule through warmth and kindly encouragement, spurring their victims into greater creative effort, better use of time, giving up smoking, glamorizing themselves, and so on.

Somewhere in every Leo is a creative streak, and it needs positive expression. Friends should encourage every effort Leo makes, because Leos more than most need encouragement. This is particularly the case with Leo children, who can crumble under nagging criticism, but blossom with constructive encouragement.

Leos in love are passionate and faithful, and will express their natural generosity towards their partners in no small way. But they are more sensitive and easily hurt than most people realize.

The Leo body-areas are the heart and spine. Many Leos suffer back pains, and should get plenty of regular exercise. Dancing is ideal for them.

Leo in friendship, love and marriage

"A little knowledge is a dangerous thing"—and that should be your answer when someone suggests that it's no good your forming a friendship or relationship with them because they're Virgoan or Cancerian, or have some other Sun-sign they've heard is incompatible with yours. The very fact that they make the statement means they know very little about astrology, and it will be up to you to put them right!

There is, however, the slightest element of truth in what they say: and I use the word "element" advisedly, because by tradition those people with Sun-signs of the same element as your own (Ariens and Sagittarians, like you with an emphasis on the Fire element) will in general be a little easier to get along with. Those of the Air element (Geminians, Librans and Aquarians) are next in order of preference, with Earth people (Sun-sign Taureans, Virgoans and Capricorns) and Water people (Cancerians, Scorpios and Pisceans) bringing up the rear.

But really, it is nonsense to take this too far, for after all it is possible that you have Mercury or Venus in Cancer or Virgo, which will go a good way to help you when you relate to people with a Cancerian or Virgoan Sun-sign. Maybe their Mars is a sign which is traditionally compatible with your own. So it is just not possible to generalize about the Sun-signs in this way, and moreover it is sad and unkind to do so, for anyone with a superficial knowledge of astrology (especially if young and gullible) can all too easily miss out on a splendid relationship in that case. It is only by a careful comparison of two fully calculated birth-charts that an experienced astrologer can make any real pronouncements, and even then no one should ever be told that a partnership is unsuitable. An astrologer can certainly point out areas of greater and lesser compatibility—of agreement and disagreement. You, as a Sun-sign Leo, for instance, want a great deal in life; you're probably

125

extravert and with a real sense of drama, a taste for luxury and for spending money. So if you fall in love with someone who is mean about money, this could be a real bone of contention between you, and if you find yourself sharing your life with a mouse, you will become even more decidedly Leo, King of the Jungle! And could the mouse cope—would a mouse *want* to cope—in that situation? And do you really not need someone you can admire, someone with hidden potential you can h 'p to develop? It might be so.

Apart from the general traditional hints about re   ..ps between signs of different elements, I have alway   .id that the best, longest-lasting relationships are betwee   ,eople with a Leo Sun or Ascendant and those with Pisces strongly stressed in their full birth-chart. You will have been able to find your own Rising-sign (from pages 225–232 of this book), and by looking at the positions of the other planets at the time of your birth you will be able to use them to consider the possible rapport between yourself and a partner. I have always found that a good foundation for stability in a relationship is an accent on your polar sign—the sign right across the Zodiac from your Sun- or Rising-sign (and see page 75 for a list of these). Your Rising-sign may be directly across the Zodiac from your partner's Sun-sign; or vice versa. The Moon has an important part to play, too: you will be "in tune" with someone whose Moon-sign is compatible with your own—and if that sign is shared there will be almost magical links between you; your feeling will be deep and individual, but you will be able to pick up each other's moods. A classic link of this sort is between the Moon and the Sun—and this is stressed in your case because the Sun rules your Sun-sign.

But really, the polarity of signs between your chart and that of a lover (or for that matter, a business partner!) is vital. With compatibility between you at this level, you will not always agree, but at least you will always *understand* each other's motives and actions. There will be a high degree of rapport between you, which is extremely important.

So in future when anyone starts talking in sweeping generalizations about astrology, put a stop to them right away—and with the full authority and dignity of your Leonine Sun-sign!

Leo friendships

Leos do not form friendships all that easily. They will have a great many acquaintances, and know and be known to a lot of people, but it will be a long time before Leo will consider someone to be a true friend. Once they do, the friendship will last indefinitely. If the two should meet after some years' separation, Leo will be well able to pick up the threads, so that it seems like only yesterday they were last together.

For you friendships are meaningful and important, and you will be sceptical of someone who calls you "friend" only an hour or so after the first meeting: you may even be rather embarrassed. You enjoy meeting new people, studying them, finding out about them. You will want to like them, for such contacts are the stuff of life as a whole, and not to be ignored. But the title of "friend" means too much to you for you to be unselective.

You will want to do a great deal for your friends, and so the closer you are to them, the harder you'll be on them. If, for instance, they are talented and you know that they are capable of a great deal more than they are actually achieving, you will do everything in your power to encourage them to additional effort. You are a very good listener, and probably find that there is often a queue of people waiting to cry on your shoulder. You carry the role of counsellor well, and they will feel much better for having made you a confidant: *you* will feel like a wet rag—but you won't mind. But do be careful when playing the role of sympathetic aunt—being very good at organizing your own life, you may tend to take over and run other people's. Someone has got to sort them out, and you are a good candidate for the job; but do show discretion and tact, and resist the temptation to take over completely.

Because you work hard and don't waste your time, you may find that as years go by you out-pace, both at work and socially, those with whom you made friends when you were all young together. Here is another area where you have to be careful. You are extremely generous, and will want to give your old friends' children extravagant presents, and take them on trips. Sometimes this may make your friends envious, and they may think you are showing off or splashing your money about with unbecoming freedom. You may find you have to be less generous than you would like, simply because others may get the wrong impression, or be made unhappy. This is a pity, because you are probably at your best surrounded by those you love and seeing them really enjoying themselves—even if this has cost you a considerable amount of hard-earned money.

Leo in love

Generally speaking, when Leos fall in love they fall very hard indeed. When they look back over their lives in old age, there will be certain relationships that were very memorable, and each one will have a distinct quality and colour which the Leo will remember with happiness, nostalgia, amusement or sometimes sadness. There will be some sad memories for Leo, because with all their exuberance for life, love and sex, they expect a great deal from their partners, and in doing so look up to them. The Leo organ is the heart, and we know that from time to time it can get badly damaged. But they are also more resilient than most Zodiac types, and they will force their Leo Sun to shine out from behind the clouds, and for therapy will turn to their many other interests.

You probably have a great zest for your partner, and will want any lover to enjoy the things you enjoy. It should not be too difficult to persuade them to do this, for your enthusiasm is very infectious. Joint enthusiasms are, I think, very important to you—more important than for many. Sharing the same thrills, looking at the same favourite painting, going yet again to a favourite film, is something special for you. You are passionate, and your creativity and exuberance can be well expressed sexually. You may well set the pace in the development of your relationships, and will organize things to that end, discreetly making sure that the atmosphere is conducive to love-making and that you aren't troubled by constant interruptions. With your sense of drama, the staging of this kind of episode will appeal to you. Having set the scene, you will be happy to relax and give yourself over to whatever the occasion has in store, knowing that you have done all you can to prepare for a memorable occasion—whether this means the beginning of a first affair, or a golden wedding anniversary. For a Leo, there may be very little difference between the two occasions.

Because you have such a strong personality, perhaps you

should ask yourself from time to time whether you are ruling the roost too singlemindedly. Many partners like to be dominated, but you could take this to extremes—so beware. Remember too that your personality can be overwhelming, and make allowances for the shy girl, or the man who may think that after all you could be a bit much for him to handle. You make a marvellous partner: you have a great deal to give, and will give it very freely. But you need a lot, too, and knowing that you are appreciated is perhaps highest on your list of priorities.

Leo in marriage

Leos have a natural capacity for enjoying marriage just like any other undertaking. They will want to "do it properly", and this may well mean the full church ceremony, the champagne reception, and the honeymoon of their dreams. So they may want to wait until they have saved up enough money to be launched in style.

Leos can be difficult to live with, and should sometimes make an effort to see themselves through their partner's eyes. Are they being too overbearing, intolerant, or just plain bossy? They should listen when criticized, though they won't like it! However, there is a great deal on the credit side too. If you are a married Leo, or one committed to a permanent relationship, you will put plenty of work, time and energy into your marriage, and give your partner all possible encouragement in the achievement of ambitions. Don't, however, overstate your point of view, or force your opinions on your husband or wife. This can all too easily happen and should your partner be less assertive than you, you could get your own way a little more often than is good for the partnership. In order to keep your equilibrium in a marriage, think of the things you like to receive—praise and compliments when you have cooked a special dish or made the family car look particularly gleaming, or a pat on the back for some achievement or other—and return them when your partner does something special for you. In your enthusiasm for life, you could get so involved in your own activities that your partner's could go unnoticed and unappreciated.

Leos never forget what it was like to be a child—what it was like not to have questions answered properly, or difficult things explained. So they treat children as people—no differently, in fact, from other people they love. Children can't help it if they are younger or smaller than other people. So Leos earn respect from children, and get a different response even from babies than the adults who coo meaningless noises at them. If they love their children they tell them so, without itchy-coos or grimaces: and it works. No baby-talk from Leo parents; a good sensible relationship will be built up from the beginning, and there is a marvellous ability to awaken the child's interest in nature, art and the world in general.

But be careful that you do not become a domineering father or mother. The mother who, because she fancied herself as a ballerina, pushes little Marianne off to ballet classes when the girl would be much happier climbing trees with her friends, may well be a Leo mother gone wrong. Leos should guide their children in the direction the child's potential suggests, and not where their own longing lies. Good Leo parents encourage their children to do their own thing, and don't use them as extensions of their own egos.

Leo careers and money matters

When assessing the Leo potential in careers and financial ability we must consider not only the psychological motivation and mode of expression attributed to Leo but also the thinking processes of Mercury, and how these two factors combined can be best used in both areas. Then there is the influence of Venus, a planet as strongly related to finance and possessions as to relationships. The latter aspect is also important in this sphere as it will affect how a person will get on with colleagues, in business partnerships, and so on. Mars may well give some hint as to the direction of energy and will most certainly influence the physical element—the drive and energy put into the day's work. As we shall see, the influence of the combined Sun- and Rising-sign is interesting and very personal: but if your birth-time is not available and you cannot find out your Rising-sign, do not be too disappointed; you should be able to glean plenty of information about this sphere of your life from the more general paragraphs.

Whatever the choice of career, it is important for any Leo to have the chance to shine in some way: if they work in a department store, they must take pride in their particular department and in the products they sell, if at a hotel reception desk they will be particularly good at welcoming guests and making them feel at home, if in the theatre they will literally take the centre of the stage. Basically, they need a job in which they can extend their self-expression into their work, and there should be some opportunity to "show off" (in the nicest way), whether it be to show off what they themselves make, or what they have to sell, or whatever. Most Leos would not be happy working in isolation or in a job where they had to hide their light under a bushel. They draw their nourishment from the admiration and appreciation shown by others—a perfectly healthy attitude provided that it is employed in a positive way. Society needs those who thrive on the limelight just as much as those who prefer to take a more back-room role.

Of course Leos are found in every walk of life, but the Leo message is "Here I am—this is what I have to offer—isn't it good?" or "This is what I can do—I enjoy doing it or making it—I hope it will give you pleasure!" and of course for "give you pleasure" we can substitute many other phrases: "make you well—or happy—or less hungry—or more relaxed . . ." depending on what Leo actually does.

Putting all these indications together, it seems that one of Leo's chief motivations is to make life a bit easier, more enjoyable and rewarding, through their efforts and considerable energy. They need to succeed in their own eyes, and to their own satisfaction; if they think they aren't succeeding, they will be very unhappy. An unfulfilled Leo is like a lion with a headache—sad, restless and miserable. But after a dreary period which won't last long by comparison with other Zodiac types, they will gather themselves together and take action. They know that it's no good sitting about moping and waiting for something to happen: one has to make things happen. Then others can take advantage of what the individual Leo has to offer—and that is quite a lot.

Leos like to do things properly; they hate amateurism, and in whatever they choose to do they will achieve a high standard. This trait is nowhere more obvious than in their careers, and in the search for perfection they set an example to other, less exacting folk. They strive for the best. A Leo girl working in a bakery, for instance, will arrange her cakes beautifully every morning, and she'll be noticed by her employers, in time will be manager—and woe betide any underlings who leave messy crumbs or splodges of whipped cream on the display units! The Leo secretary will run her boss's working life and be far more the head of their department than he is. She will not only want, but *need* to work well, and in doing so will express her potential to the full.

If Leos find themselves in jobs where their "superiors" are illogical, stupid or rude, yet demand "respect" and need to be sucked up to, the Leo will rebel. They abhor annoying, time-consuming, unnecessary jobs, and are not likely to shine or flourish under such circumstances. There is only one thing for a Leo to do in such a situation, and that is—get out! If suppressed by their bosses, or unable to work well for them, it may well be because the bosses are frightened, feeling threatened by the Leonine exuberance and zest for life. No Leo should stay in such a situation. Imagine a lively Leo teacher in a restrictive school where the Head is small-minded, uncreative, ruled by the Board of Governors and terrified of losing his job. The talented creative Leo wants to start a school orchestra, and produce an exciting musical or opera—but faces opposition all round: "We've never done *that* before—the parents won't approve." This would be a dreadful situation for a sunny Leo; and they should never persist under such conditions, even if the job seems otherwise desirable. They should never let style and ability be cramped by small-mindedness and weakness of character, or simply fear. Leos who do so will be going against their own grain and will regret it.

Scope of choice of career for Leos is very wide, and they have a place in many areas of life. The nature of the work itself is less important than the opportunities for self-expression within the job. This is of greater importance to Leos than to most Zodiac types. Although quite willing to knuckle under and perform all sorts of tasks, working conditions are of great importance, as are the kind of people they have to work under, and their attitudes: for they will not suffer fools gladly, and certainly won't want to be bossed by them. Nor will they tolerate a situation where they and their workmates can't speak up and make suggestions for the improvement of working conditions. If all these things are satisfactory, then the Leo will work well, and will take every opportunity to work extra hours on interesting projects. Whatever they have to do—even if it is only sweeping a road or driving a truck—will be done hard and well.

Mercury at work

Check the position of Mercury on pages 238–241

Mercury in Cancer

If Mercury was in Cancer when you were born, you will have an excellent memory. This can be very useful from a career point of view, being applicable to many kinds of work. You might well be attracted to history and the past in general, and might like to work in the antiques trade, or in a library, archive or museum.

Mercury in Cancer will increase your powers of imagination, so you could have a real flair for artistic work. You are sensitive, and have a caring, protective instinct, and could find nursing or working with children very satisfying. Rather differently, restoration work of any kind could interest you.

If your work finds you dealing with teenagers, and you yourself are a good bit older than them, I think you will need consciously to develop an interest in what involves and concerns them; otherwise you could tend always to be comparing present-day standards with those of the past, not moving with the times as much as you might.

If you are a student, you will organize the time at your disposal very well. Because your memory is good, you can prepare a long time in advance, and are not at all likely to forget those all-important facts when it comes to examination time.

Mercury in Leo

If Mercury was in Leo with the Sun, you will probably like to have a steady routine, and may find it difficult to be flexible. You like to know where you stand, and what you have to do, and, because you are a Leo, will see to those things yourself.

You will take great pride in what you do, and will not hesitate to tell the world about your work and the company you work for. You will be sympathetic towards companies that make or sell quality products. Or if, for example, you teach, you will want to work at the best school in town. Your scope is broad, but it is particularly important for you to think *quality* and always work somewhere where standards are high, and the attitude towards work is second to none, for your Leo sense of pride is very strong. Try also to have work that will use your organizing ability: but consciously fight those stubborn, fixed tendencies.

If you are a student, your attitude to your studies will be less adventurous than that of many of your fellow students, but there is a soundness about your work that will impress your tutors. You can think constructively and creatively. When it comes to examinations, if you prepare yourself to a standard as high as the one expected of you, you will do very well.

Mercury in Virgo

You will have the ability to work in great detail on tasks requiring care and resourcefulness if you have Mercury in Virgo. You could have a flair for figures, so accountancy might well suit you, and so might electronics. The computer industry too could be rewarding. You are a natural critic, and will not find it difficult to compile reports, time and motion studies, to re-organize filing cabinets and all kinds of information storage systems. Your creativity might well be turned to writing or journalism, or you could make excellent progress in scientific research. Any specialized career that is geared to discovering facts would be suitable. You would also make a good teacher or lecturer. Perhaps the field of health appeals to you: diet, vegetarianism, keeping fit, exercise . . . all these things could be your scene. You will be self-critical, and in general will leave no stone unturned in getting to the root of things.

If studying, you will surely enjoy your work. But try if you can not to get too bogged down by detail, for, if you do, you could rather easily lose the overall picture of your project. Your neatness and the way in which you present your work will impress. Still, try to get a little rest before exams, as you could be troubled by nerves and then not produce your best work.

Venus: money and rapport

Check the position of Venus on pages 242–245

Venus in Gemini
If Venus is in Gemini in your birth-chart, you will have to control a tendency to spend too much money on your clothes, which you will want to keep up-to-date. You will want to make money, but it will be by no means the most important thing in your life. You will want to spend a lot on entertaining, on travel, books, music, records. This is all very well; but do try to be practical, so that when you have to cope with a long-term commitment you'll be in a reasonably confident mood when it comes to approaching the bank manager for help.

You will enjoy investment and speculation, and could well find that chains of department stores and the retail trade in general are profitable areas for you. You like to take an interest in the companies you support, so reading their annual reports will fascinate rather than bore you.

You make a lively and delightful colleague: those near you in this sphere of your life will enjoy your company. If you are an employer, you'll have the reputation of getting on well with teenage employees; others in your firm will say of you "X knows how to handle 'em!" and they will go on to repeat some snatch of conversation or joke you had with the youngest junior last week!

Venus in Cancer
With this placing you are among the shrewdest of Leos. You have a natural business sense, and could well be clever with money. You will develop an excellent nose for business and the "good deal", so should you go into business on your own, or start a company, with all these qualities plus your Leonine organizing ability you should do extremely well. If you feel you want to start your own business at any time in your life, don't ignore the thought: but do remember that you might think a little too big, especially if Mercury was in Leo when you were born.

You may like to invest in fisheries, dairy produce, or products for mothers and children. The hotel and catering trades could also be very interesting and rewarding, and again this could provide scope for your very own business.

You will be kind, and want to look after employees, and will be liked for it. If you are an employee working with others, your colleagues may well in some way look to you as a father- or mother-figure, irrespective of age. Say, for instance, some-one injures themselves—the general tendency will be to send for you!

Venus in Leo

If Venus was in Leo with the Sun when you were born, you will need to make quite a lot of money to keep up your expensive and enjoyable lifestyle. You buy the best, and even when young your eyes will have gone straight to the most expensive toy in the shop when asked to choose a present. You can't help it: that's the way you're made. You really appreciate well-designed and beautiful things, and like to have them around to use and wear. With your liking for quality, you should invest in firms producing high-quality goods. For instance, if you are attracted to the car industry, buy into Rolls-Royce or Cadillac rather than a firm making small family cars. Gold and jewellery too will serve you well as an investment. However, remember that the insurance on them will be expensive.

To your colleagues you are probably "pack leader", and enjoy the role. And if you're the boss, you're a generous one—staff outings will be memorable, even if they cost a fortune. But your employees will thoroughly appreciate you for it.

Venus in Virgo

This placing will give you a natural ability to save and watch your money grow. You won't waste much money on fripperies, though you'll love attractive kitchen utensils and could spend quite a lot on good-quality linen, pure silk or wool, or ethnic products. Your tastes are less flamboyant than those of many Leos, which is in your favour saving-wise.

You might like to put money into a bank deposit account, or invest where there is a slow but steady growth. Farming products and industries, horticulture, will also be very suitable for you, as will communications, and newspapers and magazine companies.

You are probably the hardest-working person in your de-partment, and could well be taken advantage of from time to time, so be a little careful that colleagues, because they know you are good-natured, do not overload your work schedule so that you end up regularly doing more than your fair share.

If you are the boss, you'll be kind and generous, but might overdo the criticism at times, and seem a little fussy. If you are discontented, you have the ability to explain why you need and expect high standards—and having done so, buy your em-ployee a drink!

Venus in Libra

With Venus in Libra you are probably high in the Leonine extravagance charts. However, because you soon learn how dull life is without creature comforts, you'll equally soon learn that to make sure of them you will have to be clever at stretching your money.

By no means lacking in enterprise, you could use this quality subtly in organizing your finances: you may well be better working in a business partnership than alone, and perhaps could eventually find yourself a role as some kind of backer or sleeping partner for someone with an interesting scheme in mind, or whose work gives you confidence. Until such a time comes, I suggest a talk with your bank manager about the possibility of setting aside a regular percentage of your income—the less *you* handle it the better!—so that you have something by you, and your money doesn't all just vanish into the pockets of restaurateurs while you entertain your friends!

You have the ability to get other people to do quite a bit of work for you as your charm is irresistible. This applies too if you are an employer; you really can get the best out of your employees—and they'll like you for it!

Rising-signs and your career

First check your Rising-sign on pages 225–232

Note: Careers and the Midheaven
If you develop your interest in astrology, one of the first things you will learn about, but which is outside the scope of this book, is the Midheaven. Roughly speaking, this is the sign that was immediately over your head when you were born. It is as important in your career, outward expression and identification with objectives in life as your Rising-sign is in your personality. To combine it with your Rising-sign is complicated and would be impossible in a book of this length: but, while I cannot help you to discover yours in this book, rest assured that I have borne the various possibilities in mind when writing the following paragraphs in relation to your choice of profession or job.

Leo with Aries rising
You are ambitious and good at organization. You'd fit the armed services well, and have officer potential. If in a big company, you'll make a steady climb to the top. Architecture, science, mathematics or professional sport could feature in your scheme of things. Curb impatience: don't be too assertive.

Leo with Taurus rising
Sculpture or music are probably your art-forms if you are creative: they could even provide a career. But you have excellent commercial sense, and could run your own business. Banking, finance, real estate would suit you. Work as a beautician or in any luxury trade would be possible. You are very disciplined. You need financial security.

Leo with Gemini rising
You would do well working in the media, or as an artists' agent. The travel industry might suit you, and you certainly have the ability to sell. Post and telecommunications are possibilities, but so is any busy scene where you are mobile and there is plenty of variety. Beware of routine or boring jobs, but try not to make too many changes.

Leo with Cancer rising
If you would like to open a restaurant, do—you won't go far wrong. You'd make an excellent teacher of younger children. The nursing profession, the antiques trade, museum work are all open to you. So is work for a shipping line, or the Navy, indeed any career connected with the sea could be satisfying.

Leo with Leo rising
You need to be centre-stage and somewhere where you can show off! Not necessarily in the theatre, but perhaps as a much-respected surgeon, or chief buyer in a huge store. You could be a head waiter, a hotel manager, a guide—you choose. But don't choose anything that will cramp your style.

Leo with Virgo rising
You probably need to work behind the scenes, and let your work speak for you. You could be a writer or a journalist, but not a reporter, who has to be out and about. Though you need

security, you could run your own business, perhaps selling hand-made articles, or something you make yourself. Floristry, horticulture, health foods, farming—all are possibilities.

Leo with Libra rising

You would be good at personnel work or public relations: the Foreign Service is a possibility, but so is hairdressing! You have that special way with clients and inspire confidence. Try not to do work that cuts you off from other people. You'd be an excellent front-man or woman in any big company.

Leo with Scorpio rising

You must be emotionally involved in your work. Don't choose anything that is merely a job. Research, the medical profession, psychiatry, analysis, the wine and oil trades are all excellent. Big business and high finance, the computer industry, mining, could all fascinate.

Leo with Sagittarius rising

Teaching (arts subjects, perhaps), literature, publishing, the travel industry, translation, law and the Church are all possibilities. You need challenge, plenty of variety and freedom of expression. You'd enjoy working with animals—work as a vet might be very satisfying. Don't neglect your creativity, though.

Leo with Capricorn rising

You may end up in a lonely position, for you are ambitious and may well get to the top of some large concern. Teaching, politics at local or national level, may be suitable. Your career could veer towards the conventional, and you need financial security.

Leo with Aquarius rising

You won't want a run-of-the-mill job, your work should be spiced with originality. You'd enjoy being an air steward or stewardess, or working in some other capacity for an airline. Television (technical or studio work) could engross you, and if you're stage-struck, you might be right! You're a humanitarian, and charity work in the field might appeal—but so could archaeology, astronomy . . . and astrology!

Leo with Pisces rising

You'd probably make a marvellous photographer, for you are creative and should express this in your work. You might come to photography through modelling. You'd make a good nurse, and do well in the caring professions and social services. You might like book-design or illustration, publishing, or the shoe trade.

Virgo

Negative
Ruling planet: Mercury
Triplicity or element: earth
Quadruplicity or quality: mutable
Colours: navy blue, dark brown, green
Gemstone: sardonyx
Metal: mercury or nickel
Flowers: all brightly coloured, small flowers, such as the anemone
Trees: all nut-bearing trees (shared with Gemini)
Herbs and spices: those with bright yellow or blue flowers or colouring
Foodstuffs: vegetables grown under the earth
Animals: all domestic pets
Countries: Greece, the West Indies, Turkey, the state of Virginia, U.S.A., Brazil, New Zealand
Cities: Boston, Heidelberg, Paris, Athens

Of the 12 signs, Virgo is probably the busiest and has the most to get through during the working day. But Virgoans are not always very well organized and sometimes tend to do more than they need to achieve the necessary result.

Generally speaking, Virgoans cannot do enough to please their friends and family; sometimes they almost become slaves for their loved ones, and the tradition in astrology that says "Virgo serves" is not without truth. They do in many ways like to serve, and this is linked to a basic psychological motivation of theirs. Friends should encourage them to express their own abilities a little more freely, for there is a tendency to hide their delightful talents under a cloud of genuine modesty.

Virgoans are very critical, both of themselves and of others, and often their work allows them to express this trait—they make excellent critics, investigative journalists, teachers. They are versatile and very quick-minded, but tend to worry.

In love, Virgoans are very modest, and often there is a genuine shyness which is delightful: but the critical tendency can mar a relationship, for little habits in a partner can irritate a Virgo and assume too great an importance.

Parents of Virgoan children will know when they are worried about school problems. The stomach and bowels are Virgo body-areas, and both children and adults will suffer tummy upsets as symptoms of worry. Friends can encourage Virgos to use their practical, analytical talents to help them through difficulties.

Virgo in friendship, love and marriage

One of the things you like least about other people is a tendency to come out with sweeping generalizations. Your critical, analytical Virgoan faculties come into play, and you begin questioning them to discover what sort of basis they have for what they have just been saying. Often, of course, you find they have none!

You may already have responded in this way when someone has told you that you're unlikely to hit it off with them because your "sign" isn't compatible with theirs. Well, in the first place we are all a combination of the 12 signs of the Zodiac, stressed in a variety of ways; in the second place, any statement of that kind made on the basis of the Sun-signs alone is almost total rubbish. I say "almost", because there may well be a degree of ease between those who share Sun-signs of the same element (see page 75): in your case, Taureans and Capricorns are also of an Earth element. Those who share Water as their element (Cancer, Scorpio and Pisces) may well make an easy friendship with you—while Gemini, Libra and Aquarius (Air) and Aries, Leo and Sagittarius (Fire) are signs which have a slight tendency to be less easy when matched with Virgo.

But you see, you may have Mercury (the ruling planet of your Sun-sign) in Leo or Libra, or Venus in either of those signs; and if so, this could make for a very pleasant link between you and someone with the Sun in either sign. And surely a Geminian would be an interesting friend or lover, for Gemini shares Mercury with you as a ruling planet (although you may find them pretty infuriating from time to time!).

It is silly, and rather sad, to hold back from a relationship, or allow one to wither, simply because of this kind of alleged incompatibility, however. For it is only when a fully-calculated birth-chart is assessed and compared with someone else's that you can draw any firm conclusion—and even then, no good astrologer would ever warn you to stop seeing someone. What one can do is point out areas of compatibility and other areas where you can expect difficulty. For instance, you, as a Sun-sign Virgoan, have a natural modesty which may make you somewhat shy; you're prone to worry, too, and are rather critical. Could you cope with someone flashy or lazy, someone who wants to spend a lot on luxuries, and who likes to live it up? Could you cope with someone who made heavy sexual demands on you? This sort of thing can be evaluated by a study of the full birth-chart, and is the sort of thing an astrologer can encourage you to consider, so that you can make the necessary adjustments, perhaps developing common interests and hobbies to bring you closer together, and so on.

It is detailed study of the birth-charts that matters. Having read this book, you will understand this; and the tables in the back pages will enable you to find the positions of your own planets and your prospective lover's (or business partner's, for that matter) and find out about your and their reactions in various areas of life. By now, you will have used pages 225–232 to discover your Rising-sign, which is very important because some of the best permanent relationships are between couples with an emphasis on opposite or polar signs: signs on the opposite side of the Zodiac (see page 75). For instance, if your Rising-sign is Virgo and your partner's Rising-sign is Pisces, you are on to a good thing. Or perhaps your Moon is in Capricorn, while your partner's Rising-sign is Cancer.

Remember, too, if Virgo is your partner's Moon-sign there will be some very deep, instinctive rapport between you; you'll pick up each other's moods, and from a psychological point of view you'll have a tremendous foundation upon which to build. Mars can be a good guide to sexual compatibility, and the expression of energy. If this seems to be negative, if anger or aggression seem to intervene, maybe you can use other areas of the chart to improve the flow of rapport between you, so that it is expressed in positive mutual work, or in a lively sexual response.

Really, just comparing Sun-signs is stupidly simple-minded! With the help of this book you can do much better than that, and you will find it very worthwhile trying.

Virgoan friendships

You will work as hard to preserve your friendships as you will in other spheres of your life. You will want to make your friends happy, and won't feel satisfied until you have done everything you can to make sure that you have relieved them of as many chores and anxieties as possible.

In all this you could be so busy seeing to their creature comforts that you may not get as much enjoyment out of their company and conversation as perhaps you should. You'll tend to fidget round them, pushing a stool nearer for them to put their feet up, rushing to get a book they have expressed an interest in, making sure their cup of coffee is at their elbow, and in all this you miss out on *them*. It is lovely to be waited on, but we other Zodiac types like our Virgo friends to be with us, and to enjoy their company, rather than just watching them rush about on our behalf. Don't think you're not appreciated—you are. But, give *us* the chance to help *you*, especially when you need that help—you imagine too readily that your friends couldn't possibly spare the time or energy, and that you must battle on alone. Not true! You will be well in credit as far as most of your friends are concerned. Don't stagger on alone when you need an arm to lean on. Learn to lean, from time to time, it'll do you good.

Busy people are generally interesting, and you will be good at provoking interest in others. You will goad them into action, into learning a new skill, taking an active interest in a new sport or exercise, or whatever ... yet another reason why people like you! But do be a little careful not to be overcritical of your friends. When you are asked for your opinion, learn to develop a little tact, and consciously take a fairly soft line. Although you know that you mean nothing personal when criticizing a friend's efforts, they will almost inevitably take what you have to say personally. You have a rather special Virgoan critical ability, but though excellent and sound it is one that others may find difficult to cope with. Always aim to make your comments constructive, and say the nice things, the positive things, first.

You are a person who keeps friends for a long time—an excellent attribute. You love to have a great variety of hobbies and spare-time interests and, because these provide focal points in your life, it is important to you to have friends who share at least one of them. You'll find it easy to teach or otherwise help them, if they decide to take up a hobby similar to one of yours. But again, remember to offer praise and be constructive when you have to point out where they are going wrong. And don't always take it on yourself to provide the packed lunch—*they* may like to feed *you* once in a while!

Virgo in love

Virgo modesty could cause you to hold back a little, and underestimate yourself as far as your powers of attraction are concerned. If you find yourself assuming that nobody attractive would give you so much as a passing nod, you are more than likely doing yourself down. If you often find yourself thinking this way, you need to build up your self-confidence! Your modesty is in itself extremely attractive, and a great deal of charm filters through to help you to a rewarding love-life.

But of course things may not be as simple as that. If your reluctance to become sexually or emotionally involved really seems to prevent a relationship developing, you should go in for a little self-analysis. Are you perhaps afraid of sex itself, or its possible outcome? Is your inherent apprehension born of a misgiving that perhaps any partner is bound to think you less attractive or less good in bed than partners they may have had in the past? Would rejection finish you off completely? Try if you can to decide whether there is one predominant area of your attitudes or personality which is preventing you from relaxing into a relationship. If there is, and you can't resolve it yourself, you should talk things over with a sympathetic friend, or perhaps a professional counsellor such as a consultant astrologer.

But let us look on the bright side, and assume that you have grown out of any youthful shyness that may have bedevilled you. So let us hope that you have a normal interest in and enthusiasm for sex. In that case there are only one or two things to watch out for, the main one being that your partner is not getting bored. Experiment, explore the various possibilities of making love, and keep things lively. Any partner will be pleased if you develop your technique. You are, after all, the perfectionist of the Zodiac—so why not aim high where sex is concerned? You do already? Well, let's leave it at that!

You need security and permanence in personal relationships. Because Mercury is your ruling planet you also need a strong element of friendship to complement the sexual link.

Intellectual *rapport* is essential, to give your partnership a lively, interesting quality all the time you are together. There must be plenty for you to talk about at any time and it is good for your partner to be a little ahead of you intellectually, so that you are continually stimulated by new ideas, and won't be bored or drained—but you should still be able to give them a run for their money. You have always been the type to both ask questions *and* answer them. Keep it that way!

Virgo in marriage

Once you decide to commit yourself to marriage or a permanent relationship, you will feel a warm sense of security, an element of curiosity and slight apprehension. Try to let security predominate. You will then find that the positive feelings you have for your partner will blossom, and that you have discovered something very rewarding and fulfilling.

It is very important for you to be able to relax into marriage. Don't keep nagging to yourself about what you *ought* to have prepared for dinner if the boss hadn't kept you working on that report until the delicatessen was closed. Far better for your partner to find you relaxed and tranquil than all of a dither because some minor detail of life has gone unresolved.

I'm emphasizing all this because your Virgoan traits could well make you fussy about the appearance of your home and it could take up far too much of your time. If your partner accuses you of neglecting him or her for other, material things, accept the accusation for what it's worth.

Virgo husbands conscious of themselves as "head of the household" are just as likely to fall prey to overwork in the office, making money—no doubt in order to keep the home "nice"—as the wives are to get overinvolved in housework. If a wife feels neglected by a Virgo husband too concerned about a new contract, she is likely to become impatient: if a Virgo wife's efforts to keep the place clean go unnoticed, she will begin to nag about muddy footprints on the clean kitchen floor. Virgos in marriage must try to remember that their own passionate addiction to what seem to be urgent matters may seem far less justifiable to partners.

Virgos make stimulating parents. There will always be plenty of reference books about the house to satisfy children's curiosity, and they will be encouraged in their searches. But again I must emphasize that element of Virgo criticism which could be too harsh when directed at the kids. You'll appreciate their efforts, but if the paint has "gone over the edges" in that splendid birthday card they've so painstakingly made, you could be the first person to point it out. Try hard to ignore it, and give out a bit of real enthusiasm and praise. Keep your criticisms constructive, and they in turn will develop a positive, constructive outlook and attitude to projects and interests.

To other parents your attitude to your children could seem a little cold and clinical. Ask yourself if this is so, and if it is you might need to try to be a little softer and more emotional yourself. This is especially true if a child is rather sensitive or emotional—and perhaps has a Sun-sign which is of the Fire or Water element—see page 75. If your child has an Earth or Air sign he or she is more likely to respond well to your personality. In any event, you won't have any difficulty in achieving an excellent rapport with your children, because you are capable of meaningful friendship with them, giving a rewarding relationship spiced with lively intellectualism.

Virgoan careers and money matters

When assessing the Virgoan potential in careers and financial ability we must consider not only the psychological motivation and mode of expression attributed to Virgo but also the thinking processes of Mercury, and how these two factors combined can be best used in both areas. Then there is the influence of Venus, a planet as strongly related to finance and possessions as to relationships. The latter aspect is also important in this sphere as it will affect how a person will get on with colleagues, in business partnerships, and so on. Mars may well give some hint as to the direction of energy and will most certainly influence the physical element—the drive and energy put into the day's work. As we shall see, the influence of the combined Sun- and Rising-sign is interesting and very personal: but if your birth-time is not available and you cannot find out your Rising-sign, do not be too disappointed; you should be able to glean plenty of information about this sphere of your life from the more general paragraphs.

As is the case with all the 12 Zodiac signs, we of course find Virgos in every profession: but obviously there are some jobs in which they feel more at home than in others. A job where there is little activity is not good for them. A Virgo would soon get bored, for instance, looking after a high-class antique shop with few customers and little to do but sit around once the dusting and arranging had been done. In such a situation any Virgo would in fact find ways to avoid being idle, such as by studying: but they would probably feel some qualms of conscience about using working time for personal ends, even if there was nothing else to do, and would always feel much better if it were the job itself that made demands on their time and energy.

Virgos like plenty of hustle and bustle, and will make work if it's not there. The office Virgo is quite likely to be seen clearing out a filing cabinet while everyone else is having a coffee break. If all else fails, they will be found watering the cluster of pot-plants that gives everyone in the department so much pleasure.

The Virgo is an ideal secretary or personal assistant, and will do more than would be expected of someone else in that role. Once they know what is expected of them, Virgos are marvellously efficient: but they do have to be told exactly where they stand and precisely what they have to do. Once they have been given a precise briefing they will be away, and everyone else, from managing director to coffee-lady, can rest assured that they will always be there, running the whole set-up like a well-oiled machine, with Virgo wielding the oil-can, or if necessary carrying it for other less efficient types.

A great many Virgos work in the media as the influence of Mercury, their ruling planet, gives them a strong urge to communicate. They excel as critics, investigative journalists and writers of all kinds—the number of Virgo novelists, for example, is much above average. They are happy in a school or college environment and enjoy teaching and lecturing as this offers a positive expression of their well-developed critical faculties. Among their students or employees they often have a reputation for being strict. But this apparent strictness is really a desire for efficiency—for the neat presentation of work and the smooth running of a timetable. An insistence on such things has probably earned many a Virgo somewhat undeserved reputation as a martinet.

Virgos are happy in the open air. Although many find themselves caught up in the urban rat-race and stuck behind desks, it is really more natural for them to be working out of doors, for example in agriculture, horticulture or surveying. They like to see things grow, whether they be plants or buildings.

When Virgoans are deciding on a career they should look carefully at the field of health and medicine. Even if they are not cut out for a conventional medical career there are many other areas in which they can find satisfaction. They could, for example, train in some area of unorthodox medicine, such as acupuncture or homeopathy, methods which are becoming increasingly popular. A health club would also be a congenial environment for them to work in, whether practising some form of therapy or simply being in charge of the reception desk. Virgos enjoy serving others, helping them along the road to fitness or easing pain and distress when they are ill. This they find satisfying and rewarding.

There are many creative Virgoans, and those considering a course at art school will probably be at their best specializing in some activity where natural materials are used, such as pottery or weaving. As Virgo is an Earth sign the Earth and its products are often a considerable source of inspiration.

Virgos must remember that they are prone to worry, and are not the best leaders or organizers among the 12 Sun-signs. If early in their careers they are given a job that carries a lot of responsibility they could get extremely worried about it and their ability to cope—possibly to the point where it affects their health. In due course, when they know the ropes, all will be well: but they must always have time to acclimatize themselves to any responsible position. They must also ask themselves whether in fact they want to be boss, and to be in the limelight. Very often this simply isn't the Virgo scene.

There is no need for them to underestimate themselves and feel that a prominent position is ruled out: but neither should they feel inferior if they honestly believe they would rather labour in the vineyard than be its overseer. They may achieve far more satisfaction in their careers if they are not perched on the topmost branch of the tree. So often at the top the emphasis is on administration, and this means giving up a lot of work that a person has actually been trained to do. I have mentioned that many Virgos enjoy teaching. But as headmaster or principal they would be lucky to get two or three teaching periods a week, spending the rest of the time doing battle over budgets, chairing staff meetings and organizing timetables. That kind of thing can happen in many professions and is not something Virgos normally enjoy. They are devoted to their craft, whatever it is, and the additional financial reward may not compensate them for being removed from it.

Mercury at work

Check the position of Mercury on pages 238–241

Mercury in Leo

If Mercury was in Leo when you were born, your mind is very quick to grasp situations in a broad, overall sense. This is excellent, and I think you will also find it easier than most Virgos do to accept a prominent and responsible post if you have the opportunity. Should you find yourself in such a position you will cope with it very well. You are decisive, and this will help you along the way. Try to recognize that you might appear very stubborn at times, and remember consciously to develop flexibility, listening with care to others and respecting their opinions, not being afraid to admit it when you are wrong.

You have good organizing ability, and can use this to advantage. You can take situations into your own hands far more easily than most Virgos, and should not be afraid to do so. If you are a student with examinations approaching you should find it easy to plan and stick to a well-organized routine. Even so, you like to enjoy life and may have to be a little hard on yourself as the date draws near. Last-minute cramming is not for you. Keep plodding, in an organized way.

Mercury in Virgo

If, when you were born, Mercury was in Virgo with the Sun, you will have to be very careful that you don't get too bogged down by detail because, in crossing every *t* and dotting every *i*, you could lose sight of the overall message you are trying to convey. You will be a great asset to any organization: every set-up needs someone like you around. But at times others could get more than a little fed up with your nit-picking care over tiny things, which can after all slow up progress. You may have to compromise. Here is additional food for thought for you. Are you *over*careful? Do you sometimes fail to see the wood for the trees? As a student, you of all your year will present the best-looking, neatest essays or papers, and this of course is very much in your favour; tutors who find something easy and pleasant to read instead of an untidy and incoherent scribble will be biased in your favour. Whatever your mistakes, you'll have an advantage. But you do need, while remembering and noting facts, to be able to keep a sense of broad perspective, to be able to theorize about them. Your inner feelings and opinions have a place too: try to analyse your own reactions and discover how you would cope without the hindsight of carefully noted statistics or contemporary reports.

Mercury in Libra

With this placing you may have to develop decisiveness and could find it a little difficult to make quick decisions while working under pressure. Try to remember that others may be waiting for you to commit yourself. It may not be easy, don't attempt it when you are at all worried or flustered, otherwise it will slow you down still more. When you can, get away somewhere by yourself and think calmly in a quiet atmosphere. It will then be much easier for you to come to a definite conclusion. Having done so—stick to your guns! You'll have excellent understanding and will see every side of a problem. If you are in charge of others it is not likely that you will ever be accused of treating them unfairly when it comes to allotting work. If you are a student you could perhaps have a tendency to put off work in favour of other more enjoyable things. I'm not saying that you are living just for pleasure; but some subjects will attract you more than others, and the less appealing ones could very easily be neglected. You'll probably be able to forget them in due course, but don't ignore them until the night before the examination; it won't be worth while!

Venus: money and rapport

Check the position of Venus on pages 242–245

Venus in Cancer
You will have a pretty shrewd attitude to money if Venus was in Cancer when you were born: you will probably invest it wisely and carefully. You may be happy just at the thought of the black figures growing larger and larger in your bank statement; but you are more likely, as a Sun-sign Virgoan, to put your money to work. If you care to study antiques you would do well to make some specialized collection, which will give you great pleasure and also increase in value over the years. Silver could be particularly rewarding for you. The fishing and dairy industries or shipping would be good objects for investment; so would children's products—toys, clothes, and so on. You might be the sort to build up your own business. If so, your Virgoan ability to work hard plus Venus-in-Cancer shrewdness will go a long way towards making you successful. Try, however, to take things slowly and carefully, and without overstraining yourself; don't work a 24-hour day *every* day. You'll be considerate towards your colleagues, and will naturally express a protective and caring attitude towards them. If you are in charge, they will think well of you and your attitude. You'll be the sort to set up good medical insurance for them and make sure the staff canteen is something to write home about with its food as good as home cooking at its best.

Venus in Leo
If when you were born Venus was in Leo, you'll have to work hard to gain a good position in your firm, to make enough money for you to have all the good things in life that you enjoy so much. You may enjoy them rather sneakingly, because you could very well feel slightly guilty when spending money on something you find attractive. Try not to, and recognize that it's very much part of your nature. If you love to spend, it's good for you to have beautiful things to *use*—kitchen utensils, quality brushes and mirrors on your dressing-table, well-made tools for your various hobbies. Any gold you invest in will do you proud (but remember the insurance on jewellery is necessary but very expensive). If you want to buy stocks and shares, aim for firms producing high-quality products—those with traditions and years of experience. You'll find this interesting

and financially rewarding. At work you will be the one to organize staff outings, Christmas parties, theatre parties. You'll get the best deals for your colleagues' money, and they will make much of you because of your efforts; indeed, you'll be extremely popular. If you are an employer you'll above all want your employees to be happy and will see to it that working conditions are attractive, cheerful and pleasant.

Venus in Virgo

An eye to economy and a good deal of carefulness with money will mark anyone who has Venus in Virgo with the Sun. You'll like to spend your money on friends by choosing expensive, attractive presents and giving a great deal of thought to their choice. But you won't be one to waste money yourself on a new outfit that you like but can't afford. You will also be clever at making things, and in that way will save quite a lot. You'll be excellent at do-it-yourself projects; decorating or maintenance bills will be minimal. Should you want to invest, you might be interested to go for agricultural products, cereals or farm machinery. If you want to start a business, you might do well to consider a shop selling health foods, craft materials or artistic, hand-made products. At work it may be hard for you not to do everyone else's job as well as your own. Be careful: you'll be so willing to help out that others may take advantage of you. If you are an employer try to let people get on with their own jobs in their own way: you could find interfering far too easy. Be tactful if you have to be critical; you could sound as if you are carping at their efforts.

Venus in Libra

With Venus in Libra, a sign it rules, you will certainly want to enjoy the good things of life and won't be very conscience-stricken about spending quite a lot of money on entertaining your friends. You will enjoy owning attractive things and will want to make your home beautiful. You might like to invest in beauty products, copper and light industry. Department stores too might prove both interesting and profitable. A busy Virgo, you won't find it at all difficult to talk people into helping you out when you find you have taken on too much; indeed you'll collect a small band of helpers who will admire your skills and abilities and who will want to learn from you. Excellent: this works both ways—you will inspire them and they will help you to get through everything that has to be done. If you are an employer you will want to make quite sure everyone in your firm has a fair deal; perhaps you will be attracted to profit-sharing schemes. You may lack decisiveness, especially when it comes to the question of whom to promote; if necessary get some help from your second-in-command. You need to work in partnership more than any other Virgos. Try never to be in a lonely position.

Venus in Scorpio

If you have Venus in Scorpio, you will have excellent earning capacity, but excellent ability to spend too! You could be very clever with money, and it should work well and hard for you, just as you will work well and hard for whoever employs you (or for yourself). You will enjoy all the wheeling and dealing of investment and will probably do well in mining, the oil industry, the wine trade or any activity connected with the sea or sea-sports. Big business and insurance could also be your scene (both for investment and career), and saving schemes attached to them will give you a sense of security if you are not inclined to be adventurous with your hard-earned cash. You could become a little jealous of your colleagues if someone gets promoted over your head. Just make a little extra effort if this is the case; it won't go unnoticed. You are a grand person to have around the place, since you enjoy life and thrive on its problems. If you are an employer, you'll want to get the best out of employees, so the annual pay round and bonuses will be as generous as you can manage. Try not to be too secretive about future contracts: keep your employees informed all along the way. You may be reluctant to do so, but if you do they will feel far more part of the firm and be more loyal.

Rising-signs and your career

First check your Rising-sign on pages 225–232

Note: Careers and the Midheaven
If you develop your interest in astrology one of the first things you will learn about, but which is outside the scope of this book, is the Midheaven. Roughly speaking, this is the sign immediately over your head when you were born. It is as important in your career, outward expression and identification with objectives in life as your Rising-sign is in your personality. To combine it with your Rising-sign is complicated and would be impossible in a book of this length: but, while I cannot help you to discover yours in this book, rest assured that I have borne the various possibilities in mind when writing the following paragraphs in relation to your choice of profession or job.

Virgo with Aries rising
You have a powerful natural drive and are very ambitious. You might find work in politics, at local or national level, interesting. You'd be good in business, giving competitors a good run for their money. Architecture, real estate and the Army are also suitable careers for you.

Virgo with Taurus rising
You need financial security, and will rise steadily if gradually in your career. Banking, agriculture or horticulture would suit you. You would thrive in a large corporation, but you have good business sense and would also do well building up your own firm, if you start small and grow gradually. You could be artistically creative or have an inclination for science.

Virgo with Gemini rising
You are a natural media person and could find satisfaction in working in newspapers, magazines or broadcasting. You could also do well in education, especially as a teacher of teenagers. Aim for work that is not repetitive and does not keep you in one place—express your lively versatility by staying on the move.

Virgo with Cancer rising
You might do very well indeed in the caring professions. You would make a good doctor, nurse, probation officer or child care officer. Your Virgo characteristics could interest you in fringe medicine or homeopathy. The hotel trade or catering would also suit you. So might library work or historical research.

Virgo with Leo rising
You will work hard to get money and will do well working for yourself; but this could conflict with a need for financial security. Working in a department store with an eye on a position as buyer would suit you; so would the computer industry, accountancy and finance in general. You would make an enthusiastic teacher.

Virgo with Virgo rising
It is important for you to decide whether you want to work in the public eye or behind the scenes. Many of your group will work in the media and make excellent journalists. If you are interested, grab any menial job at your local radio station as a starting point. You could be good at selling. Work in telecommunications or as a secretary could also be suitable.

Virgo with Libra rising
You would do well in the luxury trades such as beauty culture or hairdressing. You may be very creative and be good at making, designing or modelling clothes. You are diplomatic. How about learning some languages and thinking of the foreign service or some similar job? You can work hard, but might need to develop initiative. You are probably capable of greater things than you realize.

Virgo with Scorpio rising
It is vital for you to be emotionally involved in your work. A mere money-making job is not enough. Decide carefully on your career and stick to it. You have marvellous potential. Psychiatry, medical pathology, detective work—any form of research in depth will be admirable for you. The oil and wine trades could also suit you. So could engineering.

Virgo with Sagittarius rising
You have the potential for study and possibly a flair for languages. You'd make a good teacher or lecturer at university or college level. The travel industry, publishing and selling books and stationery would also suit you. Don't hesitate to write if you feel you have a book in you. Professional sport could also be your scene, or working with animals, perhaps as a vet.

Virgo with Capricorn rising
You need security. You're something of a plodder, and would make an excellent architect, builder, estate agent—or would do well in town planning. If you are musical, develop your technique and stick at it. The political scene could attract you. You aren't afraid of hard work.

Virgo with Aquarius rising
You might do well working for an airline or in scientific research. Mathematics could well be a strong point. Engineering, mining and the steel industry are possibilities, and you will like jobs that are not run-of-the-mill. Try not to make too many changes of direction. Keep a sense of purpose as far as your career is concerned.

Virgo with Pisces rising
You should find work that is creative and has a definite end product. You would make an excellent photographer and would do well in the caring professions, especially nursing. Develop self-confidence. You have varied abilities; so don't lose them in a dead-end job. You might enjoy the publishing world or working with animals.

Libra

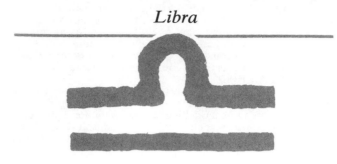

Positive
Ruling planet: Venus
Triplicity or element: air
Quadruplicity or quality: cardinal
Colour: shades of blue from pale to ultramarine; pinks and pale greens
Gemstone: sapphire, jade
Metal: copper, sometimes bronze
Flowers: blue flowers, hydrangea, large roses
Trees: ash, poplar
Herbs and spices: mint, arrack, cayenne
Foodstuffs: tomato, pear, asparagus, beans
Animals: lizards and small reptiles
Countries: Austria, Burma, Japan, Argentina, Upper Egypt, Canada
Cities: Copenhagen, Johannesburg, Vienna, Lisbon, Frankfurt, Nottingham

Years ago, astrologers used to say "Lazy Libra loathes a duster!" (who can blame Libra for that?), and Libra has earned something of a reputation for laziness. In many ways this is unjustified. Librans often work extremely hard, but they also possess the secret of really knowing how to relax. For Libra there is always time: time to get ready to go out (even if their friends and partners are waiting impatiently downstairs), time to talk, drink coffee, or just lie about—but almost always when work projects have been placed well under control.

That Librans are romantics there is no doubt, and their need for a permanent relationship is paramount. Most do not fully develop, psychologically or emotionally, until that all-important factor has been settled. This is a very basic psychological motivation, and because this is so, it can all too easily be the case that Librans rush into a relationship at an age when perhaps they are not ready to make a full commitment.

Sometimes less forthcoming types find Librans a little gushing. Their worst fault can be resentfulness; and there is, in spite of a need for total harmony, a perverse tendency to "rock the boat".

Libran children are much liked by teachers for their natural charm and good manners.

The Libran body-area is the kidneys, and sometimes slight upsets there can cause recurrent headaches. Librans may not be too keen on exercise, and if friends can encourage them to play tennis or golf they will be doing them a considerable service.

Libra in friendship, love and marriage

As a Sun-sign Libra you have a very romantic nature. You need a rewarding personal relationship, and quite rightly will do everything in your power to attain fulfilment in this all-important sphere of your life.

But you must be careful, if you think of astrology as offering some help, not to fall into the common trap of thinking that because the signs are grouped into four elements (see page 75), only the people who share your element make entirely suitable friends or lovers and that those whose element is Fire are also sympathetic to your own sign, while those of Earth and Water are not. This is a common belief, and sometimes people will go so far as to say "You're no good for me—Air and Earth don't mix."

This is very silly—though I must admit that there is something in the tradition, for it is certainly the case that if you share an element with someone you very often feel a certain ease and sympathy with them. But we should go no further than that. For the record—and again, please don't take this really very superficial tradition too seriously—the other Air signs are Gemini and Aquarius; the Fire signs are Aries, Leo and Sagittarius, and traditionally you should find people with those Sun-signs easy to get on with. Cancer, Scorpio and Pisces (Water) and Taurus, Virgo and Capricorn (Earth) are supposed not to be so easy.

But *never* hold back from a developing relationship because of this kind of tradition, based on a superficial knowledge of astrology and the elements. It is equally negative to try to force the development of a relationship just because someone shares one's own element, where the Sun is concerned. Care is needed all round, in fact.

149

In your case, remember that you could have either Mercury or Venus (the latter rules your Sun-sign) in Virgo or in Scorpio, and this will help to ease away any incompatibility between you and someone with the Sun in either of those signs. Venus will be specially helpful in that respect, because it has a strong psychological bearing on your personality. Remember, too, that even an astrologer who has worked on the fully-calculated birth-charts of you and someone else would never ever warn you to stop seeing each other. What he or she will do is point out where the relationship might be difficult, or where it should be specially rewarding. For instance, you need that special relationship with someone you love—but you can also be very indecisive, and you will also need a friend or lover who will help you reach important decisions. You need someone who is colourful and romantic; your partner should appreciate what you have to offer in the way of helping them to relax, easing strain, and so on.

Having bought this book, you have probably long since filled in page 8 with the positions of the planets at the time of your birth—the places they take up in your birth-chart. The most rewarding links between couples in a long-term relationship are those which place an accent on the polar or opposite signs in their charts: signs opposite each other across the Zodiac (see page 75 for a list). Most obviously, if your partner happens to be a Sun-sign Arien, you'll pick up the polarity of the signs in a very lively way. But is your Rising-sign perhaps opposite your partner's Sun-sign? Or is your Moon right across the Zodiac from your partner's Moon? That is a very important link, and will affect the way you pick up each other's moods, the way in which you respond to each other. If you share Moon-signs, it could be that you will entirely reflect your partner's mood, instinctively knowing what it is.

When polarities exist between a couple, there is always good understanding and excellent rapport. There won't necessarily be total agreement on every issue that comes up, but the relationship will be very lively.

Do take time out, then, to develop this particular area of astrology; the sphere of life it illustrates is of great importance (not only in friendship, love and marriage, but in business partnerships too) and will help you learn a great deal more about yourself, your needs in partnership, and your attitude towards your partner.

Libran friendships

You make a marvellous friend in many ways, but perhaps a little more participation in the friendship wouldn't go amiss. Maybe you should occasionally take the initiative in suggesting what to do. You are so easy-going that you could well leave every decision of that sort to your friends. This can get a bit tedious for them, even though you always reciprocate by showing tremendous enthusiasm for the event. Why not make your own decision about, say, a day's outing?

It is important for you to have plenty of interests which you can share with your friends. You will be a keen member of any club that you join and will enjoy helping to organize social events. You are not a loner; you like to be with others in a relaxed and easy atmosphere. Indeed this is essential to your well-being, and you should make a conscious effort to build up a set of friends with similar interests, even if you have one special friend. You are capable of spurring your friends on in their own pursuits. But you should also be prepared to let them encourage you. You could well be as good as them at, say, performing on the guitar or playing a lively game of tennis. Once hooked you could be very thankful to the friends who spurred you on.

When things go wrong between you and your friends you may harbour resentment and find it difficult to forgive and forget. Do remember that others are not necessarily as demonstrative as you: a tiny smile or nod from someone with whom you have quarrelled may be the equivalent of a small present from you. Equally, others do not always show their gratitude for kindness received quite as emphatically as you. Indeed, some people may find you a little gushing and overwhelming, just as you may find them a little cold and introverted. This is a hard lesson for you to learn, but a necessary one, for these differences can mar friendships if one does not make allowances for them.

Libra in love

Like as not you will usually be either in love, and enjoying every moment of it, or on the trail of a new love. Either state suits you.

You certainly have a great deal to offer a partner, who will enjoy the genuine affection, warmth and emotion you will lavish. You make it easier for lovers to return affection, too, for love is very infectious, and your constant thoughts about your lover will bring their own reward. Many astrologers accuse Librans of all too easily falling in love with love itself. There may be more than a hint of truth about that, and you should think about the danger of it. You will be specially vulnerable if you are young: after all, most young people tend to get a bit starry eyed during their first love-affair. If you are young and in love, try if you can to take a step outside yourself and assess your feelings objectively, however difficult it may be. Think about the long-term prospects where you and your lover are concerned; picture yourself ten years from now. Ask yourself if you are temperamentally suited, as well as being good together in bed. In your need for a permanent relationship, a strong Libran characteristic, you may tend to rush prematurely into marriage or living together on a permanent basis. You need to make extra sure that you and your partner are suited. It's also good for you to experience relationships with a variety of partners. You will gain inner strength and the ability to cope with your eventual life-partner in a far fuller and more satisfactory way if you have an experimental time first. So think of your early relationships as possible stepping-stones to the real thing. Have fun: play the field. Yes, you do need a personal relationship very much; but try hard not to make a mistake, for a mistake could damage you psychologically far more than most people. You will only learn from your own experiences, and many of the things I have said may sound pretty dull and conventional. But for older Librans they may well have the ring of truth.

You are passionate, but perhaps in a rather languid way. To enjoy sex fully you need a comfortable, relaxed atmosphere and all the time in the world. Of course in most cases you won't have all the time in the world, even if you are married or settled in together. So you may have to adjust your pace of love-making to that of your partner, and allowances will have to be made on both sides. There may be times when you are just not in the mood for sex: if so, be honest about it with your partner. Don't feign headaches or work to be done. Then ask yourself why you're not in the mood. Are you just feeling lazy? Are you feeling in a romantic but not a physical mood? Or have you some problem that is turning you off? Get to the root of any negative feelings and sort them out with your partner. This could be important.

Libra in marriage

If you have been married for some time, I think you will agree that you have developed psychologically and feel a far more complete person since you settled into a permanent relationship. Your Sun-sign does give you a strong need for a partner. But you should be careful not to submerge your personality in that of your partner. Remember you are a person in your own right and must keep your own personality and individuality, and an element of independence. It's all too easy for you to get into the habit of thinking of everything in terms of your partner. This is fine up to a point, but it can be narrowing, and if you are a woman you may be making rather too many sacrifices for your husband, submerging your own opinions and feelings and perhaps giving up your job for the sake of the partnership. It may be, of course, that you are delighted to give up the daily grind behind the counter in the department store or at the office desk: it's nice to be able to meet your friends for morning coffee, to browse through the boutiques and take ages to decide what to have for dinner. But don't overdo it. If things go wrong in your relationship, you will be the one reminding your partner of the great career you gave up so that you could make a home for him.

By the same token, if you are a man you might have given up the chance of promotion because it would have meant uprooting the household and going to live in another town, when your wife preferred to stay put. If so it may be that you are giving up too much, and that you did not put the case as strongly as you would have liked, but gave way for peace at any price. And you may have told yourself that the move would have been too demanding anyway, for you tend to make such excuses. What I'm saying to both partners is don't always take the line of least resistance!

As for your children, you need to be aware that even when they are very young they will probably be extremely good at twisting you round their little fingers. You will say no, but not mean it. Or else you will evade the whole issue by telling them to ask your partner. Remember that children need to know where they stand. They hate indecision and will go screaming up the wall if you say "Well, dear, we'll see" once too often. They know all too well that what that means is you *won't* see, at least not for ages, and that by the time you have come to a decision about, say, a school outing, the excursion will be fully booked and they won't be able to go. If you don't want them to go or you simply can't afford it, tell them so honestly. Don't be evasive—it just doesn't work and you won't increase their respect for you if you always duck out of the way of every issue.

Libran careers and money matters

When assessing the Libran potential in careers and financial ability we must consider not only the psychological motivation and mode of expression attributed to Libra but also the thinking processes of Mercury, and how these two factors combined can be best used in both areas. Then there is the influence of Venus, a planet as strongly related to finance and possessions as to relationships. The latter aspect is also important in this sphere as it will affect how a person will get on with colleagues, in business partnerships, and so on.

Mars may well give some hint as to the direction of energy and will most certainly influence the physical element—the drive and energy put into the day's work. As we shall see, the influence of the combined Sun and Rising-sign is interesting and very personal: but if your birth-time is not available and you cannot find out your Rising-sign, do not be too disappointed: you should be able to glean plenty of information about this sphere of your life from the more general paragraphs.

When we think of a Libran's needs as far as a career is concerned, we need not of course assume that they can only succeed in one kind of job or profession: as with all the other signs, they can be successful and make their mark in many occupations. There are, however, certain factors which will be very important if a Libran is to be happy at work, however trivial they may seem to other people. One is the overall atmosphere, for Librans are very susceptible to atmosphere and need a happy and acceptable one. They must have a friendly and preferably peaceful and quiet environment. If they are forced by circumstances to work in, say, a noisy factory with a constant throb of machines, they may make a successful go of it, but will never feel entirely happy. Indeed, such an atmosphere could cause them greater stress and tension, over a period of years, than they realize, and this could cause them to overreact to minor mishaps or irritating delays. They probably won't mind working against the kind of canned music that is so ubiquitous nowadays, even if it is rather loud, but some kind of constant noise could be irritating, and the less obvious it is the more distressing it may be.

If a Libran is placed in a position of authority, which may for that reason be rather lonely, he or she may be less content than in a lower position, finding that responsibility brings stress and perhaps that decision-making does not come naturally. Librans who do get to the top should make sure that they have a team of experts or trustworthy colleagues to whom they can go for information and backing when decisions have to be made. Librans are at their best when they are working closely with other people for the good of a firm—in the way architects or lawyers work. In other words they like an atmosphere in which responsibility is shared and decisions are jointly made.

Librans are usually considerate, kind, helpful and under-standing. They are always ready to listen to suggestions from colleagues, which is a great asset. Their own decisions will be all the more effective if they have assimilated advice from others. Many people these days find themselves working under stress, with deadlines to meet and work constantly piling up at every moment of the day. Two things can happen to Librans under such circumstances. Either they will not survive the pace and will have to opt out, or they will keep their cool, calming down more flustered types and helping everyone to achieve a sense of balance and an overall view of the work to be done.

Tact and diplomacy will probably be two of the Libran's greatest assets as far as their working lives are concerned, and very often we find them in jobs where these qualities are very much needed and can be most fully expressed. Indeed when choosing a career it might be as well for any Sun-sign Libran to consider the sort of job where such qualities can be used to the greatest effect, for in using them they will feel psychologically fulfilled. Librans will be found representing their countries in all sorts of capacities, from ambassador to beauty queen. In another sphere Librans do extremely well in personnel offices of big firms. Here their habitual consideration of other people and their ability to listen to what others have to say are great assets. We also find them coping very well in the complaints departments of businesses or official bodies. That kind of job, while it would seem very wearing and fraught for many Sun-sign types, provides just the sort of challenge to which Librans can successfully rise. In listening diplomatically to a grievance and then getting something done about it they are able to glide like a well-trained ice skater over difficulties and problems that would defeat others. Of course, this does not mean that they solve every tricky situation with a lot of smooth talk—they will actually get something done and will make the wronged one feel better and happier. Awareness of these useful traits is important to them.

The Libran ruling planet is Venus, and with Taurus (the other sign ruled by that planet) also on their side we find a great emphasis on beauty. So, beauty queens apart, we find that a great many Librans make the grade in the beauty professions or luxury trades. Librans of both sexes make excellent hair-dressers or make-up artists for instance. Many become models or dressmakers and designers. Others might start as a junior in the gown department of a large department store and work their way up to buyer or some similar position, helped by a good eye for what is becoming to a customer and a quick, flattering tongue to say exactly the right thing at the right moment. If they are not intimidated by their seniors in the early months of their working lives they will progress rapidly and should find their pay packets being swelled by substantial commission.

Librans generally give the impression that they have plenty of time and that there is no need to rush or get flustered. Things will sort themselves out as and when they have to. This is Libra at its best—working hard and making everyone else's job and life easier and pleasanter. The Libran office will be a haven for others to run to for a moment's relaxation, to take a deep breath and a cup of coffee (usually real coffee, not instant, and certainly not out of the abominable office machine round the corner: the Libran will have a surreptitious coffee-pot brewing in some quiet nook). In this way Librans are important in most working environments. They help to keep the balance so necessary for themselves and more necessary to the rest of us than we may realize. But to get the best of them other people must show gratitude for their time and energy and make them feel appreciated. And colleagues occasionally have to take the initiative, soothing the Libran when something goes really wrong and he or she has been forced to speak up about it.

To sum up: Librans need to relate to others both in their personal relationships and at work. The process of sharing is also very important—sharing work, sharing decisions, sharing difficulties and responsibilities.

Mercury at work

Check position of Mercury on pages 238–241

Mercury in Virgo

If you have Mercury in Virgo, you have considerable ability to think carefully and analytically. Your work will be extremely neat—an excellent advantage if you are a secretary. You'll be diplomatic and be able to work in an orderly and disciplined way.

You may tend to worry about your work and to take problems home with you—either in your mind or in a case full of papers. If you find this is happening a little too often, it will be worth looking carefully at your work schedule. A little replanning, perhaps with the help of someone who does a similar job, might be a good thing. If you are a student you will work conscientiously and well. Try to keep to an even study plan, and don't let your enjoyment of student social life spoil your chances when examinations come up. Not only will your grades be lower but you will feel guilty in the long run that you didn't work away steadily when you had the opportunity.

Mercury in Libra

With Mercury in Libra with the Sun you have probably had to develop decisiveness. You will listen to what others have to say and consider it very carefully. But do remember that eventually you will have to take one course of action, even if it means upsetting other people! Try not to dither about for too long, especially if you are in charge of other people: they could get impatient, and in the long run lose some of their respect for you. Your kindness and consideration for others will help you, but care is needed. While Mercury in Libra isn't too good as far as power of concentration is concerned, it may well be that other planets will help out. If you find it difficult to concentrate, make yourself do so for very short periods of time at first and then increase the time-span very gradually. As a student you *aren't* likely to be very fond of the motto "Never put off till tomorrow what you can do today''. No doubt that makes for a very easy life, but can you really cope with a whole term's work the week before examinations?

Mercury in Scorpio

This placing will give you additional drive and the ability to concentrate. You will also have more intellectual energy at your disposal, and if you turn this additional power towards your career you should do extremely well. Your natural charm will help you get on in whatever profession you choose, and the backing from Mercury in a strong, intensive sign will support the fact that you mean business, which will impress your superiors. You'll be very good at finding out facts. You could appear stubborn at times, and have a much greater ability to be decisive than most Sun-sign Librans. Others will know exactly how they stand with you: you'll say what you mean, even if you are pretty angry inside. If you are still a student, I think you're in the fortunate position of being able both to study and to play hard, you will pour your energies wholeheartedly into both occupations, and good luck to you.

Venus: money and rapport

Check position of Venus on pages 242–245

Venus in Leo

With this placing you will need to make a great deal of money in order to maintain your naturally extravagant lifestyle. You'll probably always spend a bit more than you should. Your taste will perhaps be a little showy, but you will buy things of quality that will last well. You probably think money is to be used, not just seen as black figures in a bank statement. If so, I'm sure you enjoy every penny you earn and see to it that others share your enjoyment. You probably love entertaining, for instance. If you have money to invest it might be as well for you to consider putting it into well-established firms that produce goods of high quality. But be careful: you could tend to overinvest, goaded on by your natural enthusiasm. So get expert advice. It is possible that if your colleagues need some favour from the boss, they will ask you to speak for them, which you will do extremely well. You could find yourself in charge of a group of people in due course, since your organizational ability is good. As an employer you are caring, and like to see your employees happy and enjoying themselves. You will see to it that there are plenty of staff outings and other benefits, and they will think you generous and considerate.

Venus in Virgo

You will work hard for your money and be less extravagant than many Sun-sign Librans if Venus is in Virgo in your birth-chart. You'll have a thrifty streak and the ability to make much of a little—a length of inexpensive material will become a Paris model under the dexterity of your hands. You probably plan your finances carefully, so that holidays are well catered for in advance. If you care to invest, you might like to try cereals, agriculture or farm machinery. You might find it interesting to start a small business, perhaps selling health foods or craft products such as hand-woven fabrics or pottery. It is just possible that colleagues might take advantage of you at times—you are the one to help everyone out of a sticky situation, or to do any explaining. If you are an employer, you'll be very considerate, always ready to listen to suggestions. However, in your employees' eyes you could be over-critical, they may even think of you as a nagger. Try to be constructive in your criticism and give plenty of real encouragement to your employees. That way you will get the best out of them.

Venus in Libra

With Venus in Libra with the Sun you might be inclined to hope that a kindly fate or a lottery win is going to drop a fortune in your lap. Get on with the job in hand and forget your daydreams. So you want to get away to a sun-drenched island in the Caribbean for your next holiday? Well, why not take up that offer of overtime to improve the savings fund? You'll enjoy the holiday even more if it's hard-earned. If you have money to invest, why not think about putting it into a chain of department stores or a firm of cosmetic manufacturers? If you are tempted to invest in metals bear in mind that copper is the Venus metal, and your Venus is very strong: so this could be a profitable area of investment for you.

You will be well liked where you work, but if your colleagues tease you about not entirely pulling your weight where dull routine is concerned, they could be right! Don't fall back on charm too often when chores have to be done. If you're an employer of others you will be admired for the way in which you are always ready to consult the work force in matters of importance, though you could procrastinate over making decisions—something you may need to learn to counter.

Venus in Scorpio

An excellent business sense generally goes with Venus in Scorpio. You probably know both how to make money and how to spend it. You have a natural business sense and you are a hard worker. You could do extremely well if you decide to set up your own business or have a money-making sideline in addition to your main career. You are the type to need some pretty demanding projects on hand and if you feel your career is not engrossing enough, an additional venture of some sort should be excellent for you. You might like to study wines, for example. Bear the wine trade in mind for investments as well. Mining and insurance of all kinds could also be good areas in which to put your money.

At work you are probably good at devising profit-sharing schemes for your employees and encouraging work by adopting lively incentives. They will appreciate your capacity to enjoy both work and play, and probably learn a great deal from you in that respect.

Venus in Sagittarius

If you have Venus in Sagittarius you could well have something of a couldn't-care-less attitude to money. If you haven't got it, you can't spend it. That's true enough, but you also have something of a gambling instinct and you may take financial risks or, worse, fall for get-rich-quick schemes. Be aware that anyone can talk you into an investment, but for goodness sake don't sign anything until you've got sound professional advice about the proposed investment. You are kind and charming yourself and could fall for schemes put to you by other charmers! You'll be especially vulnerable if you're at all emotionally involved with whoever's putting the deal to you, so think twice before doing business with your lover! You could invest in publishing, or in the travel industry. At work, you're probably the one who livens things up, amusing your colleagues in some way, especially if you all feel trapped in a rather predictable routine. You will be much appreciated for this. You could well have a philosophical streak and be capable of giving kind words of wisdom to younger people. If you're an employer, I'm sure your workers think of you as a nice, lively, approachable boss. This planetary placing might help you to exploit overseas markets.

Rising-signs and your career

First check your Rising-sign on pages 225–232

Note: Careers and the Midheaven
If you develop your interest in astrology, one of the first things which you will learn about, but which is outside the scope of this book, is the Midheaven. Roughly speaking, this is the sign immediately over your head when you were born. It is as important in your career, outward expression and identification with objectives in life as your Rising-sign is in your personality. To combine it with your Rising-sign is complicated and would be impossible in a book of this length; but, while I cannot help you to discover yours in this book, rest assured that I have borne the various possibilities in mind when writing the following paragraphs in relation to your choice of profession or job.

Libra with Aries rising
You can cope with responsibility and have high ambitions, but you are most likely to succeed if you learn to work with other people, especially if you are in business. Partnership is best for you. You could do well in the armed forces, in local or national government service, or in any large company where you can progress gradually up the ladder.

Libra with Taurus rising
You need financial security in your work. You are ambitious but could be more assertive. You probably have good business sense and money-making ability. Banking, insurance or big business of any kind would suit you. So could architecture, agriculture or science. An excellent singing voice or some other kind of musical ability often goes with Taurus. If you have a talent for music this could also lead to a career.

Libra with Gemini rising
You will certainly want to get on in the world, but at the same time will not want to feel too tied up in your career. You would do well working for an airline, for a large department store or in the media. A receptionist's job might also be suitable. You could become bored rather easily, so you need work with plenty of change and variety.

Libra with Cancer rising
Your natural instinct for looking after people could be well expressed in the hotel or catering trade. You could be attracted to nursing or some other caring profession. Work with children might also suit you very well. The antiques business, librarianship and museum work are other sound possibilities. Try not to make too many changes in your career; you could find them very unsettling.

Libra with Leo rising
Your work needs a touch of glamour, and you need to be in a position where you can show off a bit. You would be good at demonstrating and modelling, and you would enjoy any work in which you can express your organizing ability. The computer industry is a strong possibility for you. Develop any creative talent as much as you can. The harder you work, the more fulfilled you will be.

Libra with Virgo rising

You would make an excellent teacher and could do well working in the media. You will want to work hard and will thrive on it. You may be attracted to unconventional medicine and health foods. Horticulture, agriculture and the nursing profession could suit you very well. You may have considerable talent for craft work; why not try pottery?

Libra with Libra rising

It is important to decide whether you want to make your personal presence felt in your work, or whether you are better working behind the scenes. You might be very good at representing your company in some way or working in personnel. Alternatively you might prefer quietly doing research or creative work out of the public eye. You would be excellent at liaison work or in the caring professions. If you feel you have organizing ability, use it.

Libra with Scorpio rising

There is something of the sleuth about you. Police or detective work or any form of research would suit you. You might be an analyst of some kind. You probably have good business sense and would do well within a large company. You are probably at your best working behind the scenes and letting your work speak for you.

Libra with Sagittarius rising

You are likely to do extremely well in your chosen profession and need to be emotionally involved in your work. The law, publishing and university teaching are all suitable. The travel industry and the diplomatic service are also possibilities. You could have potential for writing and for languages. Don't make too many changes in your life.

Libra with Capricorn rising

Of all Sun-sign Librans you are the one to cope best with a lonely position. You might find yourself a head of some department or institution—a school for instance. Business, law, real estate and accountancy would all be possible areas for you. Keep working hard at any musical interests.

Libra with Aquarius rising

You need plenty of freedom of expression. You would be good in television or advertising or working for an airline. Astronomy, space technology and science in general are good possibilities for you. But don't neglect any artistic potential. You need work that is off-beat and slightly unusual.

Libra with Pisces rising

You have a lot of creative potential but need strong guidance. Your work should have a glamorous side. You would make an excellent photographer, and could have a flair for dress-designing. But the caring professions would also suit you well. Try to adopt a disciplined attitude to your work and develop greater self-confidence.

Scorpio

Negative
Ruling planet: Pluto (ancient ruler, Mars)
Triplicity or element: water
Quadruplicity or quality: fixed
Colour: dark reds and maroons
Gemstone: opal
Metal: steel or iron
Flower: geranium, rhododendron
Tree: blackthorn and thick bushy trees
Herbs and spices: aloes, witch-hazel, catmint
Foodstuffs: most strong-tasting foods
Animals: crustaceans, most insects
Countries: Morocco, Norway, the Transvaal, Algeria
Cities: New Orleans, Fez, Milwaukee, Liverpool, Halifax, Hull

Scorpio has a reputation for being the most forceful personality in the Zodiac. In every Scorpio, there is a strong and very intensive energy-source that needs positive direction. Sometimes we come across Scorpios who deny this. "But I'm not like that at all!" they cry, before returning to the events of their overfull day, burning up untold energy in whatever way they find most satisfying! This energy can be directed in many ways, from wheeling and dealing in high-powered industry and finance to the housewife's vigour in keeping her home impeccable for her family.

Much is written about the powerful sexual drive of the Scorpio, and often a great deal of energy is spent in that direction, though not invariably. In any event, there needs to be some important outlet for their drive, for a Scorpio without plenty of positive ways of using the sign's high emotional and physical energy level is a negative Scorpio indeed, and things can go seriously wrong if that is the case. Friends of Scorpios should be aware that a tendency to withdraw, and a brooding expression overlaying the usual intensive one, can be danger signals. As the sign is usually secretive, it can be difficult to make a Scorpio friend unburden, but if it is possible to do this by assuring them of your discretion, you will do them a great service. Secretiveness in Scorpio children should be developed in positive directions through the planning of surprises for parents on birthdays, and so on.

The Scorpio body-area is the genitals. Scorpios tend to over-indulge in good food and wine, so dieting is to be encouraged along with vigorous exercise—perhaps swimming, or any underwater sport. Boxing and karate are also popular with many Scorpios.

Scorpio in friendship, love and marriage

I don't think you would be very impressed if someone told you that their Sun-sign didn't go with yours, and so there was little point in your developing a tie of friendship or an emotional relationship. You would probably instinctively suspect that they had only a very superficial knowledge of astrology, or that they were making some silly generalization. And quite right, too.

Quite apart from that, you would be curious to know what led them to make such a statement. Well, there is indeed an old astrological tradition that says that Zodiac types sharing a certain "element" (see page 75) will naturally get on well together. That is fine as far as it goes; but far too many people take the tradition too far—especially some astrologers who write general columns in newspapers and magazines. To be fair to them, and to tradition, there is indeed a certain ease between members of signs of the same element—Cancer and Pisces share your own Water element, so you should get on well with them; Taurus, Virgo and Capricorn are Earth signs, and you should find them fairly congenial. But the Fire signs, Aries, Leo and Sagittarius, and the Air signs, Gemini, Libra and Aquarius, are traditionally said to be less so.

However, a little more astrological knowledge shows just how fallacious such statements are, except on the most superficial level. You could for instance have Mercury or Venus or both in either Libra or Sagittarius, and that would certainly help mitigate any conflicts that might arise between anyone with either sign as the home of their Sun. The position of Mars (until the discovery of Pluto, the "ruler" of your Sun-sign) will add a strong dimension to any relationship between you and someone sharing your Mars-sign—usually the accent would be on an energetic or powerfully sexual relationship.

It is only when two birth-charts are fully calculated and studied by a competent astrologer that anything can confidently be said about a possible relationship between two people. And even then no astrologer will ever be in a position to say

161

whether or not a couple should terminate or develop a relationship. That's for the couple themselves to decide. They can be told where they may clash, and where they can use their respective characteristics to dispose of difficulties. For instance as a Scorpio you really need to get a great deal out of life, to burn up in the most positive way a lot of physical and emotional energy. This energy is often expressed through sex, but it needs channelling, in a relationship, through joint interests, too. So you need a sympathetic partner who will both understand and (most importantly) *enjoy* what you have to offer; someone as energetic as yourself.

You may be able to make a good guess at whether someone is this type of person through a knowledge of the Sun-signs. But never forget that someone who has a Sun-sign that doesn't seem to "go with" yours may have the necessary qualities because of the position of other planets, or of their Rising-sign (see pages 225–232). What a pity if a potentially good relationship should be stifled out of hand before it has a chance to develop!

The most important links between couples sharing a rewarding relationship have always in my experience been based on an accent on the polar or opposite signs of the Zodiac. For instance your Scorpio Sun-sign would be beautifully complemented by someone with Taurus as their Rising-sign. Sometimes signs are shared, too. Perhaps you know and love someone with their Moon in Scorpio: if so, you certainly have a powerful and intense relationship, and one you should nurture: it is very strong, and should not be allowed to stagnate.

As is always the case with astrology, the more we discover about the subject the more fascinating it becomes. Generalizations in any subject are boring, and a superficial knowledge can lead to silly and sad decisions or actions. It is good for Scorpios to delve deeply into subjects that fascinate them, and the more work you do on this area of astrology—the comparison of charts is called *synastry*, by the way—the better; you need relationships which are powerfully meaningful, and astrology used in the right way can certainly help you towards them.

Scorpio friendships

As a Scorpio, you will probably hold on to your friends for a very long time, if not for life. You will work hard for them, and see to it that both you and they get the maximum amount of fun and enjoyment together. You will enjoy organizing communal activities of the sort that involve quite a lot of planning. You will like to organize entertainments for the old people in your neighbourhood, sporting activities, outings and celebratory dinners, all involving large numbers. You have an enormous capacity for enjoying life, and want to get as much out of it as possible. You will encourage your friends to take the same attitude, and join in the hard work of arranging events, as well as the resulting fun.

The bonds of your friendships are strong and conducive to considerable enjoyment. But you should remember that your feelings are unusually strong, and you could grow jealous if one friend seems to be getting on with another and excluding you. You suffer from slights rather more than most people, and can explode with anger as a result. You may be quite justified; but equally, you may not—it may simply be that those highly charged emotions of yours have resulted in your taking the actions or comments of one of your friends a great deal too seriously. Think it over. It could be that you lost your sense of proportion and have got things out of perspective. Say, for example, you have been a highly active member of a committee for some years, with a regular job to do. Now the committee has suddenly put forward another name for your position. The thought may be in other members' minds that it's time you had a rest or simply a change of activity; but you may suspect a direct snub and be tempted to storm out in a dramatic exit. Think again. Surely there is some compromise. Wouldn't it be quite pleasant to have a little additional time off or to turn your talents to a different sort of work? Although admittedly you are not a great one for changes this one could in fact do you good and widen your horizons by opening out new aspects of your abilities. So be careful before you start making a row and perhaps offending friends; in other words don't overreact. Think about others' feelings. Your potential is so admirable that, even if you have doubts about tackling a new and different role, you have what it takes to make it your own.

Scorpio in love

Scorpio in love makes use of the deepest, most highly charged emotion possessed by any Zodiac type. It is a wonderful force but one which needs careful channelling if the emotions are to be fully and rewardingly expressed. Otherwise it could get out of hand and perhaps even become rather frightening.

You will move mountains for your partners and want to prove your love to them as fully as possible—though at the same time you seem to be seeking means of proving to yourself how much in love you are.

The very intensity of your emotions, together with your need for sexual expression, could lead to some rather difficult situations. It might be, for instance, that you are parted from your lover for a time. While your very real passion for your partner will continue to be strong and consistent, your sexual drive is very high and could lead you into casual relationships. This could result in feelings of guilt. So you should think very carefully about your real feelings for your lovers, especially in relation to your sexual needs. A Scorpio is capable of seeking relief elsewhere while retaining a true love for a partner, but incapable, it seems, of accepting the same behaviour from others—a situation which could lead to great difficulties in view of the jealous nature of the sign. Jealousy is, of course, a very destructive emotion. You could express it when it is totally unwarranted—and even when it has some foundation it could get quite out of proportion. You might try considering whether sauce for the goose isn't also sauce for the gander! Your own little adventures will be cloaked under a typical Scorpio cloud of secrecy and deception, while you at the same time wildly resent the very possibility that your lover might be unfaithful in word or thought, let alone in deed. If you are ever accused of being jealous or even possessive, your accuser could be right.

A little self-analysis might be a very good idea in the area of love and sex. When you become interested in someone new, is it because you feel sexually attracted to them? Is sex in fact the most important factor in your partnerships? How important are other aspects of your partner, apart from sex appeal? If you are young it is quite possible that the sexual urge may be paramount with you. There is nothing wrong with that, and it is of course important for you to have a satisfactory and fulfilled sex-life. But your preoccupation may become disproportionately strong, and danger lies that way. So give some thought to the question, especially when you are considering a long-term partnership. Sexual compatibility between partners need not diminish with time; in good marriages the opposite can well be true. When you live together sex is only one element of the partnership. There must be good communication between you, a rapport, and at least some shared interests. As a Scorpio, your own interests will be dynamic and demanding, so it's obviously a good thing if your partner can be persuaded to show a certain amount of sympathy towards them.

Scorpio in marriage

Many of the comments I have made in *Scorpio in love* apply here too, and with extra force. Remember that, as a Scorpio, there will be no half-measures about you. So you expect a very great deal out of marriage as well as being prepared to put a great deal into it. You will feel very let down if your partner doesn't match you in the expenditure of energy and in your ambitions for your marriage and its success. It is therefore of great importance to you to have a partner who is as enthusiastic as you and as happy to work hard for the marriage. This applies on many levels. You will want to make money so that you can have the material comforts of a nice home, a good car, and so on. And you will expect your partner to do his or her share in contributing to the family coffers. You need a rewarding, fulfilling sex-life and you will not be at all happy with a partner who becomes uninterested in sex. You need to be well matched, to get as good as you give, in every respect. You need to be given a run for your money. A partner who lacks energy or determination to get on in life will not be for you; nor will a partner who is colourless and lacks personality. You need someone who will keep you on your toes; and in return you will be happy to support them.

Obviously you can overdo your ambition. Be careful that the lure of possible promotion doesn't encourage you to work late every night for weeks on end. This can quickly damage a marriage. Remember also that if it is your partner who is late home on several evenings in succession, he or she is probably working overtime rather than having an intrigue with a secretary or head of department! Scorpio jealousy need not only arise from a sexual cause; it can also be the result of your partner making greater progress than yourself, such as by getting promotion more quickly in his or her career or making money more easily. Whatever the reason, don't let jealousy mar your marriage.

Scorpios are assertive parents and will do everything they can to ensure that their children work hard at school and have many involving hobbies and interests at home. You will be very keen on taking them off on ambitious outings and holidays, and you will expect a great deal from them in return. This is excellent. The children will have lively and interested minds because of the various directions in which you nudge them, and they will also no doubt inherit something of your own independence of mind. But be careful not to push them too hard or to try to interest them in something simply because you once enjoyed it. Don't force piano or ballet lessons on them if they don't seem to have any leanings in that direction. They might be much happier riding ponies or playing football. If you insist you will end up with a thoroughly bored and ill-tempered child.

Scorpio careers and money matters

When assessing the Scorpio potential in careers and financial ability we must consider not only the psychological motivation and mode of expression attributed to Scorpio but also the thinking processes of Mercury, and how these two factors combined can be best used in both areas. Then there is the influence of Venus, a planet as strongly related to finance and possessions as to relationships. The latter aspect is also important in this sphere as it will affect how a person will get on with colleagues, in business partnerships, and so on. Mars may well give some hint as to the direction of energy and will most certainly influence the physical element—the drive and energy put into the day's work. As we shall see, the influence of the combined Sun- and Rising-sign is interesting and very personal; but if your birth-time is not available and you cannot find out your Rising-sign, do not be too disappointed; you should be able to glean plenty of information about this sphere of your life from the more general paragraphs.

It is important to Sun-sign Scorpios that their jobs should make heavy demands on them and that a great deal should be expected of them. This is important not only because they need and like to be kept busy and involved but also because they very quickly become bored by work that does not stretch their capacities—whether the work be digging up a road or running a gigantic financial empire. As long as the Scorpio can feel at the end of each day that some challenge has been successfully met and some progress made, then he or she can relax over the evening drink with a sense of accomplishment.

But even if the day has gone well it can take a Scorpio quite a long time to switch off mentally from his or her work and to unwind, especially if the work is of an intellectually demanding kind. Scorpios are so caught up with what they are doing that they often have to practise relaxing and freeing themselves from the ties of the day. They may have to work hard at this—as hard as they had to work to acquire the skills they needed for their job.

165

If you made a list of things that are important to a Scorpio, money would come higher up on it than with most people. Scorpios like financial security and need to build up their resources. At the same time they like to spend, because enjoyment of life is also very important to them. But money itself also fascinates them, so a Scorpio will often choose a career which not only pays well but also involves high-powered financial work. Many enjoy the stock market or large-scale accountancy. They work well in highly competitive firms in which they can attain a good position. They will enjoy bargaining and getting the best deal for their company in any transaction.

Many Scorpios like discipline and routine. Hence they are often attracted by the armed forces. (Montgomery, the British World War II general, and Rommel, his German counterpart, were both Sun-sign Scorpios, born on the same day.) But Scorpios can also thrive in a more mundane occupation, coping well with the routine of a heavy daily round of work. At the same time their tendency to become fixed in their habits can have a limiting effect and cause their lives to be unadventurous, even though they are well able to cope with adventure. In other words, they may tend to plod on in something of a rut. If a partner sees this happening, he or she should try to spur the Scorpio into more adventurous activity.

Power is extremely important in the Scorpio scheme of things, especially where the career is concerned. They cope easily with it and enjoy doing so. Sometimes they use their power mischievously to give themselves a little harmless fun, and occasionally they can, unfortunately, abuse it. But when Scorpios use power responsibly they can do so with great resoluteness, reaching decisions swiftly with the aid of knowledge that they have acquired over the years. When power is backed up with knowledge and experience in this way it can be a great force for good. As to the abuse of power, Scorpios with Pluto in Leo should be particularly aware that they can be tempted in this direction and should make sure that they use any power they have justly and with a sense of responsibility. Otherwise they could become autocratic, and many negative facets of their personality could emerge.

Tradition links iron with Scorpio, but today we also think of steel as a Scorpionic metal, and this is borne out when we consider the sort of careers that Scorpios follow. Many are attracted to engineering, mining or the construction industry. Heavy armaments can also attract them, which may be the reason why so many Scorpios are drawn to the armed services. Although of course Scorpios are found in all sorts of careers, there does seem to be an emphasis of this sort.

At the same time one must bear in mind that Scorpio is a Water sign and that liquids also often play a part in the work of Scorpios. For example the wine trade and the oil industry seem to attract them (the latter of course combines with their interest in mining). Scorpios also gravitate towards watery activities. They make good professional swimming instructors for instance. They are also to be found working as divers on oil rigs, and they have the strength and toughness to cope with such demanding work.

Scorpios are not very concerned about the atmosphere in which they work. They cope with bitchiness, whether in the office or in the hairdressing salon; they can work against noise from machines; and if there is intrusive taped music they can either enjoy it or simply cut it out of their minds. Their powers of concentration are usually excellent. They are tough enough to cope with physically demanding work, or with the kind of pressure that builds up in an operating theatre or in a television studio just before the nightly news magazine programme goes on the air.

To sum up: Scorpios have great inner strength. They will attempt much, and usually achieve much. In their careers they follow a straight path towards their aim and do not drift or allow themselves to be deflected.

Mercury at work

Check position of Mercury on pages 238–241

Mercury in Libra
If Mercury was in Libra when you were born you will be most at ease working with other people and sharing decision-making. You probably would not like working alone in a small office cut off from your colleagues, or running a whole department without any support from them. An open-plan office might suit you very well. If you have your own business you will prefer to run it in partnership. Or, failing that, you will need to know that there is one employee you can trust and confide in. Your Scorpio energy will give you all the drive you need to make good progress; but try to avoid a lonely position. You could do well in a clothes shop or a department store, for you could derive a lot of satisfaction from meeting the public and helping them to find just what they want. Hairdressing could also suit you very well. Your sympathy and ability to listen to other people are important assets which might be used to good advantage in personnel work. If you are a student, you might tend to put off studying until the last minute. Although you absorb facts easily, you need to take your time about it. Try to keep up a steady pace of study throughout the term, and don't procrastinate.

Mercury in Scorpio
Scorpios with this placing will have minds very suited to any work of an investigatory nature. So if you come into this group you are a natural researcher. You could do well as a fact-finding journalist, a research chemist, a historian, a librarian helping others in their study, or in many other fields where investigation is involved. You are capable of very meticulous work, and if you find a subject that is especially fascinating, then go for it with all your Scorpio determination and inner strength. You have the temperament of a specialist, so don't hesitate to choose a narrow field, even one which has been thoroughly worked by someone else—for unless that someone is another person with Sun and Mercury in Scorpio there is sure to be still something new for you to dig up. You will guard your discoveries with great care until you are ready to talk or write about them. If you are a student you will be keen to study in depth and could well surprise your teachers or tutors by your pronouncements on their own pet themes. But you will always be able to back your statements up, for you will have the information at your fingertips. You should do very well in examinations, since you can work intuitively but also thoroughly.

Mercury in Sagittarius
If you are a Scorpio with Mercury in Sagittarius you will have the ability to grasp situations quickly and broadly. Applying this to work, it seems likely you would be suited to a career

where mental alertness is desirable. The academic world is one possibility. You would also do well in any job requiring someone who can move with agility to cope with a sudden turn of events and is always ready to counter an unexpected move by the person he or she is dealing with. For instance, if you find yourself competing for some important deal, and your prospective client brings up the name of one of your rivals, you will at once be able to stun him with at least three instant and very convincing reasons why the other firm would be hopelessly wrong for him. You can apply yourself to any kind of study or business and make a great deal of it, so that the work, whatever it is, will become more and more important to the firm or institution you work for. If, for instance, you are a junior teacher in a large school, your efforts—perhaps in some extra-curricular activity—will be noticed, and your methods probably more widely adopted. You need challenge, and challenge is an excellent way of directing your Scorpio energy. If you are a student, you should thrive on academic work, but might have a tendency to be insufficiently oriented towards examinations. If you can take exams seriously you will do very well.

Venus: money and rapport

Check position of Venus on pages 242–245

Venus in Virgo

With Venus in Virgo you will have a prudent streak which is rather uncharacteristic of that sign. In general, Scorpios enjoy spending money as much as making it. But you will husband your money carefully so that you will have enough in the coffers to give generous presents at Christmas or buy yourself an exciting trip when the holiday season arrives. When your bank balance looks good you don't let that encourage you to go on a wild spending spree. You enjoy seeing money work for you, and invest wisely. If you invest in the dietary or health-food business you may find it pays off, for your interest in that area may be financial as well as personal. If you are one of those Scorpios who love craft work you could make that a financially rewarding hobby. You could also invest profitably in agriculture, horticulture, telecommunications or the media.

You will be a hard worker and always willing to put in a lot of effort to help colleagues. So if someone wants something done they will tend to ask you. As an employer, you could seem rather fussy; you are a perfectionist and expect others to be the same.

Venus in Libra

With Venus in Libra you'll probably have to earn rather a lot of money if you are to enjoy life according to your expectations. There are certain little luxuries you enjoy and need, and you hate to do without them. Even if you are still young, you will be no stranger to expensive tastes. If you see something attractive you will want to have it, even if it costs a bomb. But Scorpios are by no means stupid about money; they have an excellent business sense and probably a good nose for investment. So even if your Libran Venus is the source of much extravagance you could recoup through placing your money wisely. Department stores, the beauty business and the hotel trade would be possible areas for investment. A simple insurance scheme that piles up interest with the capital would also be worth consideration for you as a trouble-free means of enhancing savings.

You will be someone to whom everyone will pour out their troubles at work; you are a good listener, and kind to those in difficulty. If you are an employer you will see to it that employees get a fair deal and enjoy good social and leisure facilities. All this will be much appreciated.

Venus in Scorpio

With Venus in Scorpio with the Sun when you were born, you are likely to be very money-conscious and should have an excellent business sense. Your Scorpio caution and willingness to do plenty of background work will stand you in excellent stead when you decide what to do with your money. Of all Scorpios you should be best at building up your own business, for you are a hard worker and have the right kind of flair. You would make an excellent wine shipper (though you would have to avoid setting aside all the best wine for your own cellar). Possible areas for investment are oil, mining or heavy industry. But don't overinvest; it's just possible that you could tie up too much money and find there's not enough left for the large, unexpected bill.

You will possibly keep your social life very separate from your working life; if you get emotionally involved with anyone at work, you will try to keep it secret. As an employer you may tend to keep things so much to yourself that employees feel they are too little informed about the firm's progress. But you are a generous employer.

Venus in Sagittarius

Venus in Sagittarius will make you less concerned about money than most Scorpios. You have plenty of good sense and a philosophical attitude, so if you want something which is too expensive to go out and buy immediately you will not get too frustrated if you have to wait for a while or spend time thinking out ways of raising the necessary cash. You probably enjoy speculation, which could mean a small bet on a race or large-scale speculation in stocks and shares. You enjoy a certain amount of challenge and risk in financial matters. Should an investment fail, your reaction will be: "Better luck next time." And you may be right. But your gambling instinct is pretty strong, and, as you are a natural optimist charged with positive enthusiasm, you may need to bring your most cautious Scorpio qualities into play. You might find it profitable to invest in travel companies or in any products concerning tin and its mining. If you are in business be conscious of export markets.

You have a natural talent for cheering up colleagues, for you like to see people enjoying themselves both during and after working hours. If you are an employer, you will give great encouragement to your staff.

Venus in Capricorn

Money-making is a serious matter for you, because Venus in Capricorn at the time of your birth makes you of all Scorpios the most careful and shrewd when it comes to finance. You will take no risks, but will gradually build up your resources. This will be the case whether you are still on pocket-money from parents or the head of a large concern which you have built up over a long period of careful planning. You impress people—the right people—and naturally inspire their confidence; so you don't find it necessary to lay on expensive lunches to win over your business clients. Though this is not to say that you won't enjoy such occasions for the sake of a good meal. If you need me to advise you on investment (which is not very likely!) I would suggest real estate or any dependable savings scheme. Or you could invest in yourself by starting an enterprise of your own. Your colleagues could see you as something of a loner, a strong silent type; try not to be too distant, for you might give the impression that you are a snob. Similarly, if you are an employer an element of remoteness and unapproachability could prevent your employees from giving you their true opinions.

Rising-signs and your career

First check your Rising-sign on pages 225–232

Note: Careers and the Midheaven
If you develop your interest in astrology one of the first things which you will learn about, but which is outside the scope of this book, is the Midheaven. Roughly speaking, this is the sign immediately over your head when you were born. It is as important in your career, outward expression and identification with objectives in life as your Rising-sign is in your personality. To combine it with your Rising-sign is complicated and would be impossible in a book of this length; but, while I cannot help you to discover yours in this book, rest assured that I have borne the various possibilities in mind when writing the following paragraphs in relation to your choice of profession or job.

Scorpio with Aries rising
You need work that is demanding either physically or intellectually. Depending on your particular talents, you could be happy digging roads or doing battle in politics or big business, where your relentless drive would be used to full advantage. You could make a good career in professional sport or as a stuntman or woman.

Scorpio with Taurus rising
You need financial stability. Banking, finance and accountancy are good careers, as your business sense is excellent. The beauty trade or fashion industry would also suit you. Music could be important in your life; if so you should develop this potential. Try not to work alone—go in for partnership in any business enterprise.

Scorpio with Gemini rising
You could do well as a salesman or saleswoman and will put a lot of energy into your day's work. Working in the media might suit you, perhaps as an investigatory journalist. You might also enjoy being a receptionist or switchboard operator. You need plenty of variety and change, and could cope with more than one professional interest. Advertising is also a strong possibility.

Scorpio with Cancer rising
You would make an excellent teacher of young children. The medical profession might suit you, perhaps as a specialist in midwifery or gynaecology. You would make a marvellous chef. In fact the catering and hotel trade in general would be an excellent métier for you. Other possible areas are the antiques trade and dairy farming.

Scorpio with Leo rising
You might do very well in the computer industry. If you are creative, develop any skill you possess to the best of your ability. Also use your organizing ability in some way. Remember that you can carry responsibility and may positively enjoy showing off. If you decide on modelling or the theatre your Scorpio toughness will be on your side.

Scorpio with Virgo rising
You would do well working in the media—why not try your local radio or television station? You would also be an excellent researcher in any area or an ideal secretary. In another sphere you would make a first-rate masseur, physiotherapist, dietician or health-food expert. Horticulture and agriculture could suit you. If you think you can write a book, why not try?

Scorpio with Libra rising
Your tact and diplomacy could serve you well in the diplomatic service or in coping with difficult customers in any profession. Personnel or public relations work could give you a rewarding career. You might also enjoy working on a cruise liner or as a holiday courier. As another possibility, you would probably make an excellent hairdresser.

Scorpio with Scorpio rising
You will want either to work behind the scenes or to show off your ability to the public—no half-measures. You could be a very successful psychiatrist. Or you may need to be in a position of power, if so, be careful not to get carried away by it. Mining, the Navy, surgery and pathology could suit you. Whatever you do you need a very demanding career.

Scorpio with Sagittarius rising
Languages could come very naturally to you. You would make a good publisher or lawyer. You could do well in professional sport or teaching at university level. You need challenge and you are very versatile. Working with animals could suit you, perhaps as a veterinary surgeon. The travel industry, exports and the Church are all possibilities.

Scorpio with Capricorn rising
You have terrific potential and capacity for hard work. You can do battle in any sphere, but politics and business (especially insurance) would be excellent careers. You would also make a good architect, builder, estate manager or real estate agent. Farming could suit you, and you may have mathematical or scientific ability. You should be very successful.

Scorpio with Aquarius rising
You need to feel independent. You might enjoy work that involves the past, perhaps archaeology. Working for a large charity organization, perhaps in the field, could suit you. You could find satisfaction being an air hostess, or working in astronomy or any area concerning space. Television might be a possibility. Your career must have something to bring out the originality in your personality.

Scorpio with Pisces rising
You would be very much at home in the caring professions, provided you can control your personal feelings. You would make a wonderful nurse, social service worker or almoner. You could also enjoy working in the footwear industry, or in fishing. Don't neglect any artistic ability you may have. You need a rather off-beat career and could do well as a photographer.

Sagittarius

Positive
Ruling planet: Jupiter
Triplicity or element: fire
Quadruplicity or quality: mutable
Colour: dark blue, purple
Gemstone: topaz
Metal: tin
Flowers: pinks and carnations
Trees: lime, birch, mulberry, oak
Herbs and spices: sage, aniseed, balsam
Foodstuffs: bulb vegetables, grapefruit, currants, sultanas
Animals: horses, animals that are hunted
Countries: Spain, Australia, Hungary, South Africa.
Cities: Toledo, Stuttgart, Budapest, Cologne, Sheffield, Washington D.C.

The first impression one usually gets from a Sagittarian is of a delightful frankness and open manner, and these characteristics are linked to breadth of vision and an easy, immediate, striking and positive grasp of a project or problem. However, Sagittarians are not always good at coping with dreary details, and it is as well to avoid bothering them with anything that savours of the niggling or petty.

They are prone to considerable restlessness, which is related to two distinct characteristics: one is the feeling that the grass is always greener over the hedge; the other is a psychological need for a challenge, which they will take up and master with that lively enthusiasm they are always ready to express.

Sagittarians have a considerable capacity for love and a liveliness in their attitude towards their partners which may remind one of a youthful student (many do seem to be eternal students in some respects, for their appetite for knowledge is almost insatiable). Within relationships, they need plenty of freedom of expression, and because of this must have really understanding and tolerant partners. They simply cannot cope with possessiveness, which to them savours of claustrophobia—their worst hate.

Children of the sign are "coltish" and need to be tamed. As they grow up, they can become very involved with sport, or turn seriously to academic subjects. A balance between the two is advisable.

The Sagittarian body-areas are hips, thighs and liver. Sagittarius is another sign that likes good food, but should enjoy exercise too: friends should try to see that they get it! Intellectual stagnation should equally be avoided.

Sagittarius in friendship, love and marriage

As a Sun-sign Sagittarian you are on the whole easy to get on with, accepting people at their face value; so if someone tells you that they're unlikely to become a good friend of yours because your Sun-sign and theirs are incompatible, you'll probably think they are joking.

This belief about some signs not "going with" others is unfortunately always being touted about by popular astrological articles in magazines and newspapers. It has the smallest grain of truth in it, and is part of an ancient tradition; but it has got out of all proportion, and badly needs putting in perspective.

The truth is that there is something of a tendency for people whose Sun-signs are of the same "element" (see page 75) to find that there is a certain ease between them—a kind of relaxed accord, shared enthusiasm and outlook. Sagittarius is a Fire sign, so according to this theory you should get on well with Ariens and Leos, who share the Fire element. Air signs—Gemini, Libra and Aquarius—are also considered "good". You will be told that people of Earth signs—Taureans, Virgoans and Capricorns—and of Water signs—Cancerians, Scorpios and Pisceans—are "no good" from the point of view of friendship or a loving relationship. If you took this seriously, you would cut yourself off from half the population of the world!

Where the theory breaks down is that you may well have Mercury or Venus in either Scorpio or Capricorn, and in either case this would help to bridge any gap between you and someone with either sign as a Sun-sign. Due to the position of Mars, you may find you have a lively sexual rapport, or perhaps enjoy similar sports or exercise regimes.

Obviously, it would be very silly indeed to prevent the development of a relationship—either of friendship or of an emotional kind—just because the Sun-signs are traditionally said to be incompatible! Far too many other factors are involved. It is only when an experienced astrologer calculates and studies the full birth-charts of two people that any definite

173

conclusions can be reached—and even then no astrologer would recommend clients to terminate a relationship. That is for the individual to decide. What can be done is to suggest areas of incompatibility, so that the couple concerned can make the necessary allowances to avoid difficulties.

As a Sun-sign Sagittarian, you will find the placing of Jupiter, the ruling planet of your sign, is an important factor; the planet has special influences on you which chime in with your whole personality, as well as standing for all the usual Jupiter influences.

But what I have found most illuminating when comparing the charts of people (*synastry*, as astrologers call the process) is that there is usually an emphasis on polar or opposite signs between those with a deep and satisfactory emotional relationship. Your partner's Rising-sign (see pages 225–232) may for instance be Gemini, which is Sagittarius' polar sign (for a list of polar signs see page 75). Or your partner's Sun might be directly across the Zodiac from your Rising-sign. The Moon plays an important role too: perhaps your partner's Moon shares your Sun-sign? Or maybe there is polarity between Rising- or Sun-signs and your Moon-sign?

All this has to be worked out in detail, and the various levels of individual personality carefully studied. For instance, as a Sun-sign Sagittarius you will undoubtedly most enjoy a partner who is lively and enthusiastic. Up to that point a Fire sign person would be suitable. You have a high emotional level, and won't want a cool, undemonstrative partner; and you need someone of an equal intellectual level, too—someone who can challenge you, intellectually.

The possibilities far outreach those of the simply "good" or "bad" relationship between the elements, interesting though that may be as a starting-point, or a conversation-piece at some party or other. In this area, as in every other, the more you get to know about astrology the more fascinating it becomes. Basic Sun-sign characteristics get to be rather a bore after a time—especially for Sagittarians, who so much enjoy challenge and the exploration of all sorts of theories!

Sagittarian friendships

Perhaps your finest quality as a friend is that you are naturally able to cheer up others when they are depressed. You will always be ready to encourage them and urge them to continue their efforts. You have plenty of enthusiasm yourself, so much so that it will overflow into your friends' lives. You get tremendous pleasure when you see their renewed efforts, and watch them returning to their usual selves as a result of your help.

As an enthusiastic, lively person, you should try to be a little "low-key" at times. For instance, when friends are unburdening themselves, it is more effective if you listen quietly without butting in too much. When they have had their say then there will be time for you to add your support or encouragement to lift them out of depression or help with their problems.

Conversely, you yourself do not find it difficult to talk to your friends about your problems. You should do so, for bottling up worries does nobody any good and it goes particularly against your nature.

It is a good thing for you to be acquainted with people who are to some extent ahead of you in your interests. At the same time as being a marvellous source of inspiration to others, you need challenge in your own life. There is no better friend for a Sagittarian who is just beginning to trot a horse over nursery fences than a show-jumping champion! This can be applied to any interest. Remember that you need challenge and that accepting challenge is a basic motivation for you—it will help you make full use of your abundant potential and talent.

Your friends should be active types who lead a full and busy life, rather than the sort of people who approach everything in a lukewarm, half-hearted manner. Forget about the latter type of person, for you will be bored to tears with them in next to no time, and you need to keep boredom and restlessness at bay.

Traditionally, Sagittarius is a sign connected with far-away lands. So it may be that you get on particularly well with people from foreign countries and other ethnic groups. You could do much to foster rapport between the people of different nations. But be a little careful that, in voicing your own strong opinions, you don't upset others or clash with some political system you have to live with for a while.

Sagittarius in love

When some inner voice tells you that you are in love, another may be warning you: "It's only a passing fancy, silly." Not that this will dissuade you from pressing on with the relationship and enjoying it to the full. It is just that you are basically an extremely independent person who hates to feel tied down, so that when you know inwardly that you are smitten, another area of yourself will prompt you to wonder whether the present affair isn't just "one of those things" rather than the "real thing". Eventually there will come a time when your past experience of life and love will overcome your reluctance and you will be ready to settle into a permanent relationship.

With a lover, as with your friends, you need plenty of challenge and intellectual rapport. You are highly sexed in a lively, enthusiastic way, but could get bored with the relationship if on the one hand your partner were sexually uninventive and unadventurous, or if on the other hand sex were the only thing keeping you together. After the first sensual flurry, such a relationship could soon wear very thin. Because you are yourself versatile, you are more likely than others to succumb to boredom in any sphere of your life, and sexual boredom in a stultifying relationship is high on the danger list. You will get restless if your partner can think only about the evening's television shows or, worst of all, has nothing to talk about at all. If the sexual attraction is really strong and you both go your separate ways at other times, you may achieve a mode of living to your mutual satisfaction. But for a full and rounded relationship you need more than just sex.

The sign Venus was in when you were born can provide a variety of different colourings to your attitudes and behaviour in love, but in any case there will probably be an element of duality present so that you like to have more than one relationship at a time, enjoying both partners for different reasons. More subtly, this could be an indirect expression of your need for independence—you might take a second lover just to demonstrate to yourself that you are not tied to the first.

Perhaps you have persuaded yourself that you don't really need a permanent partner. Is this really so or are you just reacting childishly, or jumping on the "liberation" bandwagon? You should not forget that you may not always feel the way you do now, and that it would be a pity to ruin a promising relationship only to realize too late that you have missed the chance of a lifetime's beautiful and rewarding partnership and that someone with whom you could happily have shared your life has passed forever out of it.

You have a lot to give to a partner. And if you can find one who is lively and sexually demonstrative, and has other things in common with you, then you will be better able to develop and fulfil yourself and discover your true potential.

Sagittarius in marriage

It does not seem likely that a Sagittarian would ever stagnate in a marriage. They have powerful needs which appear at first to be incompatible with a permanent relationship, but by being consciously aware of the need to satisfy them they should manage to cope very well.

You will probably agree with me when I suggest that you need a husband or wife who is as busy and versatile as yourself or, if not versatile, one who possesses at least some strong interest with which you will be able to sympathize. I think this is very important, for if you are bored with your partner's preoccupations, you will soon get bored with the partner, and that would be something very difficult to cope with.

One great thing in your favour is that you will be far less likely to become jealous of your partner's outside interests than any other Zodiac type. In fact you probably can't stand jealousy at any price, even if you have Venus in Scorpio. But you will especially hate your partner to be jealous of you. This is something that must be made clear right from the start: you must both realize that you need an element of freedom within your marriage, and cannot cope with claustrophobic conditions. In return for this consideration you should exercise restraint yourself, not working too late at the office, or entertaining colleagues or clients so often in the evenings that your partner grows suspicious.

The young married Sagittarian mother will probably want a family and will love her children. But once she has got over the initial hectic stages, she should try to set aside at least a few hours every week for some kind of activity away from baby. Maybe she could take up some new and interesting hobby, or renew an old one. In this way Ms Sagittarius will happily accept motherhood and will not feel frustrated by the ties of looking after children. Even if she is tired by the demands they make on her she should try to get away occasionally. The more highly educated she is, the more necessary some outside interest is. A physically demanding hobby such as skating or riding, or perhaps some team game, should be kept up if she is to counter the trials and tribulations of being a parent and be able to appreciate the delights of motherhood.

For the Sagittarian father the problem is not usually quite so pressing, as he is more likely to get away from the child or children during the day. But his wife should remember that when he comes home he could easily be bored by a constant stream of anecdotes about what baby did or didn't do that day. Apart from this, Sagittarians make excellent parents, especially when the children are a little older. For then they will be keen to stimulate the interests of their offspring in every possible way. They will derive great satisfaction from the constant challenge of parenthood. It's not difficult for them to keep abreast of their sons or daughters, and there should be little problem with the "generation gap" in later years.

Sagittarian careers and money matters

When assessing the Sagittarian potential in careers and financial ability we must consider not only the psychological motivation and mode of expression attributed to Sagittarius, but also the thinking processes of Mercury, and how these two factors combined can be best used in both areas. Then there is the influence of Venus, a planet as strongly related to finance and possessions as to relationships. The latter aspect is also important in this sphere as it will affect how a person will get on with colleagues, in business partnerships, and so on. Mars may well give some hint as to the direction of energy and will most certainly influence the physical element—the drive and energy put into the day's work. As we shall see, the influence of the combined Sun and Rising-sign is interesting and very personal; but if your birth time is not available and you cannot find out your Rising-sign, do not be too disappointed; you should be able to glean plenty of information about this sphere of your life from the more general paragraphs.

The scope for Sagittarians as far as careers are concerned is extremely wide, for they have a very lively and varied potential. Obviously, the basic characteristics of this Sun-sign group need to be as positively expressed in their work as in any other sphere of their lives.

As is the case with every Sun-sign, we find Sagittarians in every profession and springing from all strata of society. But this is not to say they don't tend to be happier in some careers than in others. Looking broadly at the Sagittarian type, I would say that they probably need freedom of expression in any job and the possibility of doing things in their own way as far as possible. Interference or nagging from superiors, especially if in the Sagittarian's eyes they are stupid or foolish, will cause considerable disharmony in their lives and impair their performance in their work. But if they are given a reasonably free hand they will work at their tasks with great energy and enthusiasm.

The individual Sagittarian should bear in mind the fact that the greatest limitation he or she will have to cope with

177

(assessing the Sun-sign characteristics only, as we are in this section) will be an inability to cope with small detail. Sagittarians are the planners of overall schemes, the ones who will be good at deducing general reactions, rather than people who will excel at deciding in what order the paragraphs of a report will best be placed, or at putting the final small touches to a product before packing it for export.

A great deal has been written about the two types of Sagittarian—one whose energy is physically expressed and the other who tends to be intellectual by nature. There is a great deal of validity in the division, but what is often ignored is the fact that the 20-year-old sporting Sagittarian can develop into the 45-year-old intellectual Sagittarian, having understood and nurtured the growth of the mind. There does seem to be something of the eternal student about Sagittarians, and they should take this into consideration when choosing a career. They will probably think of their job, consciously or unconsciously, as a developing and creative aspect of life. They will tend not to think in terms of a career which will bring its rewards if they work hard. They will prefer to seek advancement by studying in their spare time, often contenting themselves with a menial position while they do so, believing that this scheme will lead them to better things. There will be an element of excitement, tinged by their liking for adventure and the unknown, in their approach to their career. In this sphere of life, as elsewhere, Sagittarians will create challenges for themselves and not only be ready to accept them as they occur in the natural order of things.

There is also the possibility of restlessness, which should not be allowed to get out of hand. When contemplating a change of course, Sagittarians should ask themselves whether it will be a progressive and constructive one or whether they are not simply feeling fidgety and wanting change for its own sake. Although they are versatile, members of this sign like to get to grips with one job before passing on to the next. Too many changes could lead to dissatisfaction, a state of mind which is more lethal to Sagittarians than to others.

A predictable routine is not good for Sagittarians, and those forced to work at a factory bench or on some production line should counter the danger of boredom by having engrossing spare-time interests. It is vital for them to spend their leisure constructively: working out at a gym, going to evening classes, playing football, or in any other way that will express their lively potential. The interests should be very intensive and demanding. If they can in due course be turned into a career, enabling the Sagittarian to escape from some restrictive and frustrating job, so much the better for a fulfilled future.

Often the Sagittarians will have more than one source of income. There may be a mainstream job, plus some other enterprising occupation which will be fun but also be profitable. This could be a hobby such as restoring antiques, mending clocks or doing a little translation if the Sagittarian loves languages—many Sagittarians have a genuine flair for languages, and this may be a way in which a Sagittarian could compensate for a dull job. Sagittarians should always remember that they can be good at more than one particular job, and if that means building a new skill in their spare time, they should take up that challenge. I would say to them: diversify, be versatile, find a few really rewarding interests and go at them, but don't scatter your energy too far afield, because this in turn could cause restlessness, and that could affect your health.

Mercury at work

Check position of Mercury on pages 238–241

Mercury in Scorpio

If Mercury was in Scorpio when you were born, you are well able to cope with work which is intellectually demanding. You will like finding out facts and will perhaps have a flair for research. You can keep secrets, and may be attracted to a career in the police or as a private detective. You will find it easier than most Sagittarians to cope with intricate detail, provided that this is linked to some fascinating study or some rewarding end-product. You should have an excellent memory and might well have considerable business flair. With your pleasant, open personality you could probably make a success of selling or building up your own company, for you are shrewd and would be able to deploy money skilfully within an enterprise. If you are a student you should thrive on your studies: once you are involved it will take a great deal to distract you. You should not have much difficulty when it comes to examination time since you can retain facts and have the ability to support your statements by the results of your own research.

Mercury in Sagittarius

You will think very clearly, but so broadly that you may tend to ignore difficulties and details. You have enormous intellectual potential, but you must make yourself settle calmly to work and not be too easily side-tracked into new ideas, new projects or into an even broader aspect of your career. Perhaps you should work in the export department of your firm. Or, if you feel you would like to teach, you should work with older students—you would enjoy the demanding challenges constantly thrown at you by them. This would keep you intellectually on your toes and give you the mental stimulus that you very much need. You must, I think, make allowances for others who are not as quick witted as yourself. Give them time to assimilate your statements, and if you are in a position of authority don't get irritated when you find that everyone else seems to be so much slower than you. It's just that it takes almost everyone longer to understand a problem than you. Be very careful about restlessness; you may need variety and change more than most Sagittarians, and if you skip about too much it could thwart long-term progress. If you are a student (and you are almost bound to be, in one way or another, your whole life long) your keenness and lively attitude will impress your tutors. Don't let outside interests distract you when it comes to examinations.

Mercury in Capricorn

With Mercury in Capricorn you will be able to plod along more patiently and think more constructively than most other Sun-sign types. You will make steady progress and are not likely to succumb to restlessness like so many others. You will be in many ways enthusiastic, but you will keep your liveliness well under control and will not be likely to be too easily carried away. You are among the most ambitious of Sagittarians and could cope with a powerful, and possibly lonely, position. But you are unlikely to make a pompous or remote boss. It may be that you are less versatile than most Sagittarians and will therefore have a well-developed interest in one particular sphere of your job; if you concentrate on this, you are likely to make excellent progress. Your pattern of thinking is careful, and you are never likely to make definite pronouncements off

179

the top of your head. All your statements and decisions will be very carefully considered. If you are a student you could feel rather guilty if you have been neglecting your work in order to enjoy any of the many extra-mural activities that students indulge in; and the more you have enjoyed yourself, the guiltier you will feel! In general you will have no difficulty in working hard and building up a solid foundation of knowledge that will stand you in very good stead when it comes to examinations.

Venus: money and rapport

Check position of Venus on pages 242–245

Venus in Libra

Venus in Libra with a Sagittarian Sun could give you a pretty relaxed and easy-going attitude towards money. Usually you will spend it in the best possible causes, for the benefit of friends and the happiness of your family, but you ought to give some thought from time to time not only about the way in which you dispose of your income but also about how you can increase it. You could find this rather boring, but it is very necessary for you to carry it through, simply because of your generosity and enjoyment of life. You might find investment in beauty products or the hotel trade profitable and interesting.

I think it is very important that you get good practical guidance as far as your financial situation is concerned, especially if you are self-employed. You might tend not to pay enough attention to tax requirements, and could be landed with a huge bill or miss out on some welcome rebate. So you should find a trustworthy accountant. You are likely to be very popular at work, and your presence will give a warm glow to your colleagues. You will cheer them up almost unconsciously and lighten their daily round. If you employ others, you will get the best out of them, for you will always be ready with an encouraging word and will not be unforthcoming when it comes to giving bonuses.

Venus in Scorpio

With Venus in Scorpio you will have an excellent business sense and should in general be pretty shrewd when it comes to making investments. So if you want to build up your own business you have an above-average chance of success. But remember that, while your Sagittarian Sun-sign will encourage you to accept challenges and enjoy them, it also encourages you to take a gamble. Let your deep, thoughtful Venus in Scorpio have a say in the proceedings, and in doing so you will give yourself plenty of time for careful consideration of any promising project or bright idea. If you have money to invest, you might be interested in engineering, the oil industry or the wine trade.

At work you will be the one in whom others will confide. Perhaps at times you will find it difficult to keep secrets, since Sagittarius makes you a very open person. But you must resist the temptation to spill the beans, otherwise your colleagues' opinion of you could drop, which would be a pity. If you are an employer, you will probably be excellent at making sure that your employees are able to invest in your firm on a profit-sharing basis. You will also make sure that they are generously covered by health insurance and any other scheme which you think will make their lives more rewarding and secure.

Venus in Sagittarius

If you are one of this group you need to be careful where money is concerned. It could slip through your fingers all too easily. You need to call upon all the practicality at your command to control your generosity and your enjoyment of taking financial risks and gambles. You will not want to be too tied down to any one area of investment and will enjoy playing the stock market. But don't get too carried away by the promise of future financial gain or spend too much time in dreaming about what you will do when it comes. Many people would say that you are lucky with money. Perhaps it does come your way rather easily, but it will probably melt away easily as well.

At work you will be popular, and your cheerful presence will brighten up even the dreariest of surroundings. You will boost the morale of your colleagues. If you employ others, your own *bonhomie* will infect them, and none of them will ever be able to accuse you of being stand-offish or pompous. Quite the reverse—you could tease everybody in a fun-loving and delightful way. When it comes to your having to discipline anyone you should do so directly and firmly, otherwise they will not take you seriously. But afterwards take them out for a nice friendly beer at lunchtime.

Venus in Capricorn

You are among the more serious of Sagittarians, and your attitude to money is careful. You may like to play safe and just watch it growing steadily in the hands of some investment trust. Alternatively you could find the agricultural industry rewarding and interesting for investment. Real estate or construction companies might also be a good idea. But whatever area you may invest in you will be happiest where the risk is minimal, despite your Sagittarian liking for the odd gamble. Why not give this a little thought? Find out whether you incline towards a careful attitude to money (Venus in Capricorn) or towards uninhibited enjoyment of it (Sun in Sagittarius).

At work you could, despite your Sagittarian characteristics, be thought of as something of a loner. Perhaps you thrive in some small and remote office or corner away from the general hustle and bustle. If you do feel at any level of your personality that you prefer a quieter working atmosphere you should go all out to get it, because you will probably work more effectively and happily that way. You can carry responsibility and will help resolve difficulties if they arise between employers and your colleagues. If you employ others your sense of fun will stimulate your workers into good production, but you are also able to play the role of "top person" very convincingly and impressively when it comes to dealing with customers.

Venus in Aquarius

You like to be independent, and maybe you would do well working for yourself, for then you can set about things in your own individual and original way. If you find money a bore (as far as its management is concerned) get a trustworthy accountant to cope with the financial complexities, so that you are totally free to concentrate on the business, building it up and developing it, spending your time actually earning the cash. As an employee you probably need to be a little careful with your pay-cheque, for you could be prone to impulse-buying, especially where beautiful but rather impractical things are concerned, such as decorations for the home. While you may be convinced that the objects you are buying are interesting and worthwhile they may not be satisfactory as long-term investments or even be particularly good value. You might like to invest in television, either in the manufacture of sets, or in programme companies. Airlines too could also suit you, or any company concerned with scientific development and the long-term future—the silicon chip industry, for instance.

You could appear somewhat eccentric to your colleagues, and possibly you enjoy attempting to shock them from time to time. Nothing wrong with that—it will give them something to talk about and at the same time will amuse you. If you are an employer, be a little careful not to make too obvious an effort to bridge the generation gap, for any juvenile cavortings from a middle-aged manager could embarrass the youngsters. But you will be a caring, humanitarian boss.

Rising-signs and your career

First check your Rising-sign on pages 225–232

Note: Careers and the Midheaven
If you develop your interest in astrology one of the first things which you will learn about, but which is outside the scope of this book, is the Midheaven. Roughly speaking, this is the sign immediately over your head when you were born. It is as important in your career, outward expression and identification with objectives in life as your Rising-sign is in your personality. To combine it with your Rising-sign is complicated and would be impossible in a book of this length; but, while I cannot help you to discover yours in this book, rest assured that I have borne the various possibilities in mind when writing the following paragraphs in relation to your choice of profession or job.

Sagittarius with Aries rising
It is important for you to be able to express your strong pioneering spirit and in some way to be a leader. Explore new ideas in your chosen field. You would do well in professional sport, politics or science, or working for a cause about which you feel very strongly. Try to avoid a predictable job with a very set routine, and make sure you are kept busy.

Sagittarius with Taurus rising
You need challenge and excitement, but you also need considerable financial security. Big business, perhaps the export field, would suit you. While you may of necessity find yourself working in the middle of a city, don't forget your need for fresh air. Agriculture or horticulture would suit you, and so would surveying or architecture. Don't neglect any musical talent you may have.

Sagittarius with Gemini rising
You are very versatile, so you need work with plenty of variety and change. Journalism and publishing would suit you. So would work involving travel, such as a sales representative. Working in partnership to build up a business would also be rewarding for you. Other possibilities are telecommunications or work in the postal service. Develop any writing skill or flair for languages.

Sagittarius with Cancer rising
You might do extremely well in the medical profession, especially as nurse, midwife or gynaecologist. You could be fascinated by history, and the antique trade would suit you very well. So would teaching or caring for very young children. You might be a marvellous cook, with the makings of a professional chef. Why not aim for your own restaurant? Express your caring and protective instincts where you can.

Sagittarius with Leo rising

You are probably very creative and artistic, with powers of leadership and organization. If you went into the armed forces, for example, you would rise quickly in the hierarchy. You like to show off, so could do well as a model or in the theatre. You would also make a good tour organizer or guide. Teaching would be another possible area for you.

Sagittarius with Virgo rising

The outdoors could be important to your well-being, so you might make a good horticulturist or farmer. You might like to run a business selling health foods, or to be a dietician. You would also do extremely well in the media as interviewer, journalist or researcher. If you feel you have a book in you, don't let anything or anyone discourage you from writing it down. Never underestimate your capabilities.

Sagittarius with Libra rising

You have plenty of charm and could use it to advantage in your career. You would make a good beautician or hairdresser. You could also do well in the hotel and holiday business, or working for a cruise liner. Your work needs a touch of glamour and excitement to it. Resist a tendency to laziness and procrastination.

Sagittarius with Scorpio rising

You have great business potential, but could also do well as a detective or private investigator. You might also be attracted to the medical profession and would make a good surgeon or psychoanalyst. Any form of research will fascinate you. If you are keen on sports you are likely to excel in them, and this could also provide a possible career. You need emotionally satisfying, very demanding work.

Sagittarius with Sagittarius rising

You have the capacity for very demanding work and might be attracted towards a career in religion or law. Books will fascinate you, and you might be a potential writer yourself—if so don't be held back. By the same token you would do well in publishing, bookselling or the stationery business. You are possibly fond of animals, in which case you could train as a veterinary surgeon, work in a riding stable or breed dogs. Whatever you do you need plenty of excitement.

Sagittarius with Capricorn rising

You are ambitious and have potential to get to the top, but you could be happiest working behind the scenes. One of the caring professions would suit you, for you enjoy helping others in some way and working for the good of the community. You would make an excellent osteopath, masseur, radiotherapist or dentist. You might also be attracted towards politics.

Sagittarius with Aquarius rising

You need to feel independent and to work in your own individual way. But be careful that you don't mar your progress in life by being out of step. You might do well working in the field for a large charity organization. Television, space technology or some other branch of science would provide a suitable field for you. You might also study astronomy, geography or archaeology.

Sagittarius with Pisces rising

You are probably creative and artistic and may have a poetic flair. You might make a living by selling your own creative work or could be happy working for a publisher as an illustrator or photographer. You have terrific potential and need to be emotionally involved in whatever you are doing. Don't fritter your energy away by making too many changes of direction.

Capricorn

Negative
Ruling planet: Saturn
Triplicity or element: earth
Quadruplicity or quality: cardinal
Colours: dark grey, black, dark brown
Gemstone: turquoise, amethyst
Metal: lead
Flowers: ivy, hemlock, medlár, heartsease
Trees: pine, elm, yew
Herbs and spices: hemp, comfrey, knapweed
Foodstuffs: potato, barley, beet, spinach, malt
Animals: goat, all cloven-hoofed animals
Countries: India, Mexico, Afghanistan
Cities: Oxford (U.K.) Delhi, Mexico City, and the
administrative areas of capitals

Anyone who has studied the 12 signs will at once confirm the
truth that there are two types of Capricorn—the giddy mountain goat, always climbing the mountain, and the sad domestic
animal tethered to a post down in the valley. The two types
have common traits, however—notably where grumbling is
concerned; even the most ambitious and successful Capricorn
will have a grumble given time, and one doesn't usually have to
give them much time!

More seriously, there is an element of loneliness in many
Capricorns, and it is in this sensitive area that we can help
them—sometimes without their realizing it. The achievement
of ambition often places Capricorns in the lonely position of
someone who has "made it" to the top and has to take ultimate
responsibility. They will cope very well with this, but undoubtedly it can set them apart from other people.

Capricorns can often appear hard and rather chilly, but once
committed in a relationship are very faithful. As they do like
the right thing in the right place, they can appear a little too
formal. A tendency to social climbing, the need to impress, are
often present, but we can forgive everything when that marvellous off-beat sense of humour makes its presence felt, and
they themselves grin, the corners of their mouths turned down.

Capricorns need to be aware that they may be too strict and
conventional with their children; and the children of that sign
may have to learn not to take themselves quite so seriously.

The Capricorn body-areas are the knees and shins, and there
is a tendency towards rheumatism, which can be avoided by
keeping warm and exercise. Skin and teeth and bones are also
ruled by this sign.

Capricorn in friendship, love and marriage

If you first became interested in astrology because of reading an article about it in a popular magazine, or picking up a little booklet from a news-stand, the chances are that you were told "which signs go with which". As a Capricorn, you were probably told, you will get on particularly well with Taureans and Virgoans, and be happy too with Cancerians, Scorpios and Pisceans. But you may have been warned off Ariens, Leos and Sagittarians, Geminians, Librans and Aquarians. The reason for this (whether this was mentioned or not) is that you share with Taureans and Virgoans, Sun-signs which are of the Earth element, and those of the Water element are somewhat sympathetic, while the Fire and Air signs are less so (for a list of the elements see page 75).

Well, this is all right as far as it goes, but it doesn't go very far! There is certainly something of a natural affinity between certain signs, but it would be very silly indeed, and rather sad, not to allow a friendship or a closer relationship to develop because the person concerned had a Sun-sign which is described as incompatible. Capricorns have indeed certain special needs within a relationship—needs which may seem unimportant to some other signs. You admire constancy and loyalty, but you may not express your emotions very powerfully; you'll be ambitious for your relationship, and will want your partner to back you up in this. You might or might not find those qualities in someone sharing a "compatible" Sun-sign.

Remember that it is only when an astrologer works on the fully-calculated charts of two individuals (*synastry*, this work is called by astrologers) that any real pronouncements can be made; and even then no astrologer will tell a couple whether they should or should not marry, develop or end their relationship. That is a decision for them. And after all, it is possible that you may have Mercury or Venus in Sagittarius or Aquarius, which would mean that the planets would help to mitigate any differences between you and someone with a Sagittarian or Scorpio Sun- or Rising-sign. The Moon, too, plays an important part; perhaps you will share Moon-signs with a partner, or perhaps your respective Moon-signs share elements.

Because Saturn rules Capricorn, the influence of that planet is important to you, and would be an interesting and revealing factor were your chart compared to your partner's. However, the most important indications I have found in the charts of people sharing a rewarding relationship have been an accent on the polar or opposite signs in the Zodiac (see page 75). For instance, your Sun-sign, Capricorn, would be a perfect foil for someone with Cancer as their Sun-sign, Rising- or Moon-sign. Someone whose Sun-sign is directly across the Zodiac from your Rising-sign could also be very important to you. These links really are most revealing. You won't always agree with such a person, but there would certainly be an excellent rapport between you—a natural and understanding response.

All this is far removed from the kind of generalization which goes on when people talk only about the Sun-signs, and base their pronouncements on the traditional role of the elements. It is just not possible to say anything really meaningful (or even very interesting!) about someone on the basis of the Sun-sign alone. We need a great deal more to work on than that, and as we discover more and more about astrology, we can see that the individual birth-chart is a source of many, many indications to the "profile" of a particular personality. So anyone who wants to look at the complexities of a good working relationship between two people—whether in an emotional relationship, in friendship, or in business—must look at the fully-calculated charts, and see what they have to say.

You in particular, as a Sun-sign Capricorn, will appreciate this, for if there is one generalization which can safely be made it is that someone with a strong element of Capricorn in them enjoys a searching, careful, scientific approach to any problem. And you may well benefit from it, for it will give you increased confidence in a personal relationship; if one Capricornian quality emerges in the formative stages of a partnership it is caution, natural caution!

So here is a specially rewarding area of astrology. Learn as much as you can about it: you'll soon travel a long way from that first magazine article, and its basic generalities!

Capricornian friendships

You are loyal and faithful to your friends and you have the ability to maintain friendships for many years. You will enjoy seeing your friends progress in life and you will also be able to do a great deal to encourage them along their individual pathways to success. Time does not affect your friendships: even if you are out of touch with someone for many years you will find that when you meet again you will be just as close as before. But traditionally Capricorn and its ruling planet Saturn are linked with Father Time, and time can have a bearing on your attitude to friendship in that you will be able to form a rapport with people of generations other than your own. You have the happy knack of appearing to be the contemporary of anyone you like or who interests you. This is particularly the case when you are young. You will get on very well with elderly people, who will find you considerate and kind.

But, to turn the tables, how do your friends see you? You will be thoroughly appreciated for the virtues I have mentioned: loyalty, reliability, constancy, faithfulness. You will also show immediately the kind of mood you are in when you meet a friend; they will know on sight whether you are high on a mountain peak or down in the valley. Your expression, your general appearance and your tone of voice are all great give-aways. If you are feeling miserable you will make for the nearest bar and spend an hour over coffee or a beer telling anyone who will listen all about the ghastly treatment you have just received at work or some other trying experience. In fact, you will go on to say just how downright rotten the world is in general, and how badly it has been treating you in particular. But if you are up on the sunny peak you will show it. If you have just heard that you are in line for promotion or have had some other good news you will want to share your happiness.

So remember, you need sympathetic friends who will be happy to commiserate or rejoice with you; and while you have a great deal of inner strength—far more than many other Sun-sign types—you do need a shoulder to moan and grumble, and sometimes to cry, on! One advantage of your ability to sustain a friendship over decades rather than months is that friends have plenty of opportunity to get to know you very well. Because of your fine qualities and the affection and respect they will gain for you, they will be ready to sympathize and to hand out practical advice when times are hard.

Capricorn in love

You long to be in love—yet some corner of your mind constantly hesitates to recognize the fact when you are. It may simply be Capricornian caution making its presence felt. Sexually, you tend to enjoy brief encounters of a close kind; but, when it comes to deciding whether to commit yourself to a permanent relationship or marriage, you will be very choosy indeed. As far as your Sun-sign is concerned you can seem to a partner to be cool, or even uncaring. In fact, this may well not be the case; but I think it is always worth your while considering whether you are being demonstrative enough to keep your lover happy and warm. Your practicality can in a way be an obstacle to the romantic side of your life, dampening it down, spoiling the fun because it intrudes even at the most sentimental of moments. But you can express your feelings warmly if you allow yourself the emotional freedom to do so. Obviously, the sign Venus was in when you were born will colour your attitude a very great deal (see pages 242–245); but you should try to keep in mind the fact that your reactions to your lovers can be on the cool side, and that this can be a negative factor in an affair. It may especially be true when you are very young and comparatively inexperienced, when an aloof attitude can be a cover-up for shyness, uncertainty and a difficulty in being as warm and affectionate as you would really like to be. A rebuff can hurt you very deeply, too, and you may be terrified of receiving one.

You will want to impress a lover, and it could be that in doing so you may become somewhat pompous. Draw a little mark in your mind, and be careful not to overstep it. An excellent organizer, you will plan an evening out with exquisite care. But do check with your partner in advance that what you propose is something that he or she will enjoy, and don't throw your money about too ostentatiously just in order to impress.

You will find that you want to be able to look up to and respect your partner. Choose someone who wants to scale the heights with you, who is fascinated by your own interests and who will want to help you along the path to success with love and endearment. But if you find someone just like that, ask yourself before deepening the relationship whether you are really in love or whether it is merely a question of the social advancement which the partnership could bring you. Up to a point we all want our partners to be special but don't just use them as one of the rungs of a ladder to success.

Capricorn in marriage

Without any doubt at all you will be prepared to work very hard indeed for your marriage or your permanent partner. You will want to see your relationship develop, and will watch that development over the years with a rather special fascination, reassessing it from time to time, going over in your mind the joint achievements, events and changes which have helped it to stand the test of time. Marriage is, for you, rather more significant than for most people—a partnership you will want to be proud of. But it is also a good idea for you to share this feeling with your family. Occasionally why not rest on your laurels and take time with your partner, away from the children, to share nostalgic memories of your progress together.

Capricorns of both sexes need to be careful not to overwork for their homes and families. While everyone needs sometimes to work under pressure and some strain, the Capricornian instinct to keep the nose to the grindstone can run away with them, which can be hard on the nerves. Capricornian mothers will want to get back to work as soon as possible to earn the money to buy good clothes for the kids, to give them the best possible education or to pay for lessons outside school. The Capricornian man may arrive home from the office with a bulging briefcase of work in order to impress his superiors and progress in the firm. This is all admirable, but for a marriage it can be destructive, and both sexes should consider whether they are paying enough attention to their partners and children apart from the money paid out on their behalf. Time, affection and energy are as important in human relationships as money can ever be, and the marriage will not be welded together by pounds, dollars or francs. It is very important that no member of a Capricorn's family gets the impression that father or mother is uncaring and distant because their mind is always on business or social prospects or material advancement.

In many ways Capricorns make excellent parents, but they may take a rather harder line in discipline than is always necessary. Should a child produce a painting or a poem, or appear in a school play, make an effort to take time out to look, listen or attend and remember too that you have very high standards, and may tend to judge a child by an adult's view of things. There is no need to be condescending with children, they thrive on lively encouragement. But they can be withered by damning criticism or lack of interest, so generosity of time, and enthusiasm will be very rewarding in terms of family solidarity. Remember that in the long run your own efforts will be reflected in your pride in their accomplishments.

Your innate need for quality will be emphasized in marriage. You will want an exquisite partner who is clever, with all the social graces and who is able to cope in any situation. But you are also one of the great workers of the Zodiac. You don't need to be urged to work at your marriage too, but you should remember also to enjoy it. Keep your sense of humour about it, and above all keep the lines of communication with your partner open and buzzing.

Capricorn careers and money matters

When assessing the Capricornian potential in careers and financial ability we must consider not only the psychological motivation and mode of expression attributed to Capricorn but also the thinking processes of Mercury, and how these factors combined can be best used in both areas. Then there is the influence of Venus, a planet as strongly related to finance and possessions as to relationships. The latter aspect is also important in this sphere as it will affect how a person will get on with colleagues, in business partnerships, and so on. Mars may well give some hint as to the direction of energy and will most certainly influence the physical element—the drive and energy put into the day's work. As we shall see, the influence of the combined Sun and Rising-sign is interesting and very personal; but if your birth-time is not available and you cannot find out your Rising-sign, do not be too disappointed: you should be able to glean plenty of information about this sphere of your life from the more general paragraphs.

The potential for getting to the top is an integral part of every Capricornian character, and the sign is motivated by deep and powerful drive. With Capricorns the career or profession forms a central element in their lives to a greater extent than with most Sun-signs. It needs positive outward expression, and above all total fulfilment. The Capricornian has it in his or her power to achieve all this.

But Capricornian potential can be seriously inhibited and may by no means always be properly expressed and developed. There are hurdles, especially if the Capricorn is very ambitious. Very often, when someone of the Sun-sign is not making as much progress as was hoped, it is because of a lack of self-confidence and inhibition of some kind. And when a Capricornian is depressed and grumbling about what is wrong at work, how badly he or she is being treated, this is generally a cloak for lack of self-confidence: often when one gets down to it the things which are causing the grumbling are not all that important after all. The Capricornian will seize upon some tiny niggling incident and blow it up out of all proportion, just so that it can form an excuse for a failure to make the grade. This trait often has an unnecessarily cramping effect on the extremely positive, aspiring characteristics of this admirable sign. You constantly tend to hear from a Capricorn such statements as: "Oh, well, I could have done it if. . . ." Or: "If that fool had let me know in time. . . ." But Capricorn could have coped perfectly well whatever situation arose, with sufficient push and pressure. They should realize that they have plenty of potential, and should not be afraid to take situations into their own hands a little more. Then if things go wrong they can blame themselves, at least, rather than the political situation, international affairs, the weather or other people in general.

"Doing one's duty" is a phrase always underlined in the Capricornian copybook: and it is often the case that, while they may occasionally neglect their family for career or prestige in order to get to the top (for the sake of that family), they are also quite capable of making career sacrifices for domestic reasons. A Capricornian may give up a job in order to look after an elderly parent, for instance; or will work to keep a family business together when they might really prefer to be in a totally different profession. Capricorns are loyal people, and tradition is very important to them, but sometimes these qualities will force them to stay at a humble level for domestic reasons rather than making for the top in a career, as they should. If there is any possibility of a compromise in such a situation, aim at it; lack of fulfilment in the long run can have a very depressing effect for all of us—for a Capricornian, it can be truly fearful.

Capricorn is an Earth sign, and while we find Capricornians in all kinds of careers (like every Sun-sign), they tend to gravitate to occupations with an "earthy" quality—surveying property, farming, architecture, geology or geography, for instance. But politics and local government can attract them also, and so can the ultimate jobs at the top of their chosen profession—chairman of the board, headmaster or principal. Those of this Sun-sign can cope very well with the loneliness of a commanding position when, perhaps over the years, they have succeeded in getting to the top. They will stay there in perfect security, happily accepting ultimate responsibility, making final decisions, and in short be perfectly happy that the buck stops with them. Discipline and routine offer no problem, either, though sometimes they can tend to get stuck in a rut and be somewhat inflexible in their working methods.

There is often a natural flair and love of science and mathematics, which should be encouraged by the parents of young Capricornians. If there is any inclination towards music this too should not be ignored. Should a young boy or girl of this Sun-sign express a desire to learn to play an instrument, parents should follow this up if at all possible. *But*, the desire should come from the children themselves; Capricornian music lovers should of course take their children to concerts, encourage them to play records, and so on, but there is a difference between encouraging an interest and forcing it! To apply the same criteria to adults, a Capricorn of any age who feels suddenly tempted to turn off the record-player and pick up an instrument of some kind should do so. They should consider developing whatever talent they have perhaps by taking a series of lessons and experimenting with an inexpensive instrument. Later on perhaps they may become more adventurous and spend more time and money on lessons from a good teacher. They will find not only pleasure but considerable emotional relief in music.

Mercury at work

Check position of Mercury on pages 238–241

Mercury in Sagittarius

With Mercury in Sagittarius when you were born, you should be very good at conceiving large-scale schemes and planning projects. You may not be too good at coping with detail, however; if you find this a bore, try to get out of it—and involve yourself chiefly with planning, in the broadest sense of the word. You will be glad to accept challenges, and when someone puts a suggestion to you you will feel you must get on with the job immediately. Of all Capricornians, you will be the least cautious, and you are likely to get very excited when any chance to profit comes your way. You will look before you leap, however, despite your strong measure of optimism; but all in all, your attitude of mind is so positive and forward looking that you will get the best out of any situation that comes your way. You will probably have a powerful urge to study, and a considerable capacity to do so; you will be happy writing essays, attending lectures, and contributing as much as possible to your school or college life. You might tend to work unevenly, and maybe have a finger in too many pies, so try if you can to be a little more selective. Your enthusiasm will come through strong and clear when it comes to your examination papers.

Mercury in Capricorn

If Mercury was in Capricorn with the Sun when you were born, you will work carefully and well, if perhaps rather slowly. Your natural caution will regulate your pace of work, for you will hate to make careless mistakes which would mar your efficiency and lower your well-earned reputation for reliability and care. You will quite naturally check and cross-check every reference—you are not the sort to take short cuts in any area of life, least of all in work. Indeed, if any other area of the chart nudges you in that direction, ignore the temptation—short cuts will only cause you worry in the long run. For you, the slow way is in fact the quickest way. You may fit very well into a large firm, for this will give you security, and at the same time the opportunity to make excellent, steady progress up the ladder of promotion. Any area of big business that attracts you will be suitable—perhaps insurance or accountancy. Whatever your choice of career, your progress should be gradual rather than meteoric, and you should always have some long-term ambition in view. You will be a thorough and careful student. However, if you have provocative, unusual ideas, don't hesitate to come out with them. Examinations should be no problem—natural plodders usually do well at them.

Mercury in Aquarius

The bright idea, the original thought, will come more readily to you than to others in your Sun-sign, if you have Mercury in Aquarius. Both of these of course can be a tremendous asset. But, being a cautious Capricornian, you could sometimes tend to dismiss both or either as merely "silly" and discard or bury them. Take notice of your own flashes of originality. However, though your thought patterns can throw out the occasional startling new idea you can also tend to be extremely stubborn, and if *someone else* has the idea and wants to apply it to work *you* are developing, you could be rather quick to take against it, and resent what seems to you to be uncalled-for interference. Aquarius is an Air sign and Mercury in it really makes the most of the wings on his feet. Take off with him, be positive, think kindly of others' good ideas—like as not, you are the one that really sparked them off in the first place, so give them and yourself the credit! If you are a student, you could be considerably ahead of the rest of your group. Keep things that way. You could easily lead and influence opinion.

Venus: money and rapport

Check position of Venus on pages 242–245

Venus in Scorpio
Venus in Scorpio could make you very clever with money, and you may well have an instinctive flair for business. Having acquired capital, you could make it work well for you, and you may find investment in oil companies, mining and the wine trade interesting and rewarding. But remember that any emphasis on Scorpio will make you inclined to enjoy living well and you could spend pretty heavily at times. However, your Capricorn Sun could cloud Venus with a slight feeling of guilt over, say, a large restaurant bill, or some daring outfit in which you have invested; and this may restrain you somewhat! You will be well liked at work, but could secretly enjoy going in for a little "stirring"; be careful, especially, when others take you into their confidence, because while you're a natural at keeping secrets you may at times think you can help them by dropping hints in what seem to you to be the right places. Marvellous if you are right; ghastly if you are wrong—and you could make mistakes even with the best intentions. If you are an employer, you could be something of an enigma to your employees. If you are to get the best out of them you may need to keep them in the picture rather more than you think strictly necessary—though they will thoroughly enjoy staff parties!

Venus in Sagittarius
Venus in Sagittarius will make you sympathetic towards speculation, and could lend you a flair for it! But I use the word "speculation" in the broadest sense of the word, for you could enjoy taking financial risks by putting all you own on a horse, or by the tiniest little flutter. Your Capricorn Sun-sign should enable you to control any wildness in that area of your life, and you will have the good sense only to risk what you can afford to lose—and still enjoy the excitement of the race, the football results or the ups and downs of prices on the Stock Exchange or Wall Street. This is excellent for you. Because of your innate good sense, it should be possible for you to get reasonable returns from your various financial adventures. Areas in which you might like to invest are tin, publishing, the travel industry—but you won't want to feel restricted and will find your excitement in new and different fields. You are among the jolliest of Capricorns, with the ability to cheer and warm your colleagues when the pressure of work is on. If you employ others, you will be ready to listen to their ideas and give them plenty of opportunity to work on any which may be beneficial to either the firm or its workers.

Venus in Capricorn
Having Venus in Capricorn with the Sun will probably give you a very careful attitude towards money; you will not be very inclined to spend it flippantly and wastefully and you could perhaps actually enjoy it less than you deserve, having worked hard for it, after all! Maybe you should sometimes relax and be more prepared to spend money on luxuries. But don't lash out

too much on impressive dinner parties for people who are not among your nearest and dearest; they may be impressed, but your family and friends would appreciate all that splendour much more.

If you invest, it will be as well for you to put any spare cash into well-established firms that make high-quality products; these will appeal to you personally. Long-established businesses and insurance firms—in fact, the conventional avenues of investment—will suit you best. At work, you could be seen as something of a loner; while that makes you additionally interesting, it may distance you unduly at times, when you need help either personally or for the firm. If you are an employer, make sure your employees have access to you if and when they need it. Don't forget—you chose them, and their experience can help you in the long run.

Venus in Aquarius

Even with a sound, sensible Capricornian Sun, Venus in Aquarius could entice you to spend more than you should on the latest fashion—which actually could be just a little too trendy or gimmicky to suit you perfectly. Oh yes, you will make an impact in it; but not one you will be able to repeat, and you may have to spend even more to go one up on your star-spangled entrance! Because of this tendency and other rather similar ones (a liking for somewhat spectacular lamps or ultra-glamorous mirrors for your home, for instance) money could slip rather too easily through your fingers. Of course, you will enjoy all those splashes of exciting glamour, but it might be as well to get a little help when planning your finances. If the time comes when you are able to invest, you may like to acquire some shares in TV companies—manufacturers or retailers—or airlines, or aerospace industries. You may find those areas especially interesting and rewarding. At work you will be liked for your kindness and your willingness to help others. You may not like routine, but try and toe the line to avoid disruption to the rest of your department. If you are an employer, you will have plenty of forward-looking ideas and your friendliness and kindness will not go unappreciated. And you will always be sympathetic when someone needs time off for compassionate reasons.

Venus in Pisces

You have perhaps the most practical of Sun-signs—but Venus is by *no* means practical when in Pisces. While you will work hard and save well, it will only take the appearance of a lover who needs a little extra cash, or a charity which catches your imagination, and you will give it all away! Oh, it's all very philanthropic—and no doubt you are storing up manna in heaven—but you may sometimes have to call on Capricornian firmness to insist on a more practical line. Why not commit yourself to a regular savings scheme, so that a fixed sum is spirited away by the bank when your salary cheque is paid in, and you just cannot get at it? If you want to invest it instead, you could think about a shipping line, the fishing industry, or perhaps the boot and shoe trade; these areas may be interesting and rewarding for you. At work, you are really kind! You will wait for ages for hot pies at the nearest takeaway at lunchtime, you will do a colleague's baby-sitting when she is let down, and you will come to the rescue when things go wrong. For example you will be good at covering up skilfully when someone is not around when they should be and the boss starts asking awkward questions. If you are an employer, you will be popular with your employees, and at the same time be able to keep a reasonable distance from them when necessary.

Rising-signs and your career

First check your Rising-sign on pages 225–232

Note: Careers and the Midheaven
If you develop your interest in astrology, one of the first things which you will learn about, but which is outside the scope of this book, is the Midheaven. Roughly speaking, this is the sign immediately over your head when you were born. It is as important in your career, outward expression and identification with objectives in life as your Rising-sign is in your personality. To combine it with your Rising-sign is complicated and would be impossible in a book of this length; but, while I cannot help you to discover yours in this book, rest assured that I have borne the various possibilities in mind when writing the following paragraphs in relation to your choice of profession or job.

Capricorn with Aries rising
You have terrific drive and energy to use in your career, and will be very ambitious. You need emotional involvement in your work. Politics at local or national level, engineering and science are all suitable. You can work alone and should be successful, but beware of ruthlessness and use your pioneering spirit positively.

Capricorn with Taurus rising
You need financial security and would do well in banking, finance, or any *large* firm. Beauty culture and the luxury trades could suit you. You could be successful building up your own business. What about horticulture or agriculture? And you could find the technical side of TV interesting. Don't neglect any musical talent.

Capricorn with Gemini rising
You have a need to communicate, and could do well in the media. You probably sell well, and like a busy, lively working atmosphere. You might enjoy being a sports instructor or coach; physiotherapy could also suit you, and so might social service work or chemistry. Be careful not to make too many changes of direction.

Capricorn with Cancer rising
You are better working in partnership and directly with others rather than alone. You might do well as a nurse or working with small children, but you could have culinary talent and might enjoy the restaurant trade. History, antiques and library work are all possibilities. You are shrewd and have a good business sense.

Capricorn with Leo rising
You will probably want to be boss of any firm you join, for you need a job in which you can show off and use your organizational ability. You would make a good receptionist, model, or tour organizer. What about the computer industry? You could be very creative, so you might like to make and /or sell jewellery or clothes. Big business could appeal to you, and you have the capacity to make a lot of money.

Capricorn with Virgo rising
Your potential is excellent; you are very practical, and will even work *too* hard, flourishing in the Great Outdoors—though you would make a superb secretary or personal assistant. You may be interested in diet, vegetarianism, unconventional medicine. You would do well in the media—newspapers, magazines, radio.

194

Capricorn with Libra rising
You probably need to work with people, and enjoy pleasing them; you have natural tact and can cope with tricky situations, so working in the hotel trade, in hairdressing, or in a large store, in personnel, would suit you; so would the Foreign Service, or social work at a hospital.

Capricorn with Scorpio rising
You need a demanding career and your great determination will stand you in good stead for it. The medical profession, especially where research is concerned, or work that requires great care (in any area) would suit you. So would heavy engineering, though, or the oil or wine trades, or working in the field of psychiatry or psychology. Police detective work is a distinct possibility.

Capricorn with Sagittarius rising
Don't neglect any flair for languages you may have: you would make an excellent teacher or university lecturer, could enjoy publishing or the law, and may be attracted to the priesthood. Professional sport is a possibility, too, or a career as a vet. The travel industry could be rewarding—and don't neglect any literary talent!

Capricorn with Capricorn rising
You may do well as a real estate agent or an estate manager. You can cope with tough conditions, and the construction industry or road-building are also possibilities. You would make an excellent architect or town planner, and may be interested in geology or geography. What about industrial archaeology? Dentistry and osteopathy are strong possibilities.

Capricorn with Aquarius rising
You may feel you yearn for the bright lights and a glamorous career—the stage, or modelling. You are tough enough to cope with these. But you could have scientific ability, and might like to study astronomy or meteorology. What about working for an airline, or a large charity organization?

Capricorn with Pisces rising
Don't underestimate yourself! You would do well in a caring profession, perhaps nursing, or as a chiropodist. Perhaps you could also sell shoes. You may enjoy the literary scene, so what about publishing? Or photography? Shipping lines, the fishing industry, the Navy are all possibilities.

Aquarius

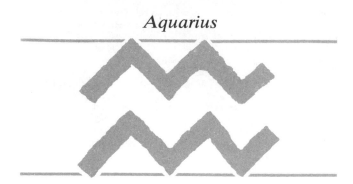

Positive
Ruling planet: Uranus (ancient ruler, Saturn)
Triplicity or element: air
Quadruplicity or quality: fixed
Colour: turquoise
Gemstone: aquamarine
Metal: aluminium
Flowers: orchid, golden rain
Trees: fruit trees in general
Herbs and spices: those with a sharp or unusual flavour
Foodstuffs: foods which preserve well: dried fruits. Food which can be deep-frozen
Animals: large birds with long-flight ability
Countries: U.S.S.R., Sweden
Cities: Moscow, Salzburg, Hamburg, Leningrad

There is no doubt that Aquarius is the individualist of the Zodiac. Tell two Aquarians the characteristics of their sign, and neither will agree to having *any* of them—which says a great deal about Aquarian perversity!

Aquarians may well agree that they are the leaders of their own generation, but conversely (a word needed a lot when describing Aquarians) they are often very rigid in their opinions, and once these are fixed, generally in youth, there has to be a terrific effort to change them in maturity. Friends of Aquarians who feel that their once-trendy acquaintances may need just a little encouragement to move with the times are probably right. While they are often emotionally cool, Aquarians are marvellous at doing good turns, and an Aquarian friend really is a friend, happy to cope with others' difficulties, and always ready to take practical action when needed.

It is very often the case that an established lifestyle is of above-average importance to an Aquarian—so much so that they will delay commitment to an emotional relationship or marriage. They love to feel free, and this can be a source of conflict when they are in love. There is a terrifically romantic streak in them, and they themselves usually have something of the glamour of a film star—beautiful but distant.

Aquarian children are usually pretty self-contained, but parents may need to tolerate an above-average involvement with current "idols".

Aquarian body-areas are the ankles: circulation too is ruled by Aquarius, so Aquarians must keep really warm in cold weather, in spite of the fact that they usually enjoy it.

Aquarius in friendship, love and marriage

The most independent of all Zodiac types, you're also the individualist among them, so it is unlikely that you will have fallen for the very common theory that one sign does or doesn't "go with" another. But you may like to know how it arose, so that you can respond if anyone ever puts it to you.

Basically, the theory (disproportionately put about in popular magazines and newspaper articles) relates to the elements (see page 75), and the fact that each sign is placed under one of four headings. Aquarius, for instance, is an Air sign, so it is said that you will get on well with the other Air signs, Gemini and Libra. The Fire signs, Aries, Leo and Sagittarius, are also said to be compatible with Aquarius, while the Earth signs (Taurus, Virgo and Capricorn) and the Water signs (Cancer, Scorpio and Pisces) are just simply said to be "no good" for you!

This is obviously silly: you are not basically incompatible with half the population of the world! But there is a grain of truth in the theory, to the extent that one usually feels immediately at ease with someone of the same element as oneself. However, the thing to remember is that there is more to astrology than the Sun-sign. You may for instance have Mercury or Venus in Pisces, and either of those planets could help to ease tension which the incompatible elements of the Piscean and Aquarian Sun-signs might throw up! So it would be silly and sad to stifle a developing relationship because of such a superficial knowledge of astrology.

The formation of emotional relationships can be tricky for Sun-sign Aquarians, because most develop an extremely independent lifestyle which really suits them; and their need for independence can often come before the need to share life with a partner. Don't allow yourself to be committed to a relationship before you feel ready for it; and don't worry if you seem to be retaining your independence longer than most people.

With this in mind, you will see that it is vital that you take no notice of the generalizations based on the popular Sun-sign notion of astrology. Remember that real pronouncements can only be made on the basis of fully-calculated birth-charts (the comparison of which is known as *synastry*). Even after looking at all the ingredients of a pair of charts, no astrologer would go so far as to say that a couple should end—or for that matter further develop—a relationship. That is a matter for them, and there will be other factors to consider than the astrological ones. But an astrologer can point out areas of compatibility and incompatibility, so the two people concerned can learn to make the necessary allowances. Your partner, for instance, will have to learn to respect your independent spirit.

I have found that relationships which stand a good chance of permanence and real fulfilment are often based on the emphases of polar or opposite signs of the Zodiac in the two charts concerned (for a list of polar signs, see page 75). Your Aquarius Sun-sign could for instance work very well indeed with someone with Leo rising. Or someone whose Sun-sign is opposite your Rising-sign would make an interesting partner. The sign the Moon is in is also very important, and that too can work by polarity. Uranus, though usually considered a "generation" influence, will have a personal effect on your chart, because it is the planet which rules your Sun-sign, and must be carefully considered when assessing your chart and that of a partner.

You see, then, that there is a very great difference between the simple assessment of the Sun-signs and a complete piece of synastry. Why not take your own astrological studies much further? Interestingly, many Sun-sign Aquarians make successful astrologers. And that takes us right back to the basic truths that are undoubtedly to be found in Sun-sign characteristics, but which should not be taken too seriously. Where all relationships are concerned, nothing can beat a close examination of the complete birth-charts.

Aquarian friendships

I think it is agreed among astrologers that Aquarians figure highly on the list of the "best friends" of the Zodiac. They have an open willingness to help, and are always ready to show interest and to listen to what one is saying. The willingness to help is interesting as it is at its purest in the Aquarian. The help will be offered not for sentimental reasons, nor on account of gushing emotion, nor even pity as such, but simply because it seems to be the logical and proper reaction. Aquarians have a powerful humanitarian streak and many of them find satisfaction in community work, or some charitable cause. On a more personal level, one gets the lively "aunt" or "uncle" who will help out weary parents by taking the children on an outing. Typically of Aquarius, that outing will not only be very original and entertaining, but probably also highly educational, and will provoke new interests in the children. Aquarians are never afraid to speak out, to make helpful suggestions and carry them out. Other people are usually happier for their actions.

You are, then, a good and faithful friend, and will maintain ties of friendship over many years. You are also capable of picking up the threads of a friendship after long separation.

But your Aquarian need for independence is never far away, and your friends may be more aware of this element of your personality than you think. It will distance you from them to a certain extent, though you may find this difficult to believe. Friends will see you as a very private person indeed. This is not necessarily a bad thing, and certainly nothing to take offence at: but remember that the time may come when you will need your friends' help and you should not be afraid to ask for it. Any decision not to invoke the aid of your friends when in real need is not so much Aquarian independence as Aquarian stubbornness. Incidentally you would be a useful member of any club or society, doing a great deal for it, and thoroughly enjoying the companionship of those who share a common interest. If you become chairman or president, your impartiality in committee would be admired. You would also cope competently with any dramas that might crop up.

Aquarius in love

The stars really shine for the Aquarian in love. You seem immediately to become more glamorous than ever and on the dreariest of November days the Sun will shine and the spring flowers burst open—if only inside your head.

Enjoy the experience—because when you have time for second thoughts you may drag yourself down to earth and begin to analyse your emotions. Do you really want to change your lifestyle and become involved in an emotional relationship that will tie you to one person? Will you be able to cope with continual compromise, thinking continually in terms of your "other half" and sharing your life at all levels with one partner? Of course, if you are really in love, you will be eager to do just that—but your need for independence is so strong that it would take a real flood of emotion and passion to enable you to give your all to a lover.

In most cases, the result will actually be a careful compromise. The lover will recognize that you are an independent, freedom-loving type, and will accept this as part of your personality. You will be able to go on taking pleasure in an interest or pursuing a career which may have no part in your partner's life. But there will be sticky moments as a result of this: compromise of this sort is not easy for anyone, not even for an Aquarian. If you feel that it will not be possible for you to adjust to the needs of another person, or to shape your life so that they can feel they play a proper part in it, maybe you should reconsider the whole relationship.

It is important that any partner of yours should have a good mind and interests with which you can sympathize and which you can encourage. You need not share every interest, but common ground helps rapport on a day-to-day level and can be as important as a sensitive and thorough understanding of each other's personality when it comes to a deep personal relationship.

Your sense of drama is pretty strong, and this will help to make special occasions really memorable. Your lover will be courted in the right atmosphere, appropriate yet excitingly "different". This colourful and entertaining talent for heightening a sense of occasion will help you to enjoy your love-life, and you should remember to do just that. Don't rebuke yourself for occasionally being sentimental and romantic, rather allow yourself to be carried along for a change. In many ways your Aquarian characteristics underline the need to allow your emotions freedom of expression, so don't make unnecessary sacrifices in this sphere of your life. Don't let a reluctance to change your way of life inhibit you.

Aquarius in marriage

The married or committed Aquarian makes for an extremely faithful partner, but you are most unlikely to enter marriage or any long-term relationship without fully weighing up the situation and deciding whether you want to lose your independence.

This kind of care and respect for your lover is something quite special. You may well joke about this in casual conversation, but deep down you will thoroughly respect your partner's principles, however different they may be from your own. You will also be very conscious of them as a person, and never be likely to think of any lover as an object that is "owned".

As is stated elsewhere in this book, the influence of the planet Venus has a strong say in your reaction in partnership and its position will colour your attitude. But basically, while Aquarian reactions and needs will vary greatly from person to person depending upon the position of Venus and to some extent of Mars, all the elements mentioned are of prime importance to you in your partnership.

It is very important to you to keep your individuality—not to lose your identity within a marriage. If you are a woman, it may be that you will have to sacrifice your satisfying and successful career for several years while you fulfil the role of mother. It is important that you should be able to accept that role without bitterness. Just how difficult it will be for you to accept it is basically a matter of personality: but as soon as possible, and certainly the moment the children are off to school, you should try to rebuild your career in the time you have available. It will be as well for you, even when the children are very young, to set aside a few hours a week during which you can get away from the house to perhaps an evening class or study group. It is important for you to have some such means of involving yourself intensively in something that has absolutely no bearing on your marriage and family.

This kind of problem may be less relevant to men, who in general still do not have to interrupt their career unduly or make similar sacrifices for the sake of their children or even for the sake of their wives. But the Aquarian husband and father could well be an exception. If he recognizes his wife's potential, he is very likely to be the one to give up his career temporarily to look after the children.

The Aquarian attitude to children is an admirable and splendid one. If you are an Aquarian parent you will not find it at all difficult to keep your children's minds alert and active. They will not crouch square-eyed in front of the television at all hours of the day and night. In your house books will be read and models made, to say nothing of the lively conversation that will keep them stimulated. In their spare time they will be Brownies or Scouts or keen members of some local drama group. In fact almost their busiest time will be after school! But, while on the subject of children, remember my comments elsewhere about you tending to become a little set in your opinions as you grow older. Many Aquarians find that there is no generation gap between them and their children. But sometimes the "fixed" quality of the sign leads to a hardening of outlook that can put the Aquarian out of sympathy with the young.

Aquarian careers and money matters

When assessing the Aquarian potential in careers and financial ability we must consider not only the psychological motivation and mode of expression attributed to Aquarius but also the thinking processes of Mercury, and how these two factors combined can be best used in both areas. Then there is the influence of Venus, a planet as strongly related to finance and possessions as to relationships. The latter aspect is also important in this sphere as it will affect how a person will get on with colleagues, in business partnerships, and so on. Mars may well give some hint as to the direction of energy and will most certainly influence the physical element—the drive and energy put into the day's work. As we shall see, the influence of the combined Sun- and Rising-sign is interesting and very personal: but if your birth-time is not available and you cannot find out your Rising-sign, do not be too disappointed; you should be able to glean plenty of information about this sphere of your life from the more general paragraphs.

The Aquarians' approach to their career is similar to their approach to other areas of their lives, and it can be summarized in one word: originality. Aquarians are of course found in all walks of life, just as are people of every Sun-sign. But to every job they take, they bring a special, individual quality and a distinctly personal approach.

Like most of us, they like to know exactly what is expected of them before getting on with the job in hand. At the same time they will want to do their work in their own individual way, and it is advisable for anyone supervising an Aquarian to keep as low a profile as possible, for Aquarians always achieve their best results without interference in their working methods. They hate having someone looking over their shoulder or giving unnecessary advice. Allowed a free rein, they will be excellent and reliable workers. Their originality and flair will contribute much to any enterprise. But if they are told that "it has never been done that way before" their reaction may well be to reject the whole task out of hand.

201

Of course Aquarians, like everyone else, will sometimes find themselves faced with boring, routine work. In such a situation their need for freedom and independence of spirit does not prevent them from buckling down and bringing enthusiasm to even the dullest task. This adaptability and willingness is a great advantage to them and helps in their advancement, whatever their career.

Aquarians should not waste their capacity for conceiving ideas in relation to their work. They should think them through properly and put them to their employers, for they have a talent for invention and may well come up with some excellent suggestions. They should apply themselves to thinking how work can be made quicker, more efficient and more interesting. If they are working, say, on a factory assembly line with no outlet for their inventiveness, they might do as well to turn their attention to the social life of their firm. They would find a great deal of satisfaction discovering common areas of interest among their workmates and setting up societies and clubs. Alternatively they might put their energies into union affairs and become hard-working shop-stewards. Such activities greatly enliven their working days. Often when a human problem is involved the Aquarian is there to help, whether by visiting a sick colleague in hospital or making sure that a retired employee is not forgotten.

Aquarians are not usually too concerned about the atmosphere in which they work. They can concentrate in a noisy room, and are good at shutting off their minds from any squabbles or arguments going on in the office. If promotion comes to them they will accept it with pleasure, and usually with the conviction that they can handle any additional responsibility. If someone behaves offensively to them Aquarians tend to rise above any personal feelings of injury and bide their time until everything is forgiven and forgotten, or the conflict is resolved in some other way.

Aquarians usually hate to waste time on any form of petty distraction from the job in hand. They will enjoy their coffee-breaks or business luncheons, but they will be equally happy to fill the entire day with work.

Aquarians tend to stand out in a crowd, and when the crowd is a collection of other workers in the same team the ability to shine and catch the eye of superiors will be even more pronounced. This can be something of a surprise to the individual Aquarian concerned, and he or she will react with honest amazement when someone says: "Of course we knew *you* would make it—you are *different!*" As the Aquarian sees it, he or she has just been getting on with the job, not interfering with or taking advantage of anyone else. What is it that prompts other people to notice them? Astrologers would say that it is a matter of the basic qualities of the Sun-sign and the influence of Uranus and the other planets. It is not easy to describe this to laymen, but as an example, consider an Aquarian who is a teacher. He or she will get pupils through the recommended syllabus on time to prepare them for examinations, but it will be the after-school talks and discussions and excursions that will be remembered by those pupils for the rest of their lives. In fiction, Muriel Spark's schoolmistress in *The Prime of Miss Jean Brodie* is, I think, the most quintessentially Aquarian character I have come across. She embodies not only the virtues but also the faults of the sign. Any Aquarian who reads the book will find plenty to identify with in this character, and will learn quite a lot about Aquarius without the bother of delving into astrological textbooks.

Mercury at work

Check position of Mercury on pages 238–241

Mercury in Capricorn

If Mercury was in Capricorn when you were born you are among the most conscientious of all Sun-sign Aquarians. You have great determination, high ambition, and a strong need to achieve your objectives. You are probably something of a plodder, and you may have developed rather more slowly than average over the years. Though you may never have reached the top of your class at school, you could well have distinct mathematical and scientific ability. If you are artistically inclined music could be your forte. You can cope with discipline, and security will be of greater importance to you in your career than to most Aquarians. You are a serious thinker, forming your opinions with great care. You can be attracted to the unconventional (because of your Aquarian Sun), but—contradictory though this may sound—your Mercury in Capricorn can also give you a sneaking sympathy for strictly conventional attitudes. So you might build a successful career within the structure of a large company or perhaps in some branch of government service. But you will probably contrive to take an independent line as far as the confines of your profession allow.

If you are a student you will work well and steadily and should be able to stick to study schedules and avoid distractions. Don't suppress your native originality when writing essays or answering examination questions that do not demand a strictly factual approach.

Mercury in Aquarius

If Mercury was in Aquarius with the Sun when you were born, you should give yourself plenty of opportunity to express your originality in your work. You may well have a brilliant mind and enjoy flashes of inspiration, and it is important that your mental faculties should be given plenty of scope in your work. It may be that some rather specialized subject will appeal to you. Archaeology would be a possible choice. Or you might go in for some challenging branch of science or technology such as radio astronomy or microprocessors. So you might in due course find yourself in a remote corner of an important university, exploring an original and interesting field of study and getting considerable satisfaction from it.

You could tend to be rather dogmatic, opinionated and fixed in your ideas. Be a little careful about that, for you could tend to overlook important new developments in your field and thus hamper your own progress. You might enjoy applying technical knowledge in a somewhat glamorous field, perhaps as a chemist concerned with the development of new beauty products—though you would probably be fiercely opposed to the use of animals to test them. No matter what you eventually decide to do, remember that it is important to exercise your excellent mind.

At college you may tend to study rather erratically, and it could be difficult for you to discipline yourself to follow a steady routine. Try to do so, otherwise your health could be affected by working all night at examination time.

Mercury in Pisces

With Mercury in Pisces, you will be among the most humanitarian of Aquarians. So you could do extremely well in medicine or in one of the caring professions. You will feel a strong need to combat social injustice and lighten other people's burdens.

You may sometimes find it difficult to marshal your thoughts clearly and precisely. Forgetfulness is a characteristic of Mercury in Pisces, and it could affect you when you are working under pressure. You will not find it too easy to cope with a really rigid discipline, but if you find yourself working flat out for a hard taskmaster, try to be calm and practical. Make a list of everything you have to do and work through the list, allowing yourself plenty of time, but sticking carefully to a timetable. If you are working within a freer ambience, use your imagination and intuition to anticipate jobs, and keep on schedule in that way. If you are at all creative, don't neglect to develop your imagination. You might discover a flair for writing stories, possibly with a rather weird and sinister touch. Your kindness and sympathy are important factors, and you would be good at counselling or at working with educationally subnormal or handicapped children.

If you are still a student, try to arrange all your rough notes into some kind of order and remember to finish essays on time. You may find revision very boring and be impatient to widen your horizons in your subject. But for examinations try to keep your mind focused on specific requirements.

Venus: money and rapport

Check position of Venus on pages 242–245

Venus in Sagittarius
Venus in Sagittarius will give you an extremely adventurous attitude to money. You will enjoy your work and the process of earning an income. You will also enjoy spending what you have earned! You could have a flair for speculation and will be attracted to seductive financial propositions. But try to develop a little more caution than you may naturally have, otherwise you could find that your enthusiasm gets the better of your good sense, especially if you like the person who is trying to sell a project to you. You are likely to enjoy games of chance, and might be a regular gambler in lotteries or horse-racing. Try not to put too much money into these activities or into more businesslike speculations. Products with a tin component might be a profitable area for investment; so might publishing or the travel industry. At work you will be capable of cheering people up and will find yourself extremely popular among colleagues. You will be good at organizing outings and other social activities. You are likely to be the one to entertain overseas buyers, since you have a gift for languages.

As an employer, you will be able to listen sympathetically to your employees and show a genuine interest in what they have to say about the running of the business. Never neglect overseas contacts or the export trade—your products might be more successful abroad than in your own country.

Venus in Capricorn
You are probably pretty careful with your money and enjoy watching it steadily grow in your bank account. Though it would be an exaggeration to call you miserly, you could be described as perhaps a little overcareful with your money. It might be a good idea to remind yourself occasionally that, since you work hard to earn your money, you deserve to enjoy it a bit! The best types of investment for you are those with a low risk, though of course these may have a lower yield than more

risky stocks. Go for security in the way you use your capital, and then you can rest assured that your money is safe but at the same time the income from it is not falling irretrievably behind the rate of inflation. Property may be the very best investment of all in your case. You like the idea of steady progress towards a substantial objective—and what better objective than the ownership of a beautiful home?

At work your colleagues may see you as something of a loner. You may give the impression that you keep yourself to yourself rather too much. Though no doubt you will be friendly enough when approached, there is a tendency for you to keep your distance rather more than many of your Sun-sign.

If you are an employer, try not to allow yourself to become a remote figure in the upstairs office. That kind of distance between you and the work-force could undermine the respect and loyalty that they will otherwise be happy to give you. Try consciously to get a little closer to your employees. When human problems arise, you will find it easy to do this, for you are good at listening and giving practical help.

Venus in Aquarius

You could be strongly attracted by glamour and might be tempted to spend quite a lot of money on attractive accessories for your home, such as mirrors and lamps. Consequently money might slip rather too easily through your fingers during visits to favourite shops. Care is necessary if you are not to find yourself broke when the time comes to decide to go off on a winter sports holiday and you are looking for a means of investing in all the right gear. A basic savings scheme of some kind would be a good idea. The answer might be to have a part of your monthly pay-cheque paid into a deposit account the moment it arrives. On the other hand it might be profitable to you to invest perhaps in television or airlines. At work you will be friendly and helpful. You will be the one to lend a colleague an outfit when he or she has planned a big night out and has nothing suitable to wear. And when a complaint has to be made to the management you will be the first choice for the task. Your smile and natural charm will come to your assistance.

As an employer you will be amiable and friendly, with the happy knack of keeping your distance without appearing aloof.

Venus in Pisces

This combination will give you strong charitable impulses, for Venus in Pisces adds pity to your Aquarian humanitarian streak. When you are moved by human suffering, you will be quite capable of sending everything you have in the bank to some TV appeal. Find a strong financial arm to lean on: someone who will give you sound advice as freely as you are willing to part with most of your hard-earned cash. You may need quite a lot of guidance when it comes to finance. Your kindness is second to none, but however admirable that may be, charity should to some extent stay at home. Be charitable to yourself and your family too. A sound savings plan would be a good thing for you: why not ask your bank manager to advise you on one? With a little money to invest, you might profitably consider the fishing industry, shipping lines or the shoe trade. Be careful that you are not unduly imposed on at work: even as an executive you might find yourself making the coffee for your secretary and doing all sorts of jobs outside your main work. This willingness to help out will make you popular.

As an employer, you could be rather soft with employees. Try to make an effort to be more severe when, for example, someone is repeatedly late for work with no good reason.

Venus in Aries

You will work hard to make money, but you may not keep it for long! The trouble is that you will always be eager to spend it, not only on enjoying life but on making those you love happy. You are one of the enthusiastic types of Aquarian, and you could be tempted by get-rich-quick schemes if they are persuasively put to you. But you will always make quite sure that such schemes are going to be profitable for you and this will help you to avoid investing your money rashly. You are enterprising and could have business interests outside your main career. You could do well investing in heavy engineering, in road-building firms or in the motor industry, but it would also be a good idea to put your money into some steadily growing investment such as a good insurance policy.

At work you will be among the more adventurous of employees. You could tend to hurry too much, lacking patience with colleagues who move more slowly than you. Don't lose your temper when the office boy spills the coffee or brings it so slowly that it's cold by the time you get it. You work hard, and if you are an employer you will expect others to do the same.

Rising-signs and your career

First check your Rising-sign on pages 225–232

Note: Careers and the Midheaven

If you develop your interest in astrology one of the first things which you will learn about, but which is outside the scope of this book, is the Midheaven. Roughly speaking, this is the sign immediately over your head when you were born. It is as important in your career, outward expression and identification with objectives in life as your Rising-sign is in your personality. To combine it with your Rising-sign is complicated and would be impossible in a book of this length; but, while I cannot help you to discover yours in this book, rest assured that I have borne the various possibilities in mind when writing the following paragraphs in relation to your choice of profession or job.

Aquarius with Aries rising

You need a career with excitement and scope for the pioneering of new ideas and working methods. Routine work would bore you. You may be scientifically minded and could do well in research of some sort. You need to be emotionally involved in your work; go for something you really care about, not just a job that will bring an adequate income.

Aquarius with Taurus rising

You need a job that gives you financial security. Routine does not bother you, but you need to be emotionally involved in your work. You could do very well in architecture, surveying or town planning. If you are artistic, sculpture or music could be your métier. You could well have financial flair and good business sense. You might start your own firm.

Aquarius with Gemini rising

Telecommunications could be your area, or you might do well working on the technical side of television or radio. You are probably good at selling. You need work that brings you into contact with people, and keeps you busy and active. For example you might enjoy working as an airline steward or stewardess.

Aquarius with Cancer rising

You have a strong caring instinct which you should exploit in your work. You could do well in nursing, midwifery or as a kindergarten teacher. You might also make a marvellous chef. You have an interest in the past that could lead you to become a historian or an antique dealer. You are also drawn towards the sea and might enjoy being in the Navy or working for a private shipping line.

Aquarius with Leo rising
You need to show off a little in your work and would do well as a receptionist for an impressive firm. You would enjoy selling jewellery or high fashion. You could be creative, in which case you should work hard and develop your potential. If you see yourself as an actor or actress, give it a try, but also learn some other trade so you can earn a living while "resting". You can carry responsibility and are a good organizer.

Aquarius with Virgo rising
You may well be interested in matters of health and diet. You would make an excellent masseur or masseuse, and might perhaps be interested in unorthodox medicine. You could do very well in the media, working perhaps as a personal assistant or researcher. If you are a secretary, your boss is lucky, for you have the ability to work hard. Agriculture might also suit you.

Aquarius with Libra rising
You are diplomatic and could do well in the foreign service or in personnel work. You could also make an excellent beautician or hairdresser. You are best working in a team with other people—a lonely position is not right for you. If you start a business, go for a partnership. You also need a pleasant working atmosphere.

Aquarius with Scorpio rising
You have the capacity to work very hard as long as you are emotionally involved in your work. You also have an excellent business sense and drive a hard bargain. You might enjoy life in the armed forces, especially the Navy. Insurance and mine engineering could also attract you, and you might find a niche in the oil industry or the wine trade.

Aquarius with Sagittarius rising
You may love animals and could well end up as a vet. Don't neglect any ability for languages or literature. The publishing world or travel industry could attract you, and you would probably enjoy lecturing at college or university level. You might possibly go in for professional sport. Try not to make too many changes of direction, in spite of your versatility.

Aquarius with Capricorn rising
You might well be attracted to politics. If so, start at local government level and see how you get on. You might also like to become an osteopath, psychotherapist or dentist. You could also have considerable business acumen. You are ambitious and will get to the top whatever you do. You would do well working for a large organization.

Aquarius with Aquarius rising
Use your originality in your work, and aim to work hard and steadily. You might do well in the social services or the caring professions. You might be attracted to science (astronomy perhaps) or to working for an airline. You may need glamour, and you could make the grade as a model or in advertising.

Aquarius with Pisces rising
If you are creative, you might like to consider photography. Alternatively you would enjoy working for a charity organization, or as a nurse. You might do well working for a publisher, perhaps as a translator. You would be quite likely to make a talented dancer or skater. If so, keep practising! Whatever you do don't underestimate yourself: your potential is terrific.

Pisces

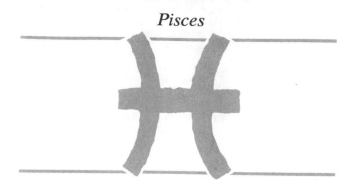

Negative
Ruling planet: Neptune (ancient ruler, Jupiter)
Triplicity or element: water
Quadruplicity or quality: mutable
Colour: soft sea-green
Gemstone: moonstone or bloodstone
Metal: platinum or tin
Flower: waterlily
Trees: willow, fig, trees that grow near water
Herbs and spices: saccharum, succory, lime (bass) flowers, mosses
Foodstuffs: cucumber, pumpkin, turnip, lettuce, melon
Animals: mammals that like water; fish of all kinds
Countries: Portugal, the Gobi and Sahara Deserts
Cities: Jerusalem, Warsaw, Seville, Alexandria, Santiago de Compostela, Bournemouth

All Pisceans have a specific Piscean look—by no means eternally sad, but suggesting that just below the surface there are tears waiting to flow: tears of positive emotion, happiness, love, and appreciation of any art form. Pisceans often underestimate themselves. They tell us they can't do a thing—when they have just created some glorious gown, thrown a fine pot, or produced a ravishing photograph they happened to take last summer but have only just got round to printing.

However, Pisceans, more than other members of the Zodiac, do need help. They have excellent potential, but must have encouragement and support to help them get the best out of it. They themselves give wonderful support to others, for example when friends are in need. They can at times be very deceptive, often for no good reason other than that it seemed at the time to be the line of least resistance, when in the long run the truth would have been much simpler. Should a Piscean have a drug or drink problem he or she will need more help to break the habit than most other signs, for there is always a tendency to pretend that the problem will solve itself of its own accord.

Pisceans fall in love very easily, and very deeply, but this sphere of their lives can be confusing—they make marvellous lovers, but learn the hard way from their mistakes.

Pisces children are very kind and gentle, but parents must not be too soft with them when dealing with the odd fib.

The Piscean body-area is the feet. They will run barefoot through the park, or live in exercise sandals or ballet shoes; or they may have a vast collection of exquisite footwear!

Pisces in friendship, love and marriage

It is a common assumption that Sun-sign Pisceans will tend to be more in harmony with those whose Sun-sign falls in the same "element" as their own—i.e., with Cancerians and Scorpios. Those whose Sun-signs are of the next element, Earth, are also reasonably compatible (Taureans, Virgoans and Capricorns); those of Fire signs (Ariens, Leos and Sagittarians) and Air signs (Geminians, Librans and Aquarians) are considered incompatible.

But in fact no astrologer would ever argue that a Sun-sign Piscean should not develop a friendship or relationship with an Aquarian just for that reason—because there are many other possible links which can cancel out a slightly negative feeling between the Sun-sign elements: you may have Venus in Aquarius, which will make for a good friendship with a Sun-sign Aquarian; or Venus in Aries, equally positive in a relationship with an Arien. Mars, too—which of course can be in any one of the 12 signs when one is born—can help you towards a very lively and satisfactory sexual relationship with someone of the same Mars-sign. So don't ever consider just the Sun-sign when you meet someone you fancy.

It's always fun to keep the characteristics of the Sun-signs in mind; it can be very amusing to watch for them, and to see how they match with or are different from those of your own Sun-sign. But it would be silly not to allow a friendship to develop because you think that someone with Sun in Libra is just never going to have the real strength to give you the support you feel you need. The Libran tendency to "gush", the slight suspicion that they may be saying rather more than they truly mean, may well be countered in other areas of their birth-chart, and there is no reason why you shouldn't find them true friends or lovers. Of course it's true that some Sun-signs are easier to get on with than others; but it would be completely unfair to let a superficial knowledge of Sun-sign astrology come between you and someone with what amateur astrologers might call an "unfavourable" Sun-sign to your own.

If you really work your way through this book, consulting the tables at the back of it, you will be able to gather enough astrological knowledge to have a much better chance of working out the possible strengths and weaknesses in a developing friendship or love affair.

Certainly it's convenient to start with what astrologers call the "triplicities" or "elements"—the division of the 12 signs into Fire, Air, Earth and Water groupings. But then, if you know your birth-time (and therefore your Rising-sign—see pages 225–232) you can take another important dimension into consideration. This is what we call "polarity"—a "polar" sign is the one directly opposite a particular Sun-sign, right across at the other side of the Zodiac. So the Piscean polar sign is Virgo—and it certainly seems to be true that a Piscean can be strongly attracted to a Virgoan he or she likes at first sight. But then again, you may strike up a memorable friendship or relationship with someone whose Sun-sign is the polar sign to *your* Rising-sign: that is, if your Rising-sign happens to be Gemini, a Sun-sign Sagittarian may come to mean much to you. Or there may be a strong pull between people whose two Rising-signs are polar opposites. To help you sort out these possibilities, there is a list of polarities on page 75.

I have done a great deal of work in the area of astrology known as *synastry*, which involves comparing the fully-calculated birth-charts of two people, in order to look at the delights or difficulties of friendship or partnership between them (you can also compare the charts of parents and children in this way, of course). I have always found that the best and most permanent relationships have been between people with important polarities working for them. There may be some allusion here to the well-known proverbial "attraction of opposites", which so often works to keep a relationship interesting and vital and alive. Between two people with a polarity of the kind I have mentioned, there invariably seems to be a strong rapport. Of course, as with any partnership, they do not always agree about everything; but one always seems able to follow the other's argument, and see an opposing point of view, even when a disagreement may be fundamental. This is important to the success of a long-term relationship.

This is, I must repeat, not the only factor that can make for long-term relationships. But polarity adds depth and tenacity. Other relationships between the birth-charts can help; but a good polarity is really excellent.

Piscean friendships

There is no doubt that you have what it takes to be a marvellous friend. You are willing to give a great deal of your time and energy to help your friends, to the point of becoming emotionally involved in their problems in the process. You listen sympathetically to their troubles, make them endless cups of coffee, go round to their place to cook meals for them when things go wrong, and so on, and on, and on. . . . You are capable of making many sacrifices for your friends and most of them will appreciate everything you do; but you could tend to be rather gullible at times, and should be extremely careful that you are not taken advantage of. For instance, you may tend to get your priorities wrong—it is marvellous to offer help where it is needed, but your employer might not take the same view if it means your coming late every day to the office. You should give your work at least as much attention as your friends.

What can your friends do in return? They should make a point of encouraging you in everything you do, for in that respect you need all you can get. To give them a fair chance to help you, you should encourage ties of friendship with people who are sympathetic to your own interests. For Pisceans a friendship bonded by common interests is particularly valuable, for you will find it easier to be close to someone who stands on the same ground as yourself. You will be less shy of showing such people your work, and they in turn can help to build your self-confidence. Friends who could not care less what you do when you are not with them tend to encourage you to remain in your shell and be reluctant to even mention your spare-time activities.

It may be that you should make a conscious effort to discipline yourself for your friends' sake. When asked out to dinner do make sure you have enough time to prepare. Don't leave the ironing to the last moment and don't forget to allow for the traffic jams. Otherwise you will arrive tense and nervous having kept your host and hostess waiting, and the dinner drying out in the oven. You are such a marvellous and kind friend that many of your faults will be excused, but some faults are more irritating than others—particularly to well-organized people who live on a tight schedule and cannot spend time waiting for you.

Pisces in love

Pisceans in love hear the sweep of lilting strings playing magical melodies in the background of every romantic scene. They will be on Cloud Nine. "Yes," they will tell their friends, "yes, this time is really *it*—at last I've found 'the one'." Do you recognize this in yourself? You probably know what I am talking about! But you may well have learned the hard way, where love is concerned. Your emotional level is so strong, so ready to spill over when a new lover is found, that once the floodgates are open it is extremely difficult for you to control your feelings. It is easy enough to throw open those gates when you are young, but as you grow older and have suffered a little in the name of love, you will tend to become rather more cautious. But it can be very difficult for you to take a practical line and be objective about your lovers: instinct and intuition will always try to rule you. Try to give yourself time to think clearly. If that means getting away on your own for a few days it will be better than making another mistake. I would strongly recommend a little quiet introspection on the subject. Absence makes the heart grow fonder, maybe, but there is also the saying, "Out of sight, out of mind." If you find it to be true you could save yourself a lot of difficulty and heartache.

You are capable of learning with experience how to control the emotional floodgates so that your really fine, caring qualities will come to the fore. Having gone through the mill, you will find yourself capable of expressing your feeling for a lover in just the way that will be most appreciated.

I think you should be careful about your tendency to make continual sacrifices for your lovers. One hears of the necessity for "give and take" in a partnership, but it is very easy for you—especially when the relationship is at an early stage—to be all give and no take. You will be the one willing to move to another town because your lover has to work there. You will be the one to give up a compelling interest or hobby because your lover demands more of your company. But that kind of attitude can become cloying. When you talk things over, your lover may not always want you to give way, may not always want you to give up your interests for them and would much rather you continued with them, even at the expense of a little less time together. So try to keep your own identity and don't get too submerged in a relationship.

I may have exaggerated these possibilities as far as you are concerned. But think about it. Unless other factors in your horoscope militate against it, it is quite likely that you will find yourself in the situation I have described. It is then that you need to be on the defensive.

Pisces in marriage

If it is important to keep your own identity in love, it is even more important in marriage. The less assertive Piscean woman can all too easily be so intent on considering her partner's needs that she just melts into his way of life. In extreme cases she will find herself becoming a mouthpiece for his views on important questions of the day—"Well, my husband always says. . . ." If you are slipping into that state of mind, it is high time to pull yourself up very sharply. Apart from anything else, you are not likely to be a very lively companion for your husband if you merely reflect his glory back at him all the time!

Tenderness and true affection are the dominant qualities of a married Piscean of either sex. In many ways you are the easiest of people to live with. Your partner may complain about your untidyness, your casual approach to life, but it is not that you are lazy—you just find it difficult to get organized. In your house routine bills may remain unpaid, but it is not wilful neglect—it is just that there are so many more interesting and rewarding things to do!

It can be the case that you sometimes project a little of the quality of your polar sign, Virgo, into your husband or wife, quite unsuspected by others. You may be overcritical of your spouse, showing more annoyance than is justified if the other half plods in dirty shoes over a newly washed floor. It is all rather petty, but *very* annoying for those on the receiving end. It is also uncharacteristic of your real Piscean self.

Children will remember Piscean parents with the greatest possible love and affection. The tendency to spoil children is always present, though in the best possible way—they will not get too many expensive toys, but they will have an abundance of love. It may be that your children simply can do nothing ill in your eyes. The disadvantage of this is that it can be a fearful shock when they do not do as well at school as you thought they would. You may give in too easily to them, allowing them to stay home with a convenient illness when there is a lesson for which they have not prepared. On the other hand a Piscean parent would very likely take the child (the headache or sore throat miraculously cured once the school bell had rung) off to the zoo or museum, where they will end up having learned far more than they would have learned at school that day!

But be careful that you do not store up difficulties for the child later in life by sapping his or her powers of self-discipline. Missing lessons may mean that they become more confused about the subject than they already are. But perhaps a well-balanced and well-loved human being is a greater benefit to humanity than a know-all! A Piscean is especially gifted at bringing up a child to become a fully "rounded" member of society and a delightful person.

Piscean careers and money matters

When assessing the Piscean potential in careers and financial ability we must consider not only the psychological motivation and mode of expression attributed to Pisces but also the thinking processes of Mercury, and how these two factors combined can be best used in both areas. Then there is the influence of Venus, a planet as strongly related to finance and possessions as to relationships. The latter aspect is also important in this sphere as it will affect how a person will get on with colleagues, in business partnerships, and so on. Mars may well give some hints as to the direction of energy and will most certainly influence the physical element—the drive and energy put into the day's work. As we shall see, the influence of the combined Sun and Rising-sign is interesting and very personal; but if your birth time is not available and you cannot find out your Rising-sign, do not be too disappointed; you should be able to glean plenty of information about this sphere of your life from the more general paragraphs.

Pisceans are a fascinating study when it comes to careers because their needs in this area tend to be very individual. They are not easily fitted into pigeonholes. All Pisceans should therefore do some careful thinking before choosing a career if they are to make the best of their lives.

I have mentioned earlier the Piscean sense of vocation. This can be very powerful. Pisceans also have a strong sense of dedication and are more capable than other Sun-sign types of concentrating on a specialized area of work.

There are many ways in which these qualities can be expressed, but the career that springs immediately to mind is nursing. The Piscean nurse will help patients not only by the careful use of skills acquired through training but also simply by being Piscean and bringing the best qualities of the sign into play. To the dedicated nurse his or her profession is not just a job performed for a salary but one in which the patients always come first.

Of course I would not go so far as to say that every Piscean man or woman has the right temperament or talents for nursing; for one thing, they will not all have the total dedication which is so indispensable for the role. But the majority of Pisceans will have something of the caring attitude which expresses itself most completely and fully in the nursing profession. Sometimes, too, Pisceans have a strong religious faith. Many become priests or nuns or else are attracted to some way of life with a priestly or monastic flavour. Another prominent Piscean concept is that of sacrifice. Every Piscean will be ready, even eager, to make sacrifices for what he or she believes in (as I have pointed out in the section on *Pisces in love*). But sacrifices can also be made for the career. A Piscean may, for instance, decide to sacrifice the whole idea of marriage for the sake of a career. An artist will, in another way, make sacrifices by putting the development of his art above the idea of a home and children. The Piscean dancer and singer will stubbornly endure the rough life of touring, in order to shape his or her career. The Piscean mother will, on the other hand, sacrifice her career to bear and bring up children. All this is part of the Piscean nature. And humanity benefits from it, directly or indirectly, by enjoying Piscean artistry and being cared for by warm-hearted Piscean doctors, nurses or mothers.

Of course one cannot expect all Pisceans to lead ideal lives of sacrifice and spectacular loving kindness! Many will get caught up in the rat-race. But Pisceans who do must realize (as they probably do instinctively) that that is really not the life for them. If circumstances force them into a noisy, tense working atmosphere where they have to work with people who are in every way different from them and perhaps insensitive to their finer feelings, they should look out for any alternative that could lead to a more sympathetic environment. Pisceans working in hostile conditions could do well to concentrate on progressing in their careers, not so much for the monetary advantages as because promotion will enable them to work in their own way and build their own quiet niche within the organization, far from the bustle of the general office. Early in a Piscean's career it should be impressed upon superiors that it pays to leave Pisceans to get on quietly with their work in their own way. Their superiors will find that it pays, for the Piscean's productivity and efficiency will greatly increase. If there is intrusive background noise or unnecessary rushing about in their vicinity their concentration will be broken and the gradual build-up of tension could be damaging.

I cannot stress too strongly the creative potential of most Pisceans. Unfortunately there are far too many cases in which it does not receive its fullest expression. Young Pisceans should try to avoid wasting it, and should seriously consider whether there is anything they deeply want to do while still at school. Don't immediately think of all the difficulties— whether parents can afford to support you in a long period of training, for instance. The important thing is to fix on some activity which *really* means something, which really cries out to be engaged in, however dissimilar it is from what everyone else may have chosen. Any real yearning for a particular career should be encouraged by every possible means. Anyone coming into contact with a young Piscean should try to be as positive as possible towards him or her, for criticism, which might have been a spur to other Sun-sign people, can deeply damage the self-confidence of a Piscean and could kill a very desirable ambition. If real encouragement is given, it is then up to the Piscean to overcome any difficulties which may stand in the way.

Mercury at work

Check position of Mercury on pages 238–241

Mercury in Aquarius

If Mercury was in Aquarius when you were born, you will be able to think quickly and produce plenty of original, bright ideas. You should do your best to exploit these, and should not be too modest to put them forward at meetings or at any other time. Your Piscean tendencies might otherwise get the better of you, leading you to dismiss your ideas as being "no good" before giving them a chance. Overcome this tendency if you can, as you have a lot to offer and may well have thought of some new line of approach which would not occur to other people. Equally you should try to remain open to the suggestions of others, to be flexible and receptive to their ideas about your proposals, for you may by nature resent other people's intervention. Try to recognize that others are often willing to offer you support and help, rather than being only concerned with criticism.

If your work is in a scientific vein, or if you are creative, your originality will stand you in good stead. Otherwise Pisces' humanitarianism and sympathy may colour your choice of career. If you are still a student, discipline yourself to regular study sessions, for you may naturally tend to work rather erratically and get unnecessarily tense and apprehensive as examinations approach.

Mercury in Pisces

Your heightened sympathy and understanding of human problems will play an important part in your career if Mercury was in Pisces with the Sun at the time of your birth. It is important for you to develop these qualities, which are very natural to you, and to make sure that they receive the fullest possible expression. Perhaps you will only exercise them as a sideline, maybe by helping with the welfare services of the firm you work for; on the other hand you may be drawn towards the caring professions, nursery education, or the care of animals. Your thinking processes will always be pre-eminently *caring*, and there may well be a voice within you which always asks "What can *I* do about it?" whenever a personal problem comes to your notice.

It will not be so good for you to be involved in work which relies too much on precision, or one in which you have to produce extremely neat and fastidious work very quickly. You may be much more at ease in a job which allows you some flexibility and diversification. You will probably have to discipline yourself not to be careless.

If you are a student, it is advisable for you to keep up a really steady pace of study throughout the term. Never give in when you think "I don't feel like doing that *today*." Revise constantly and work right up to the last minute. Never allow complacency to set in.

Mercury in Aries

Mercury in Aries may make you more assertive and more progressive than many of your fellow Pisceans. You will be more able to cope with the rigours of the rat-race, and be less likely to feel totally overwhelmed when pressure builds up. However, the sensitive, caring element of your personality still contributes much to your character, so that even when you have to cope with the toughest and most trying of colleagues you will intuitively understand them. Your stronger characteristics will, on the other hand, prevent you from being so overcome by your sympathy for their problems that you give too much ground in argument, or let business opportunities slip through your fingers. You may positively enjoy a good fight in matters of business and have what it takes to strike a firm, fair bargain. You can cope with competitiveness in any area, whether at work, in sport, or on the chessboard.

Decision making should cause you no problem, but, if you do find yourself hesitating about which line to take, you must simply reconcile yourself to taking your time. Quite a lot of abstract thought may have to go on before you suddenly realize precisely which line of action to take. In general you will not be wrong.

If you are still a student, you need regular, disciplined study periods each day but will also benefit from last-minute cramming—especially when you intuitively feel that you will be asked some specific questions about your subject. You will be able to think quickly under pressure, and a little tension is by no means a bad thing in your case.

Venus: money and rapport

Check position of Venus on pages 242–245

Venus in Capricorn
If you have Venus in Capricorn, you probably have a sensible, practical attitude towards your money. You realize that you can be something of a "soft touch" in many respects, so, to avoid getting into financial difficulty because of overkindness and generosity, you have probably arranged to contribute to some kind of savings scheme. This will force you to save regularly, so that there will be money available for travel or any important future expense. No matter how young you are it would be wise for you to begin to make provision for the day when you are ready to start looking for a house. Regular saving with this in mind might be an excellent idea for you.

You have considerable inner strength and your colleagues will speedily recognize the fact for, when they come to you with their problems, you will not only give them all your Piscean sympathy and support, but practical help as well. You will make sensible suggestions which will at once make them feel better, and show them a way through their most complex difficulties.

If you are an employer you might occasionally try to save money on your employees' comfort or welfare. Beware of false economy on cheap goods that will only wear out the quicker. You yourself love quality, so do your employees proud, as you would your home and family. Apart from this trait, you will understand and show great kindness to your staff.

Venus in Aquarius
With Venus in Aquarius, you will be very attracted to beautiful things, especially for use in your home. You will like very modern table-lamps and mirrors, attractive glassware, and so on. This could be a fatal attraction for you, for you could spend rather a lot of money on such things. Jewellery, too, could be a great fad of yours—however, it can be an excellent investment.

You may also find investment in television or airlines interesting and rewarding. Because you will be attracted to glamorous and expensive things, you should take professional advice when you have any extra money to dispose of, before it all too easily slips through your fingers.

At work your colleagues see you as having an independent streak, but they will not hesitate to turn to you when they want something done which requires the help of a good friend—the sharing of a work-load, or some favour outside working hours. You help because you see the position in a practical light, as well as because you are naturally kind and helpful. If you are an employer you will be a popular boss—friendly and kind when your employees have domestic problems, not to mention any difficulties in the day-to-day work of the firm.

Venus in Pisces

For goodness sake watch your money, if you have Venus in Pisces with the Sun! You are so kind and generous that, perhaps more than any other combination of signs, you are likely to give too much of it away, finding any charitable appeal absolutely irresistible! This is of course splendid and no doubt the world could do with a great many more people like you, but do be a little careful, because you could be too generous at times and one day there could be some emergency in your own life which could need a little extra cash. If your firm has a company savings scheme, or some kind of profit-sharing arrangement, do take part in it.

You could find shipping and the footwear industry rewarding and interesting for investment. But always be cautious and take professional advice, especially if someone puts what sounds like a fine money-making scheme to you. You are easily caught up in enthusiasm and could part with your money too readily, not only on yourself but in other ways, too. "Lend us a buck?" a workmate will say, and you will lend him ten, then remember that he has a large, growing family, and it hardly seems fair to ask for it back. . . .

Your kindness will not go unnoticed by your colleagues; they really should give you a generous gift when you retire! You do so much for them, in every possible way—you do anybody's dirty work, whatever your status. As an employer you will be the kindest of bosses, quite spoiling your employees in your concern for their welfare. Try not to be too soft, however, when coping with work-shy employees.

Venus in Aries

With Venus in Aries, you will enjoy making money, but will also spend it freely—on friends and lovers—for the sheer pleasure of it. You will never hesitate to find some excuse to throw an expensive party, for instance. Your personal motto may well be "Have it now—afford it later!" and your credit card accounts will all too often be at their limit. You may have to work very hard and force yourself to be more materialistic than you would really like, on account of these generous inclinations. But Venus is in an enterprising mood in Aries, so you may well be able to take on some money-making scheme in addition to your main job. You may find investment in engineering firms, or perhaps the car industry, worth while.

At work you show great kindness to your colleagues, giving them encouragement when they feel depressed. They will readily catch your very useful enthusiasm, so make sure you express it. If you are a boss, your enthusiasm for whatever you make or sell will stand you in good stead. You should have no problem in selling what you produce, and you will also see to it that the social life of your employees is lively.

Venus in Taurus

Of all Pisceans, you are the type for whom money and financial security matters the most. While in many ways you may seem not to care about them, the feeling of security you get from your possessions and from a healthy bank balance is really important to you, and will do a lot to stabilize you. It is important for you not have to worry about money, and you probably have little need to do so, for you have a strong element of caution and a lively enough business sense to manage your affairs well even on a small income. Do not let your generosity run away with you, however, when moved by someone else's predicament, or you may tend to give away or lend more money than you can really afford. Even if being cautious makes you feel a little guilty you should not forget this. You will do well to invest in agriculture, real estate or property. If that is not possible, put your savings into some reputable financial institution.

You are a steady, reliable worker, who does not mind a little overtime. You love good living, and you will be the one to buy cakes and goodies on a colleague's birthday or book the restaurant on more formal festive occasions. If you are an employer, you will be very keen to plan bonus and savings schemes for your workers, and your excellent business sense should do you proud.

Rising-signs and your career

First check your Rising-sign on pages 225–232

Note: Careers and the Midheaven
If you develop your interest in astrology, one of the first things which you will learn about, but which is outside the scope of this book, is the Midheaven. Roughly speaking, this is the sign immediately over your head when you were born. It is as important in your career, outward expression and identification with objectives in life as your Rising-sign is in your personality. To combine it with your Rising-sign is complicated and would be impossible in a book of this length; but, while I cannot help you to discover yours in this book, rest assured that I have borne the various possibilities in mind when writing the following paragraphs in relation to your choice of profession or job.

Pisces with Aries rising
While there are some powerful and assertive traits in your personality, you will still be at your best working behind the scenes, where your concentration is uninterrupted. You could do well in some specialist form of engineering (perhaps working in the pits at a race-track, or restoring old machines). Science, politics or professional sport could attract you. Alternatively you could cope with mentally retarded children or young delinquents.

Pisces with Taurus rising
You have good business sense and need to make money and feel secure; accountancy might suit you. You could enjoy architecture, town or garden planning, horticulture or agriculture. Don't neglect any musical talent, especially for singing. The beauty or cosmetic trades are a possibility and you might also have a flair for pottery or sculpture.

Pisces with Gemini rising
You need to be emotionally involved in your work, and are ambitious, with good powers of communication, so can probably sell well. The advertising trade or telecommunications could attract you. If you want to write, don't hesitate to have a go at it. You might also enjoy working in a large department store, a florist's, or as a speech therapist.

Pisces with Cancer rising
Plan your career very carefully. You really need much more than just any old job. You would probably do well in the catering and hotel trades and probably have a flair for cooking. If you are attracted to the medical profession, nursing would suit you and you could specialize in gynaecology. You would make a first-rate nursery school teacher.

Pisces with Leo rising
You are a natural boss, and should make excellent progress. You are probably very creative. If you want to train as an artist, or develop any skills as dancer or actor, then work hard at it. You have organizing ability and should take basic training in some more practical, down-to-earth job too. You might do well in the computer industry.

Pisces with Virgo rising
You work hard and make a marvellous secretary or personal assistant. You could be attracted to the media, so make a start in the typing pool at your local TV centre or radio station, and see what happens. Health foods, diet, physiotherapy and unorthodox medicine could also attract you. You would do well in any form of research.

Pisces with Libra rising
You should do very well in the beauty trade, preferably as a hair stylist. You would make a delightful receptionist, looking after the doctor *and* his patients! You should also be happy working for a cruise line or for the holiday trade. But try hard not to drift in your career.

Pisces with Scorpio rising
The medical profession, the mining industry, the wine trade—these could provide suitable work for you. You would also make a good analyst, detective or social-service worker. You probably need a colourful and demanding career and can cope with "difficult customers" in a quite remarkable way.

Pisces with Sagittarius rising
Languages could come easily to you, and you'd thoroughly enjoy the experience of working abroad for a time. You have the makings of a teacher, at your best working with older students rather than young children. You might be attracted to the law or to publishing, and may well have literary talent. Alternatively you could make the grade as a vet, and might well have a religious vocation.

Pisces with Capricorn rising
Politics at any level could attract you, and you wouldn't mind coping with a lonely and very responsible position. Foreign service is also a possibility. Don't neglect any musical talent. Insurance might be worth looking into as a career. Archaeology and mineralogy could fascinate you; you could also do well as a surveyor or real estate agent.

Pisces with Aquarius rising
No run-of-the-mill job would do for you. Try to find a niche in which you can express your originality. You could make the grade in fashion, perhaps in design or modelling, but you would have to work very hard. Astronomy could fascinate you, and the airlines and television trades are also suitable. What about the book trade?

Pisces with Pisces rising
You are probably very creative and have the makings of an excellent photographer, or might like to work on the technical side of the cinema or television industry. The caring professions could also suit you, and you may be attracted to a job which keeps you well behind the scenes. The shoe trade, or chiropody, are also possibilities.

Recognizing the signs

Many people have a natural talent for recognizing another person's Sun-sign. This is certainly possible (since one's image is usually allied to one's Sun-sign), but it is worth remembering that people can often look like their Rising-sign and that any planet that was *about* to rise at the time and place of their birth can subtly influence their appearance, giving them the look of the sign which that planet rules.

For instance, someone who was born at the time when the Moon was about to rise will have a Cancerian look. If at parties you are asked to suggest what someone's sign is, you will find the descriptions below useful. Experienced astrologers, should they guess incorrectly, will say; "In that case, you were born at *x* o'clock." This takes practice; but if you are wrong. I suggest you might say: "Well, I think you have an awfully strong . . .", and then name the ruling planet of the sign you think they resemble. Whether or not they understand the allusion you will usually be right, and it is an easy trick to study.

Aries

Ariens are not difficult to recognize. The glyph for the sign, ♈, can often physically be seen in the Arien's face, shown by the line of the eyebrows, usually fairly well arched, joining the line of the nose. The complexion is ruddy, and Ariens tan rather well. Men tend to baldness, and generally speaking the skull is seen to be rather round when this occurs. Ariens have a springing walk and a thrusting stride. They have a clear, pleasant and ringing laugh, and look good in casual clothes, particularly red sweaters.

Taurus

Quite often Taureans have curly hair that tends to fall over their foreheads, which are rather low. They have fairly short, thick necks, and can easily put on weight. Their ruling planet, Venus, very often bestows good looks and ample charm. They have somewhat deep-set eyes and a nice, low-pitched voice. Very often the women will tend to wear rather too many frills and floral designs, a large floppy bow or scarf around their necks. There's a hint of expensive formality in older Taureans, and the younger ones will probably buy the most expensive jeans on the market.

Gemini

The easiest way to recognize Geminians is by their walk. It is so jaunty and springing that they seem to travel vertically as much as horizontally! Geminis are usually very slim—they live on their nerves and are somewhat restless. "Quickness" could well be a keyword; it permeates their personality and their movement, action and conversation. They gesticulate more than most, irrespective of race. Gemini is also flirtatious, and you will soon get the message! They are pretty up-to-date in fashion and like a great variety of colours, especially yellows.

Cancer

Cancerians' faces are round, and their foreheads so smooth they shine almost like their ruling planet, the Moon. Very few Cancerians can take the Sun; their skins are so sensitive they turn a delicate shade of beetroot. They sometimes wear lovely, floating clothes, but all too often the overall effect is ruined by a slipping shoulderstrap, uneven hem or petticoat showing where it shouldn't. The men tend to wear *precisely* the wrong shirt, tie or shoes to match the rest of their outfit.

Leo

Leos usually have a lion's mane of hair, whatever their age or sex. They walk upright, making themselves appear taller than they really are. Leo women, also lion-like, have small waists. Both sexes have a look of the lion about their faces, which with practice you can easily recognize. They also have rather large, regal noses, which they tend to look down. Leos love jewellery, which is usually real rather than "junk". Their clothes are fashionable, glamorous and expensive. They like furs, but caring Leos who love animals now go for simulated fur rather than the real thing.

Virgo

Virgoans are seldom still; they move quickly about, breaking off in the middle of a conversation to help the hostess clear away empty glasses. They are superbly neat, and a physical characteristic that usually stamps them is a widow's peak of hair, nearly always present though sometimes disguised by the hair-style. Virgoans love small, floral patterns, spots and polka-dots, perhaps in navy blue and white. The girls sometimes favour a "country look" with hints of the Victorian children's book illustrations—always pretty, charming and very, very modest. The men will often wear a floral tie or shirt.

Libra

There is something of a fey look about the Libran face, as though an artist has drawn it and then gone over the sketch, delicately shading it with a soft, pale pencil. The hair is usually fine, and both sexes are good-looking and very charming. The women dress rather prettily, and often favour see-through fabrics. One give-away is that during conversation Librans will listen holding their heads first on one side and then the other.

Scorpio

An intensive expression and the ability to concentrate on every word you say will give you the most obvious clue to a Scorpio. The eyes are always piercing, and sometimes there is a weightiness to the body, though another Scorpio type is wiry, slim and active. Both types and sexes have interesting speaking voices. Often leather clothes are worn—and to Scorpio's advantage, since the sexiness of the sign is expressed in the overall image. The women look good in plunging necklines or generally exotic, dark, but not uncolourful clothes. The deep red connected with the sign is popular.

Sagittarius

Informality is generally the key to Sagittarius. There is an element of the "eternal student" about most of them which influences their image. Physically, they have strong bodies, usually fairly striking figures, and nearly always a wide-open, "intellectual" forehead and straight eyebrows. Men of the sign hate wearing ties, and when they have to, will take them off as soon as possible. They very often have beards—whether these are in or out of fashion. A lively enthusiasm is a striking feature of both sexes, as is a delightful flirtatious warmth, and a keenness to develop new relationships.

Capricorn

Capricorns are usually tall and slim, and may have a slight stoop. They have a dark expression, and nearly always in the men there are distinct lines running from the side of the nose to the corners of the mouth. Both sexes look their best in, and usually wear, dark colours—and the more formal the cut the better. Capricorn women favour a "little black dress" regardless of fashion, and usually have beautiful legs. Restraint is a good adjective for both sexes, and sometimes they will wear some quietly expensive piece of jewellery or accessory to complete a deceptively quiet image.

Aquarius

One physical characteristic nearly always present in Aquarians is droopy eyelids. The lids turn sharply downwards from about the middle of the eyes, so consistently that we can call these "Aquarian eyes". When Aquarians are young they are rather ahead of fashion; but they are not too inclined to move with the times as they grow older. However, they are usually interestingly dressed and glamorous—favouring pale colours like eau-de-nil. All ethnic groups will have paler than average skins and fine hair. Aquarians are friendly, talkative and original—but slightly distant. They walk upright and carry themselves with a good bearing.

Pisces

Pisceans often stand with their feet crossed, fish-like, and nearly always wear eccentric or very glamorous shoes or no shoes at all. Their eyes have a melting quality. The women of the sign can look marvellous in anything from a Paris original to a length of fabric into which they have just sewn themselves. Both sexes favour velvet or shiny fabrics. They can look very original, but sometimes their hair is a bit of a mess, in an attractive sort of way. The men often wear beards.

Glossary

Ascendant or Rising-sign   The sign crossing the eastern horizon at the time of birth.

Aspect   The angle formed between two planets as seen from the earth.

Benefics   The planets which, in traditional astrology, were thought to exert a good influence, namely the Sun, Moon, Jupiter and Venus. The "malefics", Saturn and Mars, were thought to exercise an evil influence. Today most astrologers consider that any planet can have either a good or bad effect depending on its placing and aspects.

Cardinal signs   See page 75.

Cusp   The dividing line between one sign and another.

Detriment   See rulerships.

Dignity   See exaltations.

Ecliptic   The path which the Sun appears to trace around the earth during the course of a year.

Elements   Fire, Earth, Air and Water. See page 75.

Ephemeris   A set of tables giving planetary positions for a particular year, used by astrologers in making the calculations for a horoscope.

Equinoxes   The points at which the ecliptic crosses the equator.

Exaltations   Each planet has a sign in which it is said to be "exalted", meaning that its influence will be strong and favourable. The opposite sign is referred to as the planet's "fall" and denotes weakness. The Sun is said to be exalted in Aries, the Moon in Taurus, Mercury in Virgo, Venus in Pisces, Mars in Capricorn, Jupiter in Cancer, and Saturn in Libra. There is disagreement among astrologers as to the exaltations of the three "new" planets. In the older terminology the word "dignified" was used instead of exalted.

Fixed signs   See page 75.

Friendly planets   Certain planets are said to be "friendly" to one another, whereas others are "inimical". For example, Venus and the Moon are friendly because the Moon rules Cancer, which is a Water sign, and the element Water complements the Earth element of Taurus, which is ruled by Venus.

Glyph   The traditional "shorthand" symbol used to represent a sign or planet.

Horoscope or birth-chart   A chart of the heavens drawn up for the time and place of the person's birth.

House   See solar chart.

Midheaven   The sign directly overhead at the time of birth.

Mutable signs   See page 75.

Natal   Relating to the time of birth. A planet's natal position is the one it occupies in the birth-chart.

Planet   One of the bodies of the solar system. In astrology the Sun and Moon are called planets.

Polar signs   Signs at opposite sides of the Zodiac to one another. See page 75.

Positive and negative signs   See page 75.

Progression A method of making predictions by symbolically moving the planets forward in the natal chart.

Rising-sign See Ascendant.

Rulerships Each sign is said to be "ruled" by a planet. The influence of a planet is particularly strong if it is placed in the sign over which it rules. The opposite sign in the Zodiac to the one which it rules is known as its "detriment". If a planet is in its detriment its influence is, by tradition, weak.

Sign One of the 12 divisions of the sky formerly corresponding to constellations.

Solar chart An astrological chart set up for sunrise for a person whose birth-time is unknown. Also the astrological chart used to work out "predictions" for any specific period. The chart is based on a system of 12 "houses", each governing a different sphere of everyday life, but only the Sun-signs are used. This system is used by astrological columnists. The houses also have an important bearing on the individual birth-chart.

Transit The present movement of a planet in the sky which brings it into relationship with another planet as placed in the birth-chart.

Zodiac The belt of sky through which the Sun appears to pass during the course of a year.

Astrological Societies

If you wish to know more about Astrology, or need a consultant astrologer, any of the following bodies will give you guidance:

American Federation of Astrologers Inc.,
PO Box 22040,
Tempe,
Arizona 85282,
U.S.A.

Astrological Association of Great Britain,
B.M. Astrology,
London WC1N 3XX,
England.
(Send S.A.E. or international reply coupon.)

Faculty of Astrological Studies,
Registrar: Geoffrey Hayward,
Hook Cottage,
Vines Cross,
Heathfield,
Sussex TN21 9EN,
England.

ISAR (International Society for Astrological Research),
PO Box 6874,
Torrance,
California 90504,
U.S.A.

Rome 41° 54′ N

time of day

am   noon   pm

12 1 2 3 4 5 6 7 8 9 10 11 12

ascendant

Dec Nov Oct Sep Aug Jul Jun May Apr Mar Feb Jan Dec

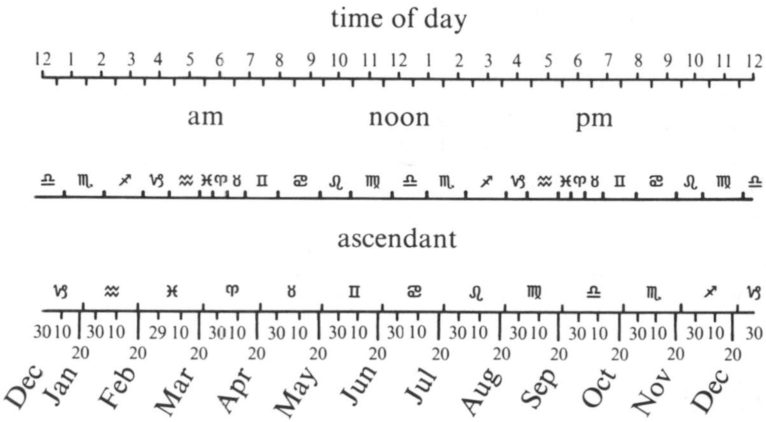

Barcelona 41°21′N
Boston, Mass. 42°18′N
Chicago 41°50′N
Detroit 42°22′N
Dubrovnik 42°39′N

Mukden 41°50′N
Oporto 41°8′N
Saragossa 41°39′N
Tashkent 41°7′N

Toronto 43° 40′ N

time of day

am   noon   pm

12 1 2 3 4 5 6 7 8 9 10 11 12

ascendant

Dec Nov Oct Sep Aug Jul Jun May Apr Mar Feb Jan Dec

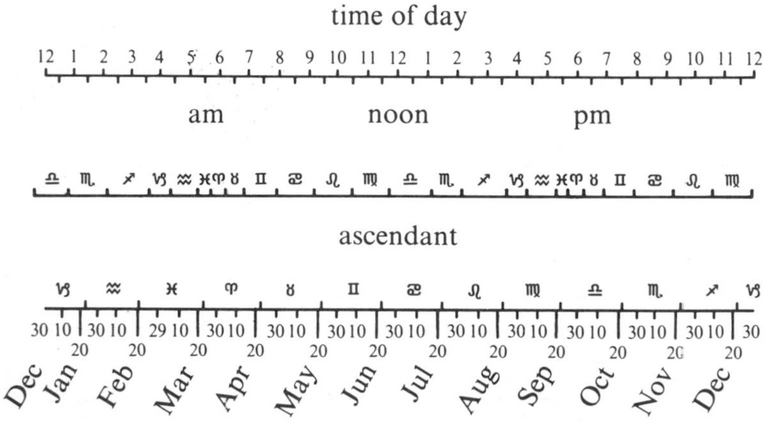

Belgrade 44°50′N
Bilbao 43°16′N
Boise 43°38′N
Bordeaux 44°50′N
Bucharest 44°27′N

Halifax, Canada 44°45′N
Marseilles 43°18′N
Milwaukee 43°9′N
Toulouse 43°37′N
Vladivostok 42°58′N

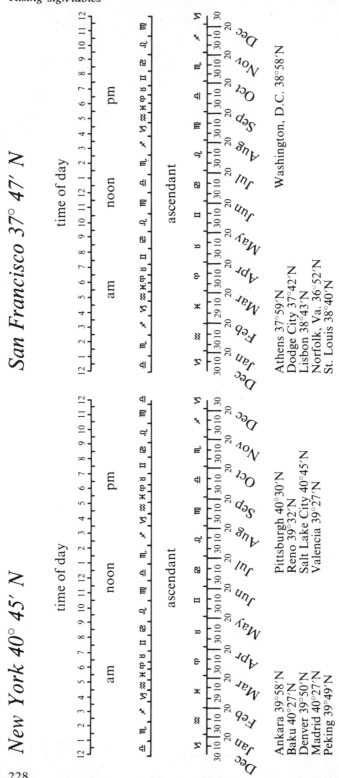

New York 40° 45′ N

San Francisco 37° 47′ N

Ankara 39°58′N
Baku 40°27′N
Denver 39°50′N
Madrid 40°27′N
Peking 39°49′N

Pittsburgh 40°30′N
Reno 39°32′N
Salt Lake City 40°45′N
Valencia 39°27′N

Athens 37°59′N
Dodge City 37°42′N
Lisbon 38°43′N
Norfolk, Va. 36°52′N
St. Louis 38°40′N

Washington, D.C. 38°58′N

Tokyo 35° 41′ N

New Orleans 29° 57′ N

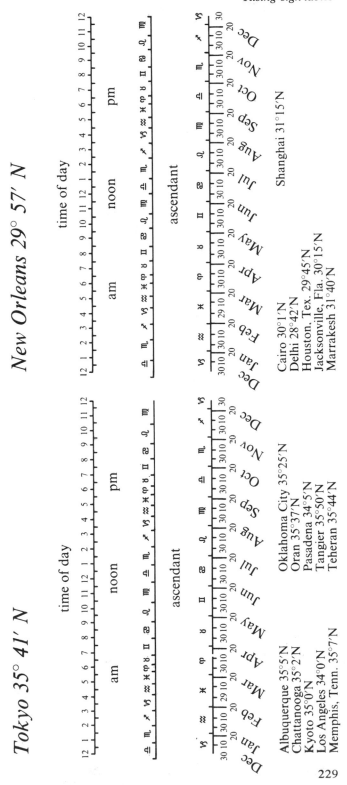

Shanghai 31°15′N

Cairo 30°1′N
Delhi 28°42′N
Houston, Tex. 29°45′N
Jacksonville, Fla. 30°15′N
Marrakesh 31°40′N

Oklahoma City 35°25′N
Oran 35°37′N
Pasadena 34°5′N
Tangier 35°50′N
Teheran 35°44′N

Albuquerque 35°5′N
Chattanooga 35°2′N
Kyoto 35°0′N
Los Angeles 34°0′N
Memphis, Tenn. 35°7′N

Mexico City 19° 26′ N

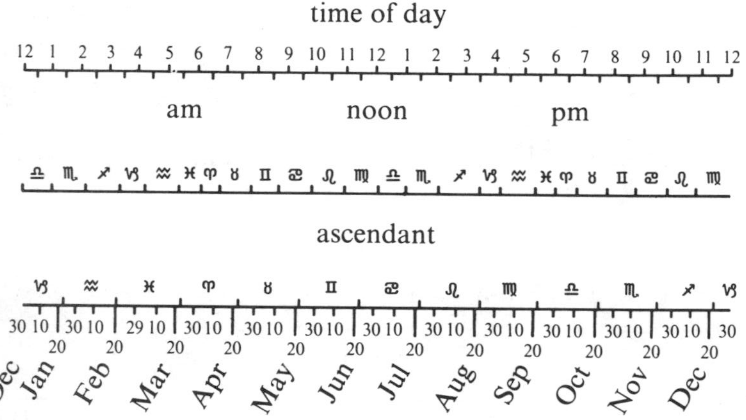

time of day

am   noon   pm

ascendant

Guadalajara 20°40′N
Haiphong 20°55′N
Mecca 21°30′N
Pachuca 20°10′N
Puebla, Mex. 19°0′N

Bombay 18° 55′ N

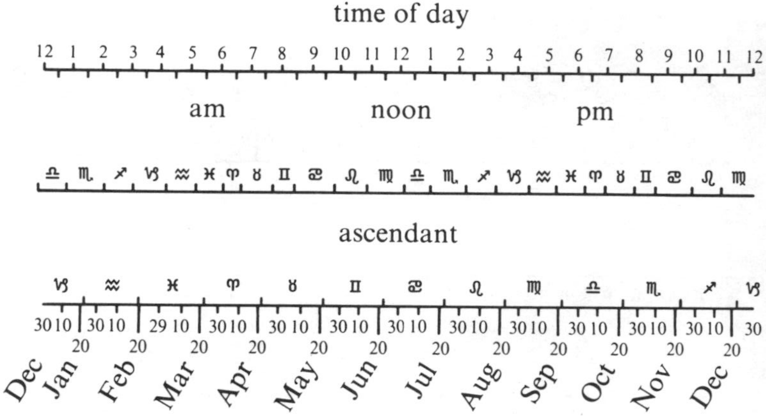

time of day

am   noon   pm

ascendant

Madras 13° 8′N

Asmara 15°19′N
Bangkok 13°45′N
Dakar 14°34′N
Guatemala City 14°40′N
Khartoum 15°31′N

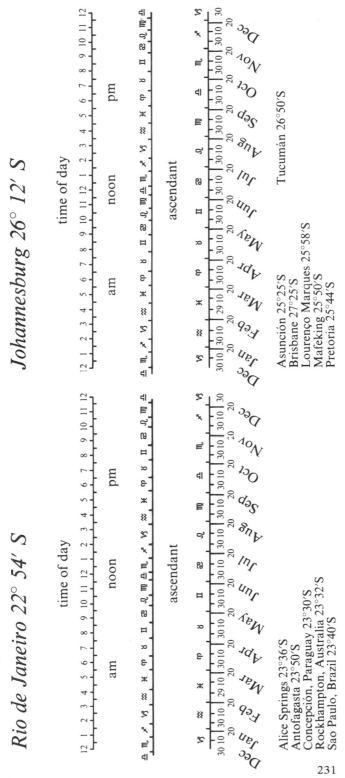

Rio de Janeiro 22° 54′ S

time of day

am   noon   pm

ascendant

Alice Springs 23°36′S
Antofagasta 23°50′S
Concepción, Paraguay 23°30′S
Rockhampton, Australia 23°32′S
Sao Paulo, Brazil 23°40′S

Johannesburg 26° 12′ S

time of day

am   noon   pm

ascendant

Tucumán 26°50′S

Asunción 25°25′S
Brisbane 27°25′S
Lourenço Marques 25°58′S
Mafeking 25°50′S
Pretoria 25°44′S

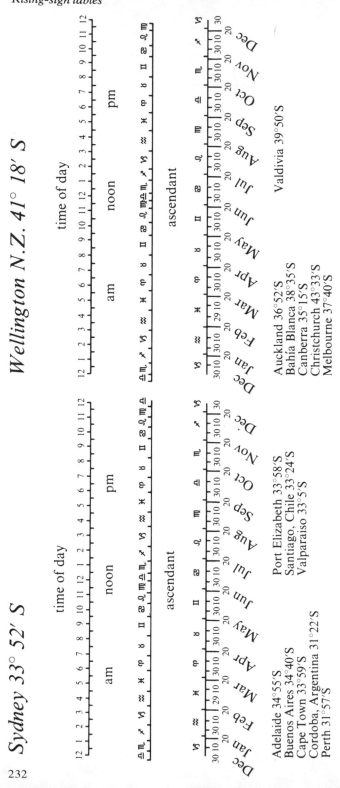

Sydney 33° 52' S

Wellington N.Z. 41° 18' S

Adelaide 34°55'S
Buenos Aires 34°40'S
Cape Town 33°59'S
Cordoba, Argentina 31°22'S
Perth 31°57'S

Port Elizabeth 33°58'S
Santiago, Chile 33°24'S
Valparaiso 33°5'S

Auckland 36°52'S
Bahía Blanca 38°35'S
Canberra 35°15'S
Christchurch 43°33'S
Melbourne 37°40'S

Valdivia 39°50'S

How to use the planetary tables

The tables on the following pages are designed to enable you to chart the positions of the planets by a simple procedure. In order to find the position of Mercury, Venus, Mars or Jupiter in your birth chart, first find your year of birth on the top line of the appropriate table and then your month of birth in the columns numbered 1 to 12 at the left-hand side of the page. Each set of figures shows which sign of the Zodiac the planet was in on the first day of each month and also any date during that month when it moved into another sign.

Suppose, for example, you wanted to find out the position of Venus on July 16, 1932. You would run your finger down the 1932 column until you reached a point opposite number 7. From the row of numbers and glyphs at that point you would see that Venus was in Cancer on the 1st, entered Gemini on the 14th and moved back into Cancer on the 28th. So on the 16th Venus was in Gemini.

The tables of Saturn, Uranus, Neptune and Pluto consist simply of a table of dates with the relevant Zodiac signs at the right-hand side.

Key to glyphs for the planets

☉ Sun	♃ Jupiter
☽ Moon	♄ Saturn
☿ Mercury	♅ Uranus
♀ Venus	♆ Neptune
♂ Mars	♇ Pluto

Key to glyphs for the signs of the Zodiac

♈ Aries	♎ Libra
♉ Taurus	♏ Scorpio
♊ Gemini	♐ Sagittarius
♋ Cancer	♑ Capricorn
♌ Leo	♒ Aquarius
♍ Virgo	♓ Pisces

How to find your Moon-sign

The Moon takes about two and a half days to travel through each sign of the Zodiac. Although its *exact* position at any given moment cannot be obtained without reference to an ephemeris (see *Glossary* page 223), it is possible to estimate the sign the Moon was in on the day when you were born. To do this, refer to the tables on the following pages. They will show you the sign in which the Moon was on the first day of every month from 1916 to 1980. First of all, make a note of the sign in which the Moon stood on the first day of the *month* of your birth. Then consult the table on this page, which lists the days of the month with a number against each: this shows the number of signs you have to count on through the Zodiac to reach that in which the Moon stood on the day of your birth.

Example One: To find the Moon-sign for someone born on October 10, 1936. First look up the Moon-sign for October 1, 1936. This was Aries (♈). Now look up the date—the 10th—in the *Moon table* printed here. Against it is the number four. So the Moon-sign we seek is Aries plus four signs: and we count Aries, Taurus, Gemini, Cancer—*Leo*. This subject will have Moon in Leo.

Sometimes you will have to count 'through' Pisces and start the Zodiac again in Aries, as in—

Example Two: To find the Moon-sign for someone born on March 21, 1943. First look up the Moon-sign for March 1, 1943. This was Sagittarius (♐). Now look up the date—the 21st—in the *Moon table* on this page. Against it is the number nine. So the Moon-sign we seek is Sagittarius plus nine signs: and we count Sagittarius, Capricorn, Aquarius, Pisces, Aries, Taurus, Gemini, Cancer, Leo—*Virgo*. This subject will have Moon in Virgo.

Moon table

Number of signs to be added for each day of the month

Day	ADD (signs)	Day	ADD (signs)
1	—	16	7
2	1	17	7
3	1	18	8
4	1	19	8
5	2	20	9
6	2	21	9
7	3	22	10
8	3	23	10
9	4	24	10
10	4	25	11
11	5	26	11
12	5	27	12
13	5	28	12
14	6	29	1
15	6	30	1
		31	2

Note

It must be remembered that by this method we cannot be absolutely sure of accuracy, so it is essential to read the characteristics of the previous and the following signs, and note the characteristics which are listed. Those with which you seem to have most in common will indicate your Moon-sign, if there is any doubt in your mind.

Moon-signs – first day of every month 1916–1938

	1916	1917	1918	1919	1920	1921	1922	1923	1924	1925	1926	1927	1928	1929	1930	1931	1932	1933	1934	1935	1936	1937	1938
1	♏	♎	♌	♑	♉	♍	♒	♊	♏	♎	♌	♐	♎	♍	♑	♉	♍	♓	♋	♏	♎	♌	♑
2	♑	♊	♍	♒	♋	♐	♎	♌	♐	♉	♍	♒	♊	♏	♓	♋	♐	♎	♌	♑	♉	♍	♒
3	♒	♊	♍	♒	♌	♐	♎	♌	♑	♊	♍	♒	♋	♏	♓	♋	♐	♉	♍	♑	♊	♍	♒
4	♓	♌	♐	♎	♍	♑	♉	♍	♓	♋	♏	♎	♍	♑	♉	♍	♒	♊	♎	♓	♌	♐	♋
5	♉	♍	♑	♊	♎	♒	♋	♏	♎	♌	♐	♉	♎	♒	♊	♎	♓	♋	♐	♎	♍	♑	♉
6	♊	♎	♓	♋	♏	♎	♌	♑	♊	♎	♒	♋	♏	♓	♋	♐	♉	♊	♑	♊	♍	♒	♌
7	♋	♏	♎	♌	♐	♉	♍	♒	♋	♏	♎	♌	♐	♋	♍	♑	♊	♋	♓	♋	♏	♋	♎
8	♍	♑	♊	♎	♒	♋	♏	♎	♌	♐	♉	♍	♒	♊	♏	♓	♋	♐	♎	♌	♍	♉	♍
9	♎	♓	♋	♏	♎	♌	♐	♉	♍	♒	♋	♏	♎	♍	♐	♎	♍	♒	♊	♎	♓	♋	♏
10	♐	♎	♍	♌	♉	♍	♏	♊	♏	♋	♌	♐	♉	♑	♏	♉	♎	♓	♋	♏	♋	♌	♑
11	♑	♊	♍	♒	♋	♐	♎	♊	♐	♌	♍	♑	♋	♏	♒	♋	♐	♎	♊	♑	♊	♍	♒
12	♓	♋	♏	♓	♌	♑	♉	♍	♒	♊	♎	♓	♌	♐	♎	♌	♑	♉	♍	♒	♋	♏	♓

235

Moon-signs – first day of every month 1939–1961

	1939	1940	1941	1942	1943	1944	1945	1946	1947	1948	1949	1950	1951	1952	1953	1954	1955	1956	1957	1958	1959	1960	1961
1	♉	♍	♒	♊	♍	♓	♌	♐	♎	♍	♑	♊	♍	♓	♋	♏	♎	♌	♑	♉	♍	♒	♋
2	♊	♏	♎	♌	♐	♉	♍	♑	♊	♍	♓	♋	♐	♎	♍	♑	♉	♍	♒	♊	♏	♎	♌
3	♋	♐	♎	♌	♐	♉	♍	♒	♊	♏	♓	♋	♐	♉	♍	♑	♊	♏	♓	♋	♏	♎	♌
4	♌	♑	♉	♍	♒	♋	♏	♓	♌	♑	♉	♍	♒	♊	♍	♓	♋	♐	♎	♌	♑	♊	♍
5	♍	♒	♊	♏	♓	♌	♑	♉	♍	♒	♊	♍	♓	♋	♐	♎	♍	♑	♉	♍	♒	♋	♏
6	♏	♎	♌	♑	♉	♍	♒	♊	♏	♓	♌	♐	♎	♍	♑	♊	♍	♓	♋	♐	♎	♌	♑
7	♑	♉	♍	♒	♊	♏	♓	♌	♐	♎	♍	♑	♊	♍	♓	♋	♏	♎	♌	♑	♉	♍	♒
8	♒	♋	♏	♓	♌	♐	♉	♍	♑	♊	♏	♓	♌	♐	♎	♍	♑	♉	♍	♒	♊	♏	♎
9	♎	♌	♑	♉	♍	♒	♋	♏	♓	♌	♐	♎	♍	♑	♊	♍	♒	♋	♐	♎	♌	♑	♊
10	♉	♍	♒	♊	♍	♓	♌	♐	♎	♍	♑	♊	♍	♓	♋	♏	♓	♌	♑	♉	♍	♒	♋
11	♊	♏	♎	♊	♐	♉	♍	♑	♊	♏	♓	♋	♏	♎	♍	♑	♉	♍	♒	♊	♏	♎	♌
12	♌	♑	♉	♍	♑	♊	♍	♒	♋	♐	♎	♌	♑	♊	♍	♒	♊	♏	♓	♌	♐	♉	♍

Moon-signs – first day of every month 1962–1980

	1962	1963	1964	1965	1966	1967	1968	1969	1970	1971	1972	1973	1974	1975	1976	1977	1978	1979	1980
1	♏	♓	♌	♐	♎	♍	♑	♊	♎	♒	♋	♐	♎	♌	♑	♉	♍	♒	♊
2	♐	♉	♍	♒	♊	♏	♓	♋	♏	♈	♍	♑	♉	♎	♒	♋	♏	♈	♌
3	♐	♉	♎	♒	♊	♏	♈	♌	♐	♉	♍	♑	♊	♎	♓	♋	♏	♈	♍
4	♒	♋	♏	♈	♌	♑	♉	♍	♒	♊	♏	♓	♋	♐	♈	♍	♑	♊	♎
5	♓	♌	♐	♉	♍	♒	♊	♎	♓	♋	♐	♈	♍	♑	♉	♎	♒	♋	♏
6	♉	♍	♒	♊	♏	♓	♌	♐	♉	♍	♑	♊	♎	♓	♋	♐	♈	♌	♑
7	♊	♏	♓	♌	♐	♈	♍	♑	♊	♎	♓	♋	♐	♈	♌	♑	♉	♍	♒
8	♌	♐	♉	♍	♒	♊	♏	♓	♋	♏	♈	♍	♑	♉	♎	♓	♋	♏	♈
9	♍	♒	♋	♏	♓	♋	♐	♉	♍	♑	♊	♎	♓	♋	♐	♈	♌	♐	♊
10	♏	♓	♌	♐	♈	♍	♒	♊	♎	♒	♋	♐	♈	♌	♑	♉	♍	♒	♋
11	♐	♉	♎	♒	♊	♎	♓	♋	♐	♈	♍	♑	♉	♎	♓	♋	♏	♓	♌
12	♑	♊	♏	♓	♋	♐	♈	♌	♑	♉	♎	♒	♊	♏	♈	♌	♐	♉	♍

Mercury 1916–1932

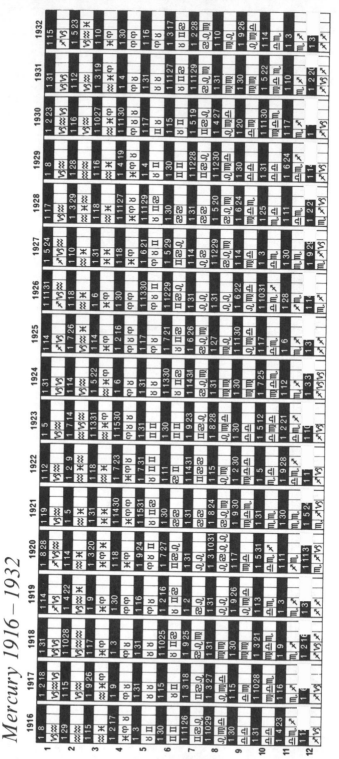

238

Mercury 1933 – 1949

Mercury 1950 – 1966

	1950	1951	1952	1953	1954	1955	1956	1957	1958
1	1 2 15 ♑♒♑	1 31 ♑♑	1 13 ♐♑	1 7 26 ♐♑♒	1 18 ♑♒	1 11 ♑♒	1 4 ♑♒	1 31 ♑♑	1 14 ♐♑
2	1 15 ♑♒	1 10 28 ♑♒♒	1 3 21 ♑♒♓	1 12 ♒♓	1 5 ♒♓	1 28 ♒♒	1 3 15 ♒♑♒	1 13 ♑♒	1 7 25 ♑♒♓
3	1 8 25 ♒♓♈	1 16 ♓♈	1 8 ♓♈	1 3 16 ♓♈♓	1 31 ♓♓	1 18 ♒♓	1 11 29 ♒♓♈	1 4 21 ♒♓♈	1 13 ♓♈
4	1 8 ♈♉	1 2 ♈♉	1 30 ♈♈	1 18 ♓♈	1 13 30 ♓♈♉	1 7 22 ♓♈♉	1 13 30 ♈♉♊	1 5 ♈♉	1 3 11 ♈♉♈
5	1 31 ♉♉	1 2 15 ♉♈♉	1 15 31 ♈♉♉	1 8 23 ♈♉♊	1 15 31 ♉♊♋	1 7 ♉♊	1 31 ♊♊	1 31 ♉♉	1 17 ♈♉
6	1 15 ♉♊	1 9 24 ♉♊♋	1 15 30 ♊♋♌	1 6 26 ♊♋♌	1 30 ♋♋	1 30 ♊♊	1 30 ♊♊	1 13 29 ♉♊♋	1 6 20 ♉♊♋
7	1 3 17 ♊♋♌	1 9 28 ♋♌♍	1 31 ♌♌	1 29 ♌♋	1 31 ♋♋	1 14 31 ♊♋♌	1 7 21 ♊♋♌	1 13 30 ♋♌♍	1 5 26 ♋♌♍
8	1 2 28 ♌♍♎	1 31 ♍♍	1 31 ♌♌	1 12 31 ♋♌♍	1 8 23 ♋♌♍	1 15 31 ♌♍♍	1 6 27 ♌♍♎	1 31 ♍♍	1 24 ♍♌
9	1 11 ♎♍	1 30 ♍♍	1 7 24 ♌♍♎	1 16 ♍♎	1 8 29 ♍♎♏	1 30 ♎♎	1 30 ♎♍	1 30 ♍♍	1 11 29 ♌♍♎
10	1 10 27 ♍♎♏	1 3 20 ♍♎♏	1 12 31 ♎♏♏	1 5 31 ♎♏♏	1 31 ♏♏	1 31 ♎♎	1 11 31 ♍♎♏	1 6 24 ♍♎♏	1 16 ♎♏
11	1 15 ♏♐	1 8 ♏♐	1 30 ♐♐	1 7 ♐♏	1 5 11 ♏♎♏	1 8 27 ♎♏♐	1 19 ♏♐	1 12 ♏♐	1 5 ♏♐
12	1 [illegible] ♐♑	1 2 13 ♐♑♐	1 3 [illegible] ♐♐	1 11 31 ♏♐♑	1 4 23 ♏♐♑	1 1[illegible] ♐♑	1 [illegible] ♐♑	1 2 29 ♐♑♐	1 3[illegible] ♐♐

	1959	1960	1961	1962	1963	1964	1965	1966
1	1 11 31 ♐♑♒	1 4 23 ♐♑♒	1 15 ♑♒	1 8 ♑♒	1 2 20 ♑♒♑	1 31 ♑♑	1 13 ♐♑	1 8 27 ♐♑♒
2	1 17 ♒♓	1 9 ♒♓	1 2 25 ♒♓♒	1 28 ♒♒	1 15 ♑♒	1 11 29 ♑♒♒	1 3 21 ♑♒♓	1 13 ♒♓
3	1 5 ♓♈	1 31 ♓♓	1 18 ♒♓	1 15 ♒♓	1 9 26 ♒♓♈	1 17 ♓♈	1 9 ♓♈	1 3 22 ♓♈♓
4	1 30 ♈♈	1 16 ♓♈	1 10 27 ♓♈♉	1 3 18 ♓♈♉	1 10 ♈♉	1 2 ♈♉	1 30 ♈♈	1 18 ♓♈
5	1 13 29 ♈♉♊	1 5 19 ♈♉♊	1 11 29 ♉♊♋	1 3 ♉♊	1 3 11 ♉♊♉	1 31 ♉♉	1 16 ♈♉	1 10 25 ♈♉♊
6	1 12 29 ♊♋♌	1 3 30 ♊♋♋	1 30 ♋♋	1 30 ♊♊	1 15 ♉♊	1 10 25 ♉♊♋	1 2 16 ♉♊♋	1 8 27 ♊♋♌
7	1 31 ♌♌	1 6 ♌♋	1 31 ♋♋	1 11 27 ♊♋♌	1 4 18 ♊♋♌	1 9 27 ♋♌♍	1 2 31 ♋♌♍	1 31 ♌♌
8	1 31 ♌♌	1 11 27 ♋♌♍	1 4 19 ♋♌♍	1 11 30 ♌♍♎	1 3 27 ♌♍♎	1 31 ♍♍	1 3 ♍♌	1 31 ♌♌
9	1 5 21 ♌♍♎	1 12 ♍♎	1 5 27 ♍♎♏	1 30 ♎♎	1 17 ♎♍	1 30 ♍♍	1 9 25 ♌♍♎	1 17 ♍♎
10	1 9 31 ♎♏♐	1 2 ♎♏	1 22 ♏♎	1 31 ♎♎	1 11 29 ♍♎♏	1 3 20 ♍♎♏	1 13 ♎♏	1 6 30 ♎♏♐
11	1 25 ♐♏	1 30 ♏♏	1 11 30 ♎♏♏	1 5 24 ♎♏♐	1 16 ♏♐	1 8 30 ♏♐♐	1 2 ♏♐	1 13 ♐♏
12	1 1[illegible] ♏♐	1 8 27 ♏♐♑	1 20[illegible] ♐♑	1 1[illegible] ♐♑	1 [illegible] ♐♑	1 1[illegible] ♑♐	1 3[illegible] ♐♐	1 12 31 ♏♐♐

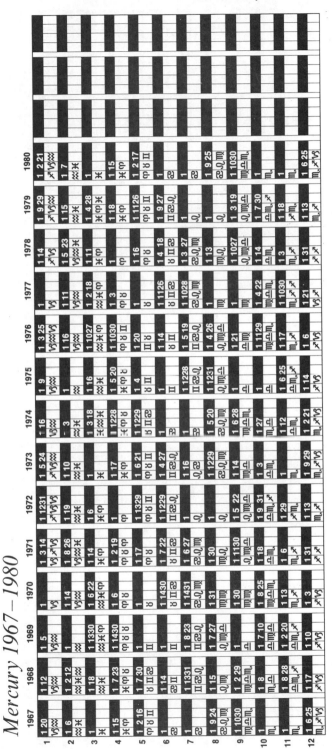

Mercury 1967–1980

Venus 1916–1932

242

Venus 1933 – 1949

	1933	1934	1935	1936	1937	1938	1939	1940	1941	1942	1943	1944	1945	1946	1947	1948	1949
1	1 15 ♐ ♑	1 ♒	1 9 ♑ ♒	1 4 28 ♏ ♐ ♑	1 7 ♒ ♓	1 24 ♑ ♒	1 5 ♏ ♐	1 19 ♒ ♓	1 14 ♐ ♑	1 ♒	1 9 ♑ ♒	1 4 29 ♏ ♐ ♑	1 6 ♒ ♓	1 23 ♑ ♒	1 6 ♏ ♐	1 19 ♒ ♓	1 14 ♐ ♑
2	1 8 ♑ ♒	1 ♒	1 2 26 ♒ ♓ ♈	1 23 ♑ ♒	1 2 ♓ ♈	1 17 ♒ ♓	1 7 ♐ ♑	1 13 ♓ ♈	1 7 ♑ ♒	1 ♒	1 2 26 ♒ ♓ ♈	1 22 ♑ ♒	1 3 ♓ ♈	1 16 ♒ ♓	1 7 ♐ ♑	1 12 ♓ ♈	1 7 ♑ ♒
3	1 4 28 ♒ ♓ ♈	1 ♒	1 23 ♈ ♓	1 18 ♈ ♓	1 10 ♈ ♓	1 12 ♈ ♓	1 ♑ ♈	1 28 ♈ ♈	1 3 ♈ ♓	1 ♒	1 22 ♈ ♈	1 18 ♈ ♓	1 12 ♈ ♓	1 12 ♈ ♈	1 6 31 ♈ ♓	1 9 ♒ ♈	1 2 27 ♒ ♈ ♈
4	1 21 ♈ ♉	1 7 ♒ ♓	1 17 ♈ ♓	1 12 ♉ ♈	1 15 ♉ ♈	1 6 30 ♈ ♉ ♊	1 26 ♓ ♈	1 5 ♉ ♊	1 21 ♈ ♉	1 7 ♒	1 16 ♈ ♉	1 11 ♉ ♈	1 8 ♉ ♈	1 6 30 ♈ ♉ ♊	1 26 ♓ ♈	1 5 ♉ ♊	1 20 ♈ ♉
5	1 16 ♉ ♊	1 7 ♓ ♈	1 12 ♈ ♉ ♊	1 6 30 ♈ ♉ ♊	1 ♈	1 25 ♊ ♋	1 21 ♈ ♉	1 7 ♊ ♋	1 15 ♉ ♊	1 7 ♓ ♈	1 12 ♊ ♋	1 5 30 ♈ ♉ ♊	1 ♈	1 25 ♊ ♋	1 21 ♈ ♉	1 8 ♊ ♋	1 15 ♉ ♊
6	1 9 ♊ ♋	1 3 29 ♈ ♉ ♊	1 8 ♋ ♌	1 23 ♊ ♋	1 5 ♈ ♉	1 19 ♊ ♌	1 15 ♉ ♊	1 ♊ ♋	1 9 ♊ ♋	1 3 28 ♈ ♉ ♊	1 8 ♋ ♌	1 23 ♊ ♋	1 6 ♈ ♉	1 18 ♊ ♌	1 14 ♉ ♊	1 30 ♊ ♋	1 9 ♊ ♋
7	1 3 28 ♋ ♌ ♍	1 24 ♊ ♋	1 8 ♌ ♍	1 18 ♋ ♌	1 9 ♉ ♊	1 15 ♌ ♍	1 10 ♊ ♋	1 6 ♊R ♊	1 3 28 ♋ ♌ ♍	1 24 ♊ ♋	1 8 ♌ ♍	1 18 ♋ ♌	1 14 ♉ ♊	1 9 ♌ ♍	1 ♊ ♋	1 ♊	1 3 28 ♋ ♌ ♍
8	1 22 ♍ ♎	1 18 ♋ ♌	1 ♍	1 12 ♌ ♍	1 4 31 ♊ ♋ ♌	1 10 ♍ ♎	1 3 28 ♋ ♌ ♍	1 2 ♊ ♋	1 22 ♍ ♎	1 18 ♋ ♌	1 ♍	1 11 ♌ ♍	1 5 31 ♊ ♋ ♌	1 10 ♍ ♎	1 3 27 ♋ ♌ ♍	1 4 ♊ ♋	1 21 ♍ ♎
9	1 16 ♎ ♏	1 12 ♌ ♍	1 ♍	1 5 29 ♌ ♎ ♍	1 26 ♌ ♍	1 8 ♎ ♏	1 21 ♍ ♎	1 9 ♋ ♌	1 16 ♎ ♏	1 11 ♍R ♎	1 ♍	1 4 29 ♍ ♎ ♍	1 25 ♌ ♍	1 7 ♎ ♏	1 20 ♍ ♎	1 9 ♋ ♌	1 15 ♎ ♏
10	1 12 ♏ ♐	1 6 30 ♍ ♎ ♏	1 ♍	1 24 ♏ ♐	1 20 ♎ ♏	1 ♎ ♏	1 ♍ ♎	1 8 ♌ ♍	1 22 ♎ ♏	1 ♍	1 23 ♏ ♐	1 20 ♏ ♐	1 17 ♎ ♏	1 14 ♎ ♏	1 7 ♎ ♏	1 ♌ ♍	1 11 ♏ ♐
11	1 7 ♐ ♑	1 23 ♏ ♐	1 10 ♍ ♎	1 17 ♐ ♑	1 13 ♏ ♐	1 16 ♏ ♏	1 8 ♏ ♐	1 2 27 ♍ ♎ ♏	1 7 ♏ ♐	1 22 ♍ ♎	1 10 ♍ ♎	1 17 ♐ ♑	1 13 ♏ ♐	1 ♎ ♏	1 7 ♏ ♐	1 2 27 ♍ ♎ ♏	1 6 ♏ ♐
12	1 5 ♑ ♒	1 11 ♐ ♑	1 9 ♎ ♏	1 12 ♑ ♓	1 7 31 ♐ ♑ ♒	1 ♏	1 2 26 ♏ ♐ ♑	1 21 ♏R ♐	1 6 ♏ ♐	1 16 ♎ ♏	1 9 ♑ ♒	1 7 31 ♏R ♐ ♑	1 ♐	1 25 ♎ ♏	1 12 ♏ ♐	1 ♏	1 ♐

Venus 1950–1966

	1950	1951	1952	1953	1954	1955	1956	1957	1958	1959	1960	1961	1962	1963	1964	1965	1966
1	1 ≈	1 8 ♑ ≈	1 3 28 ♏ ♐ ♑	1 6 ≈ ♓	1 23 ♑ ≈	1 7 ♏ ♐	1 18 ≈ ♓	1 13 ♐ ♑	1 ≈	1 8 ♑ ≈	1 3 28 ♏ ♐ ♑	1 5 ≈ ♓	1 22 ♑ ≈	1 7 ♏ ♐	1 18 ≈ ♓	1 13 ♐ ♑	1 ≈
2	1 ≈	1 25 ♓ ♈	1 22 ♑ ≈	1 3 ♓ ♈	1 16 ≈ ♓	1 7 ♐ ♑	1 11 ♓ ♈	1 6 ♑ ≈	1 ≈ ℞	1 25 ♓ ♈	1 21 ♑ ≈	1 2 ♓ ♈	1 15 ≈ ♓	1 6 ♐ ♑	1 11 ♓ ♈	1 6 ♑ ≈	1 7 26 ≈ ♑ ≈
3	1 ≈	1 22 ♈ ♉	1 17 ♈ ♉	1 15 ♈ ♉	1 12 ♈ ♉	1 5 31 ≈ ♓ ♈	1 9 ♈ ♉	1 2 26 ≈ ♓ ♈	1 ≈	1 21 ♈ ♉	1 17 ♈ ♉	1 31 ♈ ♈	1 11 ♈ ♉	1 5 30 ♈ ♓ ♈	1 8 ♈ ♉	1 2 26 ≈ ♓ ♈	1 ≈ ♓ ♈
4	1 7 ≈ ♓	1 16 ♉ ♊	1 10 ♓ ♈	1 ♈	1 5 29 ♈ ♉ ♊	1 25 ♓ ♈	1 5 ♉ ♊	1 20 ♈ ♉	1 7 ≈ ♓	1 15 ♉ ♊	1 10 ♈ ♈	1 30 ♈ ♈	1 4 29 ♈ ♉ ♊	1 8 ♈ ♉	1 4 ♈ ♉	1 19 ≈ ♓	1 7 ≈ ♓
5	1 6 ♓ ♈	1 12 ♊ ♋	1 5 29 ♈ ♉ ♊	1 ♈	1 24 ♊ ♋	1 20 ♈ ♉	1 9 ♊ ♋	1 14 ♉ ♊	1 6 ♓ ♈	1 11 ♊ ♋	1 4 29 ♈ ♉ ♊	1 ♈	1 24 ♊ ♋	1 19 ♈ ♉	1 13 ♊ ♋	1 ♉ ♊	1 6 ♓ ♈
6	1 2 28 ♈ ♉ ♊	1 8 ♋ ♌	1 23 ♊ ♋	1 6 ♈ ♉	1 18 ♋ ♌	1 14 ♉ ♊	1 24 ♊ ♋	1 7 ♉ ♊	1 2 27 ♈ ♉ ♊	1 22 ♋ ♌	1 6 ♈ ♉	1 18 ♋ ♌	1 13 ♉ ♊	1 18 ♋ ♌	1 7 ♉ ♊	1 27 ♊ ♋
7	1 23 ♊ ♋	1 9 ♌ ♍	1 17 ♋ ♌	1 8 ♉ ♊	1 14 ♌ ♍	1 9 ♊ ♋	1 ♊ ℞	1 2 27 ♊ ♋	1 23 ♊ ♋	1 9 ♌ ♍	1 17 ♋ ♌	1 8 ♉ ♊	1 13 ♌ ♍	1 8 ♊ ♋	1 ♊	1 26 ♌ ♍	1 22 ♊ ♋
8	1 17 ♋ ♌	1 ♍	1 10 ♌ ♍	1 5 31 ♊ ♋ ♌	1 10 ♍ ♎	1 2 26 ♋ ♌ ♍	1 5 ♊ ♋	1 21 ♍ ♎	1 17 ♋ ♌	1 ♍	1 10 ♌ ♍	1 4 30 ♊ ♋ ♌	1 9 ♍ ♎	1 26 ♋ ♌	1 6 ♊ ♋	1 20 ♍ ♎	1 16 ♋ ♌
9	1 11 ♌ ♍	1 ♍	1 4 28 ♍ ♎ ♏	1 25 ♌ ♍	1 7 ♎ ♏	1 19 ♍ ♎	1 9 ♌ ♍	1 15 ♍ ♎	1 10 ♌ ♍	1 21 26 ♍ ♎ ♏	1 3 28 ♍ ♎ ♏	1 24 ♌ ♍	1 7 ♎ ♏	1 19 ♍ ♎	1 9 ♌ ♍	1 14 ♍ ♎	1 9 ♌ ♍
10	1 5 29 ♍ ♎ ♏	1 ♍	1 23 ♍ ♎	1 19 ♍ ♎	1 24 28 ♎ ♏	1 14 ♏ ♐	1 7 ♍ ♎	1 10 ♏ ♐	1 10 ♍ ♎	1 4 28 ♍ ♎ ♏	1 22 ♍ ♎	1 19 ♍ ♎	1 ♏	1 13 ♎ ♏	1 6 ♍ ♎	1 10 ♎ ♏	1 4 28 ♍ ♎ ♏
11	1 22 ♏ ♐	1 10 ♎ ♏	1 16 ♎ ♏	1 12 ♎ ♏	1 ♏ ℞	1 7 ♏ ♐	1 26 ♎ ♏	1 6 ♐ ♑	1 21 ♏ ♐	1 10 ♎ ♏	1 16 ♎ ♏	1 12 ♎ ♏	1 ♏	1 6 30 ♏ ♐ ♑	1 26 ♎ ♏	1 6 ♐ ♑	1 20 ♏ ♐
12	1 15 ♐ ♑	1 9 ♎ ♏	1 11 ♑ ≈	1 6 30 ♏ ♐ ♑	1 ♏ ℞	1 25 ♐ ≈	1 20 ♏ ♐	1 13 ♐ ♑	1 8 ♎ ♏	1 11 ♑ ≈	1 5 29 ♏ ♐ ♑	1 ♏	1 24 ♐ ♑	1 20 ♏ ♐	1 ♐ ♑	1 14 ♐ ≈

Venus 1967–1980

	1967	1968	1969	1970	1971	1972	1973	1974	1975	1976	1977	1978	1979	1980
1	1 7 31 ♑♒♓	1 2 27 ♏♐♑	1 5 ♒♓	1 21 ♑♒	1 7 ♏♐	1 17 ♒	1 12 ♐♑	1 30 ♒	1 6 30 ♑♒♓	1 2 26 ♏♐♑	1 5 ♒♓	1 21 ♑♒	1 7 ♏♐	1 16 ♒♓
2	1 24 ♓♈	1 20 ♑♒	1 2 ♓♈	1 14 ♒♓	1 6 ♐♑	1 10 ♓♈	1 5 ♑♒	♑	1 23 ♓♈	1 20 ♑♒	1 2 ♓♈	1 14 ♒♓	1 5 ♐♑	1 10 ♓♈
3	1 20 ♈♉	1 16 ♒♓	1 ♈	1 10 ♓♈	1 4 30 ♑♒♓	1 7 ♈♉	1 25 ♓♈	1 7 ♒♓	1 20 ♈♉	1 15 ♒♓	1 ♈	1 10 ♒♓	1 4 29 ♑♒♓	1 7 ♈♉
4	1 14 ♉♊	1 9 ♓♈	1 ♈	1 3 28 ♈♉♊	1 24 ♓♈	1 4 ♈♉	1 18 ♈♉	1 5 31 ♓♈♉	1 14 ♈♉	1 8 ♓♈	1 ♈	1 3 27 ♈♉♊	1 23 ♓♈	1 4 ♈♉
5	1 10 ♊♋	1 3 28 ♈♉♊	1 ♈	1 ♈♈	1 19 ♈♉	1 11 ♉♊	1 12 ♈♉	1 26 ♈♉	1 10 ♈♉	1 3 27 ♈♉♊	1 6 ♈♉	1 22 ♉♊	1 18 ♈♉	1 13 ♉♊
6	1 7 ♋♌	1 21 ♊♋	1 6 ♈♉	1 23 ♉♊	1 12 ♉♊	1 12 ♊♋	1 6 30 ♉♋♌	1 21 ♊♋	1 6 ♉♊	1 21 ♉♊	1 7 ♉♊	1 16 ♋♋	1 12 ♉♊	1 5 ♊♋
7	1 9 ♌♍	1 16 ♋♌	1 7 ♉♊	1 17 ♊♋	1 7 31 ♊♋♌	1 ♊	1 25 ♊♋	1 15 ♊♋	1 9 ♊♋	1 15 ♋♋	1 3 29 ♊♋♌	1 12 ♊♋	1 6 31 ♊♋♌	1 7 ♊♋
8	1 ♍♌	1 2 27 ♌♍♏	1 23 ♋♌	1 8 ♋♍	1 25 ♊♋	1 6 ♋♌	1 19 ♋♍	1 8 ♋♍	1 ♋	1 8 ♋♍	1 23 ♋♌	1 8 ♋♍	1 24 ♊♋	1 8 ♋♌
9	1 10 ♍♌	1 21 ♍♎	1 18 ♌♍	1 7 ♍♎	1 18 ♌♍	1 5 31 ♋♍♎	1 13 ♍♎	1 ♌♍	1 10 ♍♎	1 2 26 ♌♍♏	1 17 ♌♍	1 7 ♍♎	1 17 ♌♍	1 5 30 ♋♍♎
10	1 2 ♍♎	1 21 ♐	1 5 28 ♍♎♏	1 7 ♎♏	1 12 ♍♎	1 25 ♍♎	1 6 ♎♏	1 3 27 ♍♎♏	1 10 ♍♎	1 14 ♎♏	1 10 ♎♏	1 8 ♍♏	1 11 ♍♎	1 24 ♍♎
11	1 10 ♎♏	1 11 ♏	1 ♎♏	1 ♏	1 12 ♏♐	1 ♎♏	1 6 ♏	1 13 ♎♏	1 ♏	1 ♐♒	1 ♎♏	1 7 ♏	1 11 ♎♏	1 ♎♏
12	1 ♎♏	1 ♑♒	1 ♎♏	1 ♏	1 ♏♐	1 ♏♐	1 8 ♏	1 13 ♏♑	1 ♏	1 10 ♒	1 4 28 ♏♐♑	1 ♏	1 ♏	1 ♏♐

245

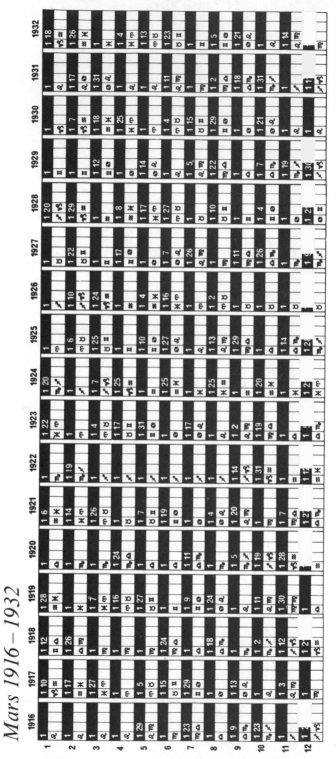

Mars 1916–1932

Mars 1933 – 1949

	1949	1948	1947	1946	1945	1944	1943	1942	1941	1940	1939	1938	1937	1936	1935	1934	1933

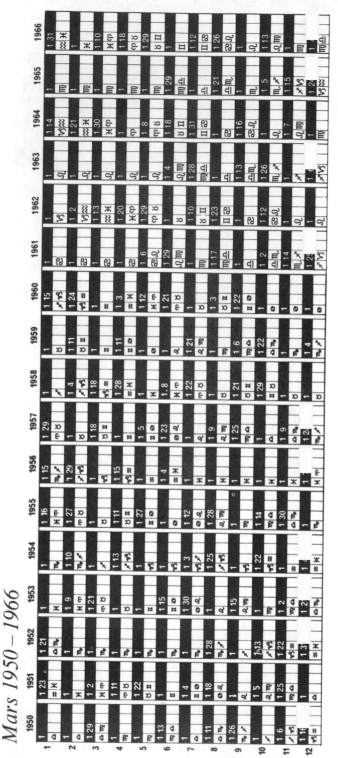

Mars 1950 – 1966

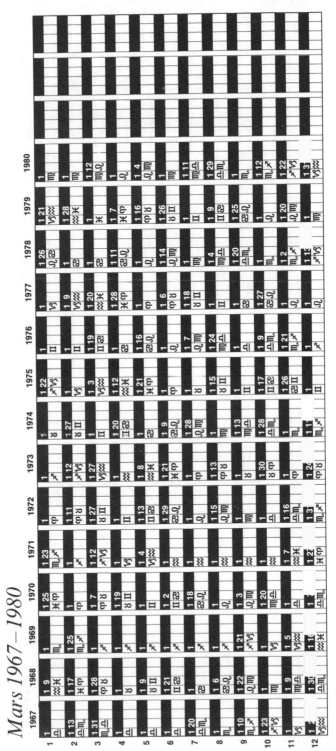

Mars 1967–1980

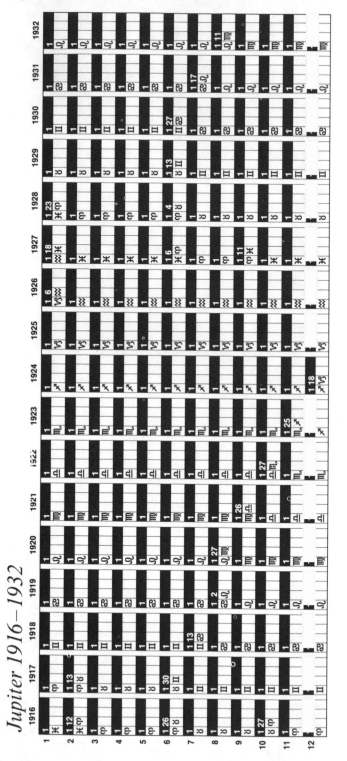

Jupiter 1916–1932

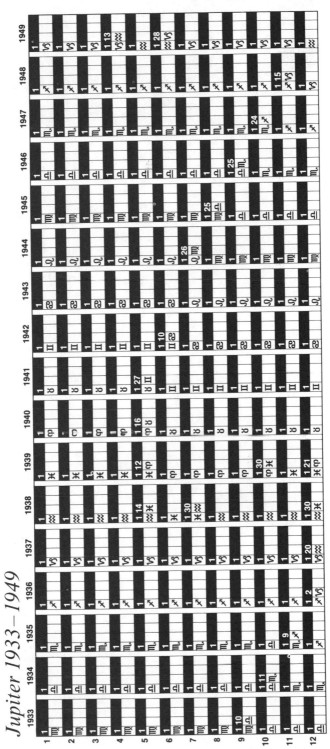

Jupiter 1933–1949

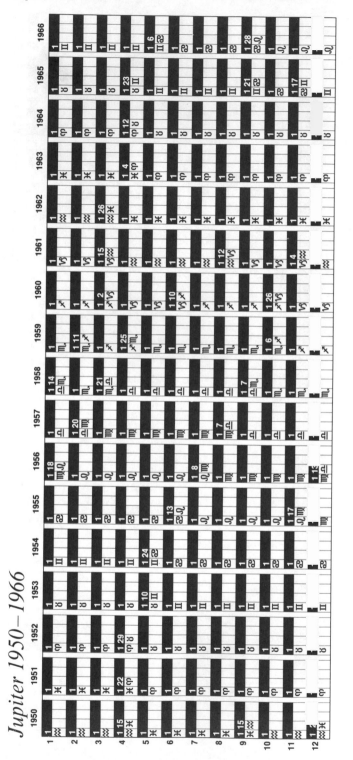

Jupiter 1950–1966

252

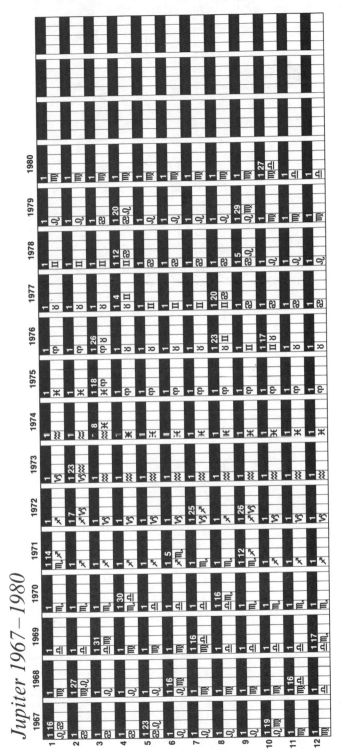

Jupiter 1967–1980

Saturn

1916
Jan 1–Oct 16 ♋
Oct 17–Dec 7 ♌
Dec 8–Dec 31 ♋
1917
Jan 1–June 23 ♋
June 24–Dec 31 ♌
1918 ♌
1919
Jan 1–Aug 11 ♌
Aug 12–Dec 31 ♍
1920 ♍
1921
Jan 1–Oct 7 ♍
Oct 8–Dec 31 ♎
1922 ♎
1923
Jan 1–Dec 19 ♎
Dec 20–Dec 31 ♏
1924
Jan 1–Apr 5 ♏
Apr 6–Sept 13 ♎
Sept 14–Dec 31 ♏
1925 ♏

1926
Jan 1–Dec 2 ♏
Dec 3–Dec 31 ♐
1927–1928 ♐
1929
Jan 1–Mar 14 ♐
Mar 15–May 4 ♑
May 5–Nov 29 ♐
Nov 30–Dec 31 ♑
1930–1931 ♑
1932
Jan 1–Feb 23 ♑
Feb 24–Aug 13 ♒
Aug 14–Nov 19 ♑
Nov 20–Dec 31 ♒
1933–1934 ♒
1935
Jan 1–Feb 13 ♒
Feb 14–Dec 31 ♓
1936 ♓
1937
Jan 1–Apr 24 ♓
Apr 25–Oct 17 ♈
Oct 18–Dec 31 ♓

1938
Jan 1–Jan 13 ♓
Jan 14–Dec 31 ♈
1939
Jan 1–Jul 5 ♈
Jul 6–Sep 21 ♉
Sep 22–Dec 31 ♈
1940
Jan 1–Mar 19 ♈
Mar 20–Dec 31 ♉
1941 ♉
1942
Jan 1–May 8 ♉
May 9–Dec 31 ♊
1943 ♊
1944
Jan 1–Jun 19 ♊
Jun 20–Dec 31 ♋
1945 ♋
1946
Jan 1–Aug 1 ♋
Aug 2–Dec 31 ♌
1947 ♌
1948 ♌

1949
Jan 1–Sep 18 ♌
Sep 19–Dec 31 ♍
1950
Jan 1–Apr 2 ♍
Apr 3–May 28 ♌
May 29–Dec 31 ♍
1951
Jan 1–Nov 19 ♍
Nov 20–Dec 31 ♎
1952
Jan 1–Mar 7 ♎
Mar 8–Aug 13 ♍
Aug 14–Dec 31 ♎
1953
Jan 1–Oct 22 ♎
Oct 23–Dec 31 ♏
1954–1955 ♏
1956
Jan 1–Jan 12 ♏
Jan 13–May 13 ♎
May 14–Oct 9 ♏
Oct 10–Dec 31 ♐
1957–58 ♐

1959
Jan 1–Jan 4 ♐
Jan 5–Dec 31 ♑
1960–1961 ♑
1962
Jan 1–Jan 3 ♑
Jan 4–Dec 31 ♒
1963 ♒
1964
Jan 1–Mar 23 ♒
Mar 24–Sept 16 ♓
Sept 17–Dec 15 ♒
Dec 16–Dec 31 ♓
1965–1966 ♓
1967
Jan 1–Mar 3 ♓
Mar 4–Dec 31 ♈
1968 ♈
1969
Jan 1–Apr 29 ♈
Apr 30–Dec 31 ♉
1970 ♉
1971
Jan 1–Jun 18 ♉
Jun 19–Dec 31 ♊
1972
Jan 1–Jan 9 ♊
Jan 10–Feb 21 ♉
Feb 22–Dec 31 ♊
1973
Jan 1–Aug 1 ♊
Aug 2–Dec 31 ♋
1974
Jan 1–Jan 7 ♋
Jan 8–Apr 18 ♊
Apr 19–Dec 31 ♋
1975
Jan 1–Sep 16 ♋
Sep 17–Dec 31 ♌
1976
Jan 1–Jan 14 ♌
Jan 15–Jun 4 ♋
Jun 5–Dec 31 ♌
1977
Jan 1–Nov 16 ♌
Nov 17–Dec 31 ♍
1978
Jan 1–Jan 4 ♍

Saturn continued

Jan 5–Jul 25	♌
Jul 26–Dec 31	♍
1979	
1980	
Jan 1–Sep 20	♍
Sep 21–Dec 31	♎

Uranus

1913–1918	♒
1919	
Jan 1–Mar 31	♒
Apr 1–Aug 16	♓
Aug 17–Dec 31	♒
1920	
Jan 1–Jan 21	♒
Jan 22–Dec 31	♓
1921–1926	♓
1927	
Jan 1–Mar 30	♓
Mar 31–Nov 4	♈
Nov 5–Dec 31	♓
1928	
Jan 1–Jan 12	♓
Jan 13–Dec 31	♈
1929–1933	♈
1934	
Jan 1–Jun 5	♈
Jun 6–Oct 9	♉
Oct 10–Dec 31	♈
1935	
Jan 1–Mar 27	♈
Mar 28–Dec 31	♉
1936–1940	♉
1941	
Jan 1–Aug 6	♉
Aug 7–Oct 4	♊
Oct 5–Dec 31	♉
1942	
Jan 1–May 14	♉
May 15–Dec 31	♊
1943–1947	♊
1948	
Jan 1–Aug 29	♊
Aug 30–Nov 12	♋
Nov 13–Dec 31	♊
1949	
Jan 1–Jun 9	♊
Jun 10–Dec 31	♋
1950–1954	♋
1955	
Jan 1–Aug 23	♋
Aug 24–Dec 31	♌
1956 Jan 1–Jan 27	♌
Jan 28–Jun 9	♋
Jun 10–Dec 31	♌
1957–1960	♌
1961	
Jan 1–Oct 31	♌
Nov 1–Dec 31	♍
1962	
Jan 1–Jan 10	♍
Jan 11–Aug 9	♌
Aug 10–Dec 31	♍
1963–1967	♍
1968	
Jan 1–Sep 28	♍
Sep 29–Dec 31	♎
1969	
Jan 1–May 20	♎
May 21–Jun 23	♍
Jun 24–Dec 31	♎
1970–1973	♎
1974	
Jan 1–Nov 20	♎
Nov 21–Dec 31	♏
1975	
Jan 1–May 1	♎
May 2–Sep 7	♏
Sep 8–Dec 31	♏
1976–1980	♏

Neptune

1913	♋
1914	
Jan 1–Sep 22	♋
Sep 23–Dec 14	♌
Dec 15–Dec 31	♋
1915	
Jan 1–Jul 18	♋
Jul 19–Dec 31	♌
1916	
Jan 1–Mar 19	♌
Mar 20–May 2	♋
May 3–Dec 31	♌
1917–1927	♌
1928	
Jan 1–Sept 20	♌
Sept 21–Dec 31	♍
1929	
Jan.1–Feb 19	♍
Feb 20–Jul 23	♌
Jul 24–Dec 31	♍
1930–1941	♍
1942	
Jan 1–Oct 2	♍
Oct 3–Dec 31	♎
1943	
Jan 1–Apr 17	♎
Apr 18–Aug 1	♏
Aug 2–Dec 31	♎
1944–1954	♎
1955	
Jan 1–Dec 23	♎
Dec 24–Dec 31	♏
1956	
Jan 1–Mar 11	♏
Mar 12–Oct 18	♎
Oct 19–Dec 31	♏
1957	
Jan 1–Jun 16	♏
Jun 17–Aug 4	♎
Aug 5–Dec 31	♏
1958–1969	♏
1970	
Jan 1–Jan 4	♏
Jan 5–May 2	♐
May 3–Nov 6	♏
Nov 7–Dec 31	♐
1971–1980	♐

Pluto*

1913
Jan 1–July 9 ♊
July 10–Dec 27 ♋
Dec 28–Dec 31 ♊

1914
Jan 1–May 27 ♊
May 28–Dec 31 ♋

1915–1936 ♋

1937
Jan 1–Oct 6 ♋
Oct 7–Nov 24 ♌
Nov 25–Dec 31 ♋

1938
Jan 1–Aug 2 ♋
Aug 3–Dec 31 ♌

1939
Jan 1–Feb 7 ♌
Feb 8–Jun 13 ♋
Jun 14–Dec 31 ♌

1940–1955 ♌

1956
Jan 1–Oct 20 ♌
Oct 21–Dec 31 ♍

1957
Jan 1–Jan 15 ♍
Jan 16–Aug 18 ♌
Aug 19–Dec 31 ♍

1958
Jan 1–Apr 11 ♍
Apr 12–Jun 9 ♌
Jun 10–Dec 31 ♍

1959–1970 ♍

1971
Jan 1–Oct 4 ♍
Oct 5–Dec 31 ♎

1972
Jan 1–Apr 16 ♎
Apr 17–Jul 30 ♍
Jul 31–Dec 31 ♎

1973–1980 ♎

*Transitional dates
are subject to a
margin of error of
about two days

256